FATHERHOOD

FATHERHOOD

RISING TO THE ULTIMATE CHALLENGE

ETAN THOMAS

with **NICK CHILES**

Foreword by **TONY DUNGY**

NEW AMERICAN LIBRARY

New American Library
Published by New American Library, a division of
Penguin Group (USA) Inc., 375 Hudson Street,
New York, New York 10014, USA
Penguin Group (Canada), 90 Eglinton Avenue East, Suite 700, Toronto,
Ontario M4P 2Y3, Canada (a division of Pearson Penguin Canada Inc.)
Penguin Books Ltd., 80 Strand, London WC2R 0RL, England
Penguin Ireland, 25 St. Stephen's Green, Dublin 2,
Ireland (a division of Penguin Books Ltd.)
Penguin Group (Australia), 250 Camberwell Road, Camberwell, Victoria 3124,
Australia (a division of Pearson Australia Group Pty. Ltd.)
Penguin Books India Pvt. Ltd., 11 Community Centre, Panchsheel Park,
New Delhi - 110 017, India
Penguin Group (NZ), 67 Apollo Drive, Rosedale, Auckland 0632,
New Zealand (a division of Pearson New Zealand Ltd.)
Penguin Books (South Africa) (Pty.) Ltd., 24 Sturdee Avenue,
Rosebank, Johannesburg 2196, South Africa

Penguin Books Ltd., Registered Offices:
80 Strand, London WC2R 0RL, England

First published by New American Library,
a division of Penguin Group (USA) Inc.

First Printing, May 2012
10 9 8 7 6 5 4 3 2 1

 REGISTERED TRADEMARK—MARCA REGISTRADA

LIBRARY OF CONGRESS CATALOGING-IN-PUBLICATION DATA:
Thomas, Etan.
Fatherhood: rising to the ultimate challenge/Etan Thomas with Nick Chiles;
foreword by Tony Dungy
p. cm.
ISBN 978-0-451-23673-9
1.Fatherhood. 2. Parenting. 3. Parent and child
I. Chiles, Nick. II. Title.
HQ756.T476 2012
306.874'2—dc23   2011045100

Set in Bembo
Designed by Patrice Sheridan

Printed in the United States of America

PUBLISHER'S NOTE
While the author has made every effort to provide accurate telephone numbers, Internet addresses,
and other contact information at the time of publication, neither the publisher nor the author assumes
any responsibility for errors, or for changes that occur after publication. Further, publisher does not
have any control over and does not assume any responsibility for author or third-party Web sites or
their content.

To my wife, Nichole,

Thank you for always believing in me, supporting me, and encouraging me to go after my passions even if they are not widely supported at the time. I respect you, admire you, and look forward to the journey of raising our beautiful kids together. You are an incredible mother, and we make a great team. I am far from perfect, but I want to be the best father and husband that I can possibly be. You have been a blessing to me and I am thankful for you.

To Malcolm,

You are an incredible son. I couldn't be prouder of you. You have a kind heart, you are thoughtful, respectful, passionate, and you have a great sense of humor. You amaze me with your intelligence, talent, insight, and courage. You are going to be something special in whatever you decide to do. I am proud to have you as my son.

To Imani,

You are not only beautiful on the outside but you are beautiful on the inside. Your determination and passion really amaze me. Your smile brings joy to my heart. Every time I hear you singing or watch you doing ballet or gymnastics, I can't help but smile from ear to ear. You have a voice like an angel. You are a sharp little girl, and you can be anything you want to be in life. I will always be here for you.

To Sierra,

My beautiful little baby. I see how you watch your brother and sister and you are constantly observing. Almost as if you are taking notes. Your little laugh and smile is absolutely precious, even if it is at 3:00 in the morning. Looking into your face, I can never be mad at the sleepless nights or broken sleep patterns you provide. You're so innocent and sweet. I am truly blessed to have the family I have. No matter what age, you all can always count on me for support and encouragement. I am blessed to have all of you.

CONTENTS

CONTENTS

CONTENTS

FOREWORD BY TONY DUNGY

Men in our society have been fooled into thinking that we can get joy and satisfaction from everything except fatherhood. If I make enough money . . . if I get enough accolades . . . if I get this contract . . . if I get whatever, that's really going to make me happy. Maybe it can, to a certain extent, but it does not give you a joy like seeing your offspring flourish. When my son Eric played in the high school state championship football game in Florida, I was way more nervous than I ever was on the sidelines at the Super Bowl. This is your son; you want him to do well. I couldn't even stand up when I was watching him play in that game. People say, "How do you compare a high school game to the Super Bowl?" Well, I'm telling you, there was no comparison—I was a hundred times more nervous watching him play in high school than I was watching my team, the Indianapolis Colts, in the 2007 Super Bowl.

When I read through the chapters of this book, I knew right away that it was something really special. I knew it was going to be a book that helped a lot of people. I am so happy to be a part of it. When I come upon the words of Coach John Thompson, talking about how hard his dad worked but that he was always there for young John, then I contrast that with the essays of guys like Malcolm Shabazz and Isaiah Washington, who talk about how much they missed and how much pain they experienced because their dads were not there, that summarizes the whole message of this book for me. Joy and pain. Dad being there; dad being gone.

I grew up really blessed, because I had the benefit of my dad being there for me for forty-eight years—he died seven years ago, when I was forty-eight. I took it for granted that he was there, because I thought everybody's life was that way. My dad was a college professor, so basically he was off when I was off. When I was home, he was always around. In the summertime when I was out of school, he was around. When I got home from school, he was home from his classes. That's how I grew up for eighteen years; until I got to college, I thought that's what all dads were like. But when I got away and had roommates and saw other guys who didn't have that, it really made an impact on me. After I began coaching and came into contact with other young men, I'd start talking to them and began realizing that for many of them, this was the first time they'd had conversations like these. I remember talking to a player who got hurt in Indianapolis, talking about his family, making sure they were set, telling him not to worry about his position because he would be coming back, and asking him to think about what the Lord was trying to say to him in all this. I was reassuring him that he was going to be fine. He looked at me and said, "I could never have a conversation with my dad like this." When he said that, I just said, "Wow." But that's clearly more the norm than the situation I had growing up, because I see so many players who have come up that way. We have a generation of young men and women growing up without that role model, who didn't see a picture of what family life and fatherhood were supposed to be like. Now they are wanting to do it right, but not really knowing how.

I saw this firsthand with Michael Vick, when I started talking to him and really getting to know him when he was in prison. In his letters and when I went to see him, when I asked him what he wanted to do moving forward, he said, "I can't tell you how difficult it is to be away from my kids." He said, "I can only talk to my kids one or two minutes a day on the phone. I went through the same thing, being away from my dad, and I don't want that to be the case with my kids." That was really the first thing we talked about; it's what was on his mind—not getting back to football or figuring out what was going to happen with his career. What we addressed first was, How do we put this back together where you can do the job with your family that you want to do?

Andre Agassi touched on this in his piece when he explored the realization that as athletes, we tend to do self-centered and self-focused things. But the act of parenting is, as he puts it, "contributing to the success of others." And that's how I define true leadership—putting the welfare of the group ahead of yourself, which will then affect your choices.

I am excited about getting this book in the hands of an entire generation of young men. I want these young men to use this book to think about the things they didn't have growing up, but also about what they need to provide their children—whether they got it from their dads or not. I think if I had just gone into corporate America, I may always have taken my dad for granted. But when I began to come across so many young men who didn't have that relationship with their fathers, it began to be clear to me how important the parenting aspect is. This book will help guys on both ends—in dealing with the effects of not having their dads around, and in thinking about how to raise their own children. It will crystallize a little bit more for them what's really important.

In the end, what's most important in life isn't going to be how much money you make, how many material things you acquire, how many sexual conquests you have. It's going to be the way you guide the young people you bring into the world. When you have to make decisions about your career versus your children, which one is it going to be? How are you going to spend the little bit of discretionary time you have? What type of message will you pass along to your children that will make a difference in their lives and the lives of their children, and on and on from there? In the following chapters, Etan does a wonderful job of laying out the point that grandfathers, great-grandfathers, the elders who surround children, they all have an impact on the message that gets passed on. It's more challenging now, because our society doesn't really stress many of the issues discussed in this book. We talk about a lot of things, but very seldom do you hear much conversation about the legacy you pass on to your kids and how that's an important part of the job of a man.

I am so glad that the spiritual aspect of fatherhood gets addressed in these pages, by people like Allan Houston and Derek Fisher. That's so critical, because when we look at the problems we're having with young people, in the education system, and the other woes that get documented here, I think much of our spiritual plight stems from the fact that men haven't done their jobs in the home. When young girls and boys see their relationship with their father as something that they can't count on, then when people start talking to them about a heavenly Father, it doesn't mean anything—or it may even be a negative thing. They say, "I couldn't trust a father I see; how can I trust a father I don't see?" They get a negative image of God simply because we haven't done what God put us on earth to do, and that's nurture our children.

One of the biggest lessons my dad tried to pass along to me from day one was to be a leader. He'd say, "There's nothing wrong with being in the crowd, as long as the crowd is going where you want to go. But don't go somewhere you don't want to go just because the crowd is going there. If you want to go somewhere different, then you have to set the tone and make the crowd follow you." I talk to teenagers all the time and I know the pressure they feel to fit in, to not stand out, to be a part of the group, is very strong. But parents have to say that the family is a group, whether it's a group of three or five or seven, however many there are in the family. We're a group and that has to be enough. If we do things the right way, there will be a big group following us.

One of the most moving aspects of this book is so many guys being willing to express the pain of not having their fathers there and what that means to them. What I took away—and this is a good thing—is that they were saying, "I got hurt in this deal and I'm not going to let my kids be hurt in the same way." So often we try to repress the pain and not think about it, put it out of our minds, and so often we end up repeating the same mistakes that caused us the pain. But the guys on these pages are saying, "No, that's not the way I wanted to grow up; it wasn't good for me, and now that I have kids I'm going to be there for them."

As Etan says so eloquently, there is no such thing as the perfect father. Perfection is not what our kids want or need. It's expected that you won't have all the answers, won't always make the right decision, but you have to be there and show that you care. As I said earlier, I would define a leader as a person who puts the welfare of the group above himself. It's the same thing with fathers. You may not have all the answers; you're going to make mistakes. As a coach, I made the wrong call many times, but my guys knew where my heart was, that I was in it for them. I wasn't in it for myself, trying to make myself look good or make people say, "Look how smart he is." If I made the wrong call, it was sincere and it was honest, me thinking I was doing the best thing for the team. If I made a bad call, they were going to go out there and make it work, because they believed in the head coach. It's the same thing with a dad. He's not going to have all the answers; he's not going to be right every time. Sometimes he might say, "If I could do that over again, I would do it this way." But when your kids know that you're in it for them and have their back, that's what's most important. Everybody will learn from it. You could have had the perfect role model—or maybe you didn't have one at all—but you're still not going to have all the answers when you start the process of parenting.

When I was in Tampa, I worked with an organization called All Pro Dads. We called it that because everybody can relate to what it takes to be an All-Pro football player: Yes, you have to have talent, but more than that, you have to work hard, you have to have consistency, you have to do it day in and day out, on the practice field and on the game field. That's how you get to that high level. It takes the same work ethic, same energy, and same drive to be an All-Pro dad. It's hard work. But it's important.

Showing love and affection to your kids, which is a major part of the message Etan is conveying, was probably the biggest thing I've had to learn. Guys my age grew up with dads who didn't believe you were supposed to show affection. You were supposed to be the tough guy. It was just like the movies and media we saw. My dad grew up with John Wayne. That's the way you were supposed to be—getting the cattle from Kansas City to Dodge City, no matter what happened. If you got that done, you were a man. Men didn't cry, didn't show affection. You didn't love on your kids; you provided for them. Well, now we know how much of a misconception that was. In Stuart Scott's piece, he recognizes the joy of showing affection to his daughters but realizes that's not what most of us men have been taught. But he has chosen to break that cycle and show his daughters the kind of manly affection they should crave. That's powerful! I had to learn that it was good to show affection. You know where I saw it? On the athletic field and in the locker room. If you won a big game and came back into the locker room, guys weren't just shaking hands and patting one another on the back and saying, "Good game." No, you saw that brotherly love. You'd see that coach hug the guy who scored the game-winning touchdown. To say it's okay in that situation but you can't ever let your kids see that doesn't make sense. That's a very important lesson—and one that our society is doing a better job now of getting across. We're letting young people know that failing to show affection is not what being a man is all about; there's a very proper and appropriate way of showing affection. Your kids have to see both sides—they have to see you be strong and protect them and stand up for them, but they have to see you loving them as well.

I'm glad that Etan included a chapter on single mothers. More than half our kids are growing up that way; it's the reality of where we are right now. When Derek Fisher said he felt like he had to pick sides as a kid when his parents split up, I had never thought of it that way, but I can see how that would happen. How do you as a single mom try to raise your kids but not have them take sides? Trying to keep the dad involved is a hard way to go, a difficult line to balance on, but that's what you have to do, because the kids do need to know that Dad loves them. As much as it may not be happening for the two of you, how can you make sure he's not totally out of the kids' lives? Etan does a great job in tackling some of these issues. When guys came into the NFL and I'd sit down to talk to them, I'd ask them a lot of questions. Who impacted your life? Who shaped you? The answer would always be, "Mom," "Grandmom," "My high school coach," "My junior high coach." That made me start thinking, It's great what these moms have done, raising such high achievers, but what about the kid—boy or girl—who isn't in sports and doesn't have Mom or the high school coach pushing him? Who's reaching that kid, helping him grow and flourish? What is he missing?

Etan talks at length about going into the prisons to reach out to some of the guys in there. I've also done quite a bit of that. In 1996, when I got the head coaching job at Tampa, I met with a guy who runs a prison ministry who invited me to go in because he thought I'd be an inspiration to some of them. I was apprehensive at first, but when I went in and saw how young some of them were, all my apprehensions were gone. I was forty at the time, and some of them were eighteen, nineteen, not hardened criminals but young kids. When I started talking to them, I saw two common threads: There was no dad in the home, and they dropped out of high school. I felt that the two were often tied together—there was no dad around to stress to them the importance and necessity of their education. Especially for African-Americans, leaving school early is clearly a formula for incarceration. I would tell them that it was up to them to break the cycle; I would tell them it's not too late. I would always equate it to football—you may be down in the third or fourth quarter, but you can still come back and win the game. When we went to the Super Bowl in 2007, we had to beat the Patriots in the AFC Championship when we were ahead for only one minute in the whole game. But it was the last minute. Being behind for fifty-nine minutes, we didn't let that stop us. I tell these guys that right now they're behind, but that doesn't mean their lives are over. They have to come out and break the cycle. Get back to their kids and not let them fall into the traps.

I think this project is critically important, bringing much-needed attention to the role of dads. I hope young men and young women will read these words by Etan and by the many other wonderful men gathered in these pages, and they will have for the rest of their lives a powerful standard for fatherhood.

INTRODUCTION

I'm not a fatherhood expert. I don't want to give you the impression in this book that I'm trying to lecture you. In a sense, this book has been as much of a learning process for me as I hope it will be for you. This is the book that I wish I had when I was a young boy. That was a huge part of my motivation in writing it. The things I talk about on these pages, the subjects we explore, were almost therapeutic for me. Because I wanted the book to be as broad and inspirational and educational as possible, I called upon a wide range of men to assist me, to write essays about their own experiences with fatherhood and about how they were able to overcome fatherlessness as young men. I don't feel qualified to tell a story as important and meaningful as this one by myself; that's why I leaned heavily on a large fraternity of men to help me.

As I entered the fatherhood realm myself, my thoughts and opinions about a lot of these subjects grew more passionate, but I still had many questions I wanted answered. This book is my attempt to go out and seek some of those answers, whether we're talking about the power of a father's love, the importance of elders, the impact of history, the corrosiveness of anger, the destructiveness of stereotypes, or the burden on single mothers. I was a brand-new parent when the barrage of scorn was thrown at Dr. Bill Cosby for challenging the black community on its failure to take responsibility for many of its actions, its failure to adequately parent so many black children. Although I didn't agree with everything he said, I am thankful that he brought this topic to life. I learned a lot from the Cosby debate, but I felt like too many of his points got lost in the melee that ensued. So I wanted to revisit the issues Cosby raised and ask some brilliant minds, such as Dr. Cornel West, Russ Parr, John King, Ed Gordon, Kareem Abdul-Jabbar, and Malcolm-Jamal Warner, to help me in dissecting the controversy.

Before I go on, let me say that I wouldn't have been able to complete this project without the loving support of my wife, Nichole. She was extremely encouraging to me throughout the entire process, providing me with a sounding board when I needed it, or a timely opinion. At times it was a bit time-consuming tracking down all these busy men, but not once did I get anything but encouragement from her, because she believed in the importance of this project.

I want this book to be a prod to young people, to let them know that even if they grow up in a single-parent household, they can still be wildly successful and achieve anything they want to achieve. Perhaps they might find some help on these pages to enable them to get past the anger they may have about their situation and not let it affect their entire lives. I want this book to show men the beauty and manliness in showing love and affection toward your kids, how you can feel a love so strong that you'll struggle sometimes to put into words how meaningful it is. I want this book to be something that men automatically consult when they begin having kids, or perhaps when they are going through divorce. If it's something you've never been taught or never seen modeled, you may not be familiar with the joys of fatherhood—but in these pages, you will have the experience modeled for you by some of the most prominent, successful, interesting men of our time. Just like an entire generation of women and men run to the book *What to Expect When You're Expecting* when they get that exciting news of impending parenthood, I want this book to serve as a manual for fathers new and old. I made the decision to focus the book exclusively on men because I wanted it to be a place where men could come together and shine a spotlight on our role. Yes, I certainly need and pray for the support of women for this project, but I wanted this to be about fathers taking a stand, doing what's best for our families and ourselves. And as you will see from skimming through the table of contents, we went out of our way to include a cross section of different races, backgrounds, cultures, and religions on these pages. As I've gotten older, it's become so clear to me that we're all in this together. Being a good father is an issue that crosses color lines. The challenges are the same, whether they are being tackled by Yao Ming, Howard Dean, Andre Agassi, or Ice Cube. When I am out in public with my kids and I pass another father pushing a stroller, we will automatically exchange a look, a nod, a recognition of the fatherhood bond. As I said before, it is a fraternity. Even if you're a different race or from a different part of the country, you understand each other and know exactly what the other guy is going through. Whether you're rich or poor, Democrat or Republican, we all have to deal with many of the issues we explore in these pages, from the struggle to be a presence in your child's life as much as possible to the anger so many of us are still grappling with from our own childhoods.

For young men, I hope you are able to open your minds and hearts and hear the accounts of so many men who went through the exact same things you are going through now. Men who made it out successfully on the other side and want to tell you how you can, too. Sometimes, by reading some of their stories, you also are able to put yours into some context—to see that maybe your situation isn't as bad as you thought, because so many others had it much worse than you do. I challenge you to delve into Baron Davis's account of growing up with drug-addicted parents and a father in prison, surrounded by family members who were in gangs, and see if you aren't able to view your own troubles from a new perspective. You might discover that you don't have as much to complain about as you thought you did. And then there's always the ultimate fatherlessness success story—President Barack Obama. I never get tired of using his tale to prove my point that the sky is the limit.

I would like young people to use this book as a shield to combat the negativity you hear as a young person growing up without a father, whether you have somebody throwing statistics at you, or maybe using the disturbingly negative term "broken home" to describe your situation. I would like for these pages to prove both inspirational and educational.

When I first embarked on this project, I thought it would be on a much smaller scale. I had no idea that so many men of such caliber and prominence would be eager to participate. I've been blessed to play in the NBA for a long time, and during those years I have met many different people in many different fields. As I started asking people about adding their voices to the project, I was overwhelmed by the responses. Nearly every man I approached said he was happy to do it, happy to work time into his schedule to write an essay, because the topic was so important. Nearly every single person said this was a book he would love to have read when he was young. Or he'd love to read it right now so he could keep learning about fatherhood. I am extremely grateful to each of them for helping me bring this project to life. I hope you will conclude that it was worth the effort.

FATHERHOOD

CHAPTER ONE

GOT TO BE THERE: SPENDING TIME WITH YOUR CHILDREN

My oldest child, Malcolm, is just five years old as I write this, so I'm fairly new to the state of fatherhood. I can talk for days on end about that thrill you get in the morning when your little one, wearing a grin bright enough to light the neighborhood, bursts through your bedroom door, well in advance of your carefully set alarm clock, and presents you with enough joy to get you through the new day. I can go on about the way your heart skips when he wraps his little arms around your neck as you carry him to his room for bedtime. But I can't say a thing about the nerves that accompany his first driving lesson. Or the sadness when he waves good-bye on the first day of his freshman year of college. For me, those moments will come soon enough.

What I would like to say is something so simple that it can be done in just two small words: Be there. Those seven letters encompass the Tao of fatherhood. That's it. I'm not a child psychologist or some kind of parenting expert. I can't tell you the precise psychiatric terms to describe what happens to your child when you aren't there, when she cries herself to sleep at night because you missed another birthday. Rather than academia, the places I speak from might be called pain and longing. I have had a lifetime with these, watching them inflict damage on kids all around me. Feeling them in my own life. Knowing that tightness that forms in the chest when you desperately need to tell something to your dad, but you don't have the type of father-son relationship where you would feel comfortable seeking his advice.

Woody Allen memorably said that 80 percent of success is showing up. I don't know whether he was thinking of fathers when he said this, but in my mind his words give us a brutally honest way to consider the simplicity of fatherhood. On the whole scale of human achievement, fatherhood won't rank very high. There are many tasks humans endeavor to accomplish that most of us would consider far more complex than being a father. Designing an electric car battery. Finding a cure for AIDS. Stopping a massive oil leak in the Gulf of Mexico. That's not to say that fathers aren't faced with difficult decisions on a regular basis, or that we're always going to know what to do because our jobs are so easy. But what most of us will find is that our kids are remarkably forgiving. They aren't expecting perfection. They don't even want perfection. They just want us to be there.

I think this message gets lost so easily precisely because it is so simple. We humans have a tendency to make everything a lot more complicated than it needs to be. It's like when you take the SAT and they tell you to stick with your first choice, because that's usually the right one. But instead of going with the gut, which is really our education and experience whispering in our ear, we find a dozen reasons why the answer must be D and not A, primarily because A just seems too obvious. I think life is like that. If A feels right to you, then pick A. In his bestselling book *Blink*, Malcolm Gladwell says humans are innately suspicious of our gut instincts because "we live in a world that assumes that the quality of a decision is directly related to the time and effort that went into making it."

We make fatherhood more complicated than it needs to be whenever we choose another option over being there. It doesn't even matter what the other option is; if it involves our being somewhere else, it's the wrong choice. That's not to say that we don't go out there and make a living. I'm a professional basketball player. By definition, half of my workdays occur out of town at away games. As you can probably imagine, I know all too well what it's like to hear that front door close behind you as your children are calling out, "Bye, Daddy!" It's a horrible feeling. But in my line of work, I have no other choice. When I get home from a road trip and I'm faced with the option of hanging out with the fellas or taking my son to the park, it isn't hard to rationalize the need to hang out: It's fun, relaxing, a way to relieve some of the stress of being a professional athlete. All of that may be true, but it's not being there.

Howard Dean, former six-term governor of Vermont and onetime Democratic presidential candidate, was about as busy as a man could be while his kids were growing up, but he knew how important it was for him to be there for them. In the following piece, Dean tells us why.

I'm the father of a daughter and a son, both now out in the world in their mid-twenties. I came relatively late to the parenting realm, but I think that ultimately made me more patient as a parent—and, believe me, I'm not a patient person.

My life has been a busy one, but I tried to make time to do things with my kids that would be fun and memorable—things like camping, hiking, canoeing, and watching a ton of hockey and soccer games. As the kids got older, they didn't want me around them as much, but I didn't let that deter me. I was going to be there and they knew it. I came home two nights before the Wisconsin primary just to see my son's last high school hockey game. I knew there would always be another speech to give, but never another "Senior Night."

Still, I wish I had sometimes been even more patient. Time is the most important thing with kids. But it has to be good time. Time on the phone with someone else while they are in the room, which was my biggest problem, doesn't count. Time yelling at them doesn't count unless it's quick and followed by an explanation. The explanation is the thing. It builds respect and understanding, even when they don't act like they hear you. And believe it or not, it builds a vocabulary and a sense that things can be solved with words, not verbal or physical violence. You learn as much by being a parent as you teach by being a parent. The first time I really understood my own father was after I became one myself.

My favorite story about parenting took place when my daughter was in middle school. Believe me, the horrors of middle school parenting are not exaggerated.

We were in the car driving somewhere when my daughter started complaining about her math homework. I gave her a lecture that included the phrase, "If something is worth doing, it is worth doing well." She gave me a lot of sass in return. We lapsed into silence. A half hour later, we got into another tiff. In her most sarcastic tone, she repeated the entire lecture from half an hour earlier, word for word. I started to get mad, but then I realized she must have listened to every word of it if she was able to repeat it verbatim. I smiled and shut up.

Take pleasure in small steps forward and love every moment of being a dad. And to get it right, you have to work at it. It is worth every minute.

Now, I know that I'm hardly the father ideal. I struggle with selfishness and confusion and powerful career ambition just as much as anyone else. I have to remind myself on a regular basis of the importance of being there. I think that's one of the reasons I always try to bring Malcolm along with me, even when I'm heading someplace where having a five-year-old in tow isn't exactly convenient. Someplace like basketball practice. He loves to dribble the ball around the gym and try his hand shooting at the basket, no doubt trying to imitate me. And when I'm out on the court, he will "take a knee" on the sidelines and watch. The joy of watching his dad play is powerful enough to tame even a five-year-old. But as soon as I stop, it's his turn. "Daddy, look at me!" he says, as he dribbles and shoots, showing off his stuff.

At home, when it's time to work out in my basement exercise and weight room, I take him down there with me. We recently went out and found a set of plastic dumbbells for him. He had been trying to pick up my real weights, and my wife, Nichole, was worried that he might get hurt. So now he has his own. They are dark blue and they sit next to mine. He even makes a little noise when he's lifting them, again imitating me. Before we lift, we do stretches together. He loves it. I enjoy seeing the pleasure on his face when I tell him we're about to go work out. Is there anything more fun than the face of an excited five-year-old?

It's interesting how technology has changed the landscape for a traveling father, giving us a false sense of security, of being there when we really aren't. Whereas traveling dads in previous generations had to depend on the telephone to keep in touch, I have videoconferencing on Skype. So I get to witness the changing expressions on my son's little face when he tells me about his day at school, or his T-ball game. I might close down the screen and convince myself that my absence at his game was of no consequence, since we just had a meaningful conversation about it. But I would be wrong.

There are many self-help guides on the market that advise folks to live without fear and guilt, to go out there and grab life by the horns and tackle it to the ground. I can understand the attraction of such a life philosophy. Who wouldn't want to hear encouragement to do whatever you please in a frantic pursuit of personal fulfillment and happiness? That surely sounds wonderful, doesn't it? No guilt, no doubts, no fear, no responsibility. However, in my view, such a philosophy is inconsistent with fatherhood. If you want a life without guilt and responsibility, that's fine. Just don't have children. Then when you grow older and are forced to slow it down, you can comfort yourself with grand memories of thrilling adventures. I'd prefer to have a loving family around me. But that's my choice.

I present it as a stark choice—adventure versus fatherhood—but in reality the two things don't have to be mutually exclusive. Nobody understands that more than extreme skateboarding legend **Tony Hawk**, who brings his children with him on his adventurous travels as much as he can. Hawk knows that the travels with Dad will be memorable for his children—just as he will always remember a trip he took with his own father that he reflects on in the following essay.

The most important lesson I learned from my father is to be actively involved in your child's life. My dad was not the most communicative, nurturing, or friendliest person around. But he took an interest in what I did, and gave me endless support. Considering I chose to do something different and generally frowned-upon (skateboarding as a career path was definitely not applauded in the early eighties), this was huge. He drove me to the skate parks and most of the skating events in Southern California, and eventually he formed a professional competition series when there was none. Compared to the dads of my friends who skated, my dad was a hero; their parents didn't want them skating at all. My dad and I had plenty of disagreements during our years together, but I always knew how lucky I was, and I didn't take his support for granted. In fact, it set me up to be an effective father in my own way.

One of the best memories I have of my father was when I wanted to get my first skimboard (a skimboard is what you use to skim along the wet sand at the beach to hit an oncoming shorebreak). I had saved up enough to buy a decent board, and my dad took me to a good surf shop in San Diego to pick one up. The shop didn't have the brand I wanted (Victoria Skimboards were considered the best at the time), so we asked what store carried them. They said no store in San Diego (skimboarding was relatively underground at the time), but that we could get one at the Victoria factory in Laguna Beach, an hour's drive away. Without hesitation, my dad said, "Well, let's go!" I was excited, but I realize now that I was happier about my dad going to such lengths to help me than about getting the actual skimboard. In fact, my memories of skimming are pale compared to the memory of my dad's generous offer. It showed his true devotion to his kids. I can only hope to pass it on.

Having four children, I have learned a few things over the years. No parenting regimen universally works, but taking interest in whatever your kids choose to do gives them a sense of self-confidence that sometimes they can't find anywhere else. This can be as simple as building LEGOs with them, or watching their favorite TV show together. Participate; don't just observe. Quote funny lines, even if it's not your favorite type of humor. The feedback can be tremendous. The value of sharing inside jokes and basic experiences together has greater resonance than taking them to Disneyland or buying them cotton candy.

I do not see my kids every day, due to divorce and an extensive travel schedule. But I devote my attention to them when we are together. I have learned that just because you are physically present doesn't mean that you are there for them. Hanging around your kids while fixated on your iPhone/BlackBerry is not participating. Take interest, learn the rules, join the fun, and encourage trying different things together. While some may disagree, I believe it is possible to be their friend and still have parental authority.

A valuable lesson I've learned from my kids is not to be afraid of personal humiliation. Kids love it when you are human and fallible. Let your guard down and enjoy the ride. My kids know I'm not perfect, but they appreciate that I am the first to admit it. And *it gives them courage to try new things, even if they know they will fail at first. Humility by example can go a long way.*

My dad made us go on lengthy road trips when we were young. While this seemed like a burden to my young mind, I realize now that it gave us a better perspective on the world and taught us a new level of patience. This was, of course, in the days before backseat DVD/Nintendo entertainment. I have carried on that tradition by taking my kids on as many trips as possible. It is challenging at first—especially when they are very young—but it becomes infinitely easier the more you travel with them. Nowadays, my oldest son doesn't blink when I tell him we are going to South Africa (which can be a thirty- to forty-hour trip from California). And they learn to enjoy the adventure. The cliché is true: Sometimes it's about the journey, not the destination.

There are many lives that illustrate the difficulty of fatherhood in the midst of boundless exploration and adventure. Or even the repercussions of single-mindedness. These cautionary tales abound. After his son Cameron was sentenced to five years in prison for dealing meth, legendary Hollywood actor Michael Douglas admitted that much of his son's troubles was due to his being absent during his son's early years, trying to build a career. Douglas recognized his errors, but the recognition came many years too late to help his son.

In my own sport, NBA Hall of Fame legend Rick Barry should have been the proudest father in the land when not one but *three* of his sons wound up playing in the NBA. But upon closer examination, we found out that Barry's relationship with his sons was severely strained after Barry left their mom when they were young, and they barely saw him. In major league baseball, slugger Prince Fielder and his father, Cecil Fielder, a great slugger in his own right, have been feuding for years instead of enjoying the amazing fact that the son has been able to follow in his father's footsteps.

Some people may find it odd that these warnings about being

there are coming from a guy who can't always be there himself. But I plead for your indulgence. This is an issue that has brought me more than a little pain since I became a dad. If I can convince just one father who is reading this to change his priorities, to make different decisions about how he spends his time, then I can at least feel like something useful has come out of my pain. You might think that "pain" is too strong a word when describing the so-called "glamorous" lifestyle of a professional athlete. After all, we make a lot of money and spend a lot of time in fancy hotels. In response, all I can do is remind you of how quickly children change, how rapidly they grow. I have had occasions where I've returned from a road trip and felt like Malcolm looked different. I missed his first steps because I was away. When I left, he was at that stage where he was constantly standing up and trying to keep his balance. When I came back, he was taking steps. It happened that quickly, almost overnight. When you're not there, you don't even realize all the things you miss. Every tiny, minute change feels enormous in my eyes, because I wasn't there when it happened. I can't hit rewind and get it back. The closest I get is listening to my wife, Nichole, describe it to me. Fun, but not the same.

Once I came home from a West Coast swing that had lasted for ten days and my daughter Imani, who was about six months old, didn't remember me. Can you imagine that? I got down on the floor with her to play, but I could see the expression in her eyes. She was trying to figure out who I was, as though I looked familiar to her but she couldn't quite place me. So she crawled back to Mom. She had to relearn me all over again. And that was just from a ten-day absence!

When Malcolm started talking, the separation was even more difficult, because he could verbalize that he didn't want me to leave. "You just got here—you have to leave again?" he'd say, his words slowly breaking my heart. His face would start to crumple and he'd begin acting differently, dropping his toys, walking around with a sad expression. The first time he cried when I left tore me up. We were in the living room. I put my bags down, gave him a hug, wiped his tears away, and said, "It's all right; Daddy will be back soon. No worries." That's a little expression we would say to each other: "no worries." But he wasn't trying to hear it. All of a sudden I was no longer worried about running late. Everything just stopped. That's the thing with kids: Time stops when they're not happy. When I was driving away, waving to him, I could still see the tears running down his face. I didn't want to leave. I kept thinking about it the rest of the day. It was a picture that played over and over in my head.

If I want to remind myself of the sublime joys of fatherhood, all I have to do is go back to the day Malcolm came to us. I was extremely fortunate, because he was born in June, after the NBA season had ended. I've seen players miss the birth of their children because of its happening in the middle of the season, so I knew my presence at the birth was not something I should take for granted. Believe me, the June birth was not something my wife and I had meticulously planned out. We just got lucky. It was truly a gift. I was amazed by the whole process—the labor, racing to the hospital, the delivery, holding new life in my hands. Leading up to the fateful moment, I was like Steve Martin in the movie *Parenthood*—I had the bags packed, various routes to the hospital mapped out depending on traffic scenarios. I was ready, on top of it. It seemed like it took forever, but when Malcolm finally came out, so many different thoughts and feelings rushed through me. It really is a moment that you can never fully prepare yourself for. In that one precise instant, everything in your life changes. You are holding an extension of yourself. You're wondering what he's going to look like when he's ten, how he's going to grow up. And most of all, you become a different person. You think differently; you eat differently; what you watch on television changes. You become mature. Well, you should become mature. I admit it doesn't happen to everyone. Maybe we are having so many problems with absent fathers because not enough of us are there in that delivery room when the baby comes out. I have heard some men say that the nursing staff was actually surprised to see them in the delivery room, because it was such an unusual sight. You know that's wrong when a nurse is so used to the father not being there at birth that she would actually verbalize her surprise.

From the day Nichole and I first learned we were pregnant, I was thoroughly engaged, reading *What to Expect When You're Expecting* and every other baby book I could get my hands on. I was thrilled when I found out that the first child was going to be a son, knowing that we'd be starting out with a little miniature version of me. But now that we've also had two daughters, Imani and Sierra, I see that a father's love for his daughters is just as profound as that age-old need for a man to have a son; it's a different love— more protective, more sensitive, more affectionate. And our priorities change so much that soon we don't even look like the same person. Before my kids arrived, I used to drive around in a Cadillac Escalade with giant speakers in the back. It was a crazy sound system; you could hear me coming from a mile away. But when the kids came along, the speakers had to go. After all, they needed someplace to sit. Now, instead of speakers, I have a booster seat and two car seats in the back. My entrance on the block is a lot quieter now.

The power of a father's strong presence in his son's life is perfectly illustrated by **Coach John Thompson** in the following piece. Thompson was the first black coach to win a national championship, in 1984 with Georgetown, and has had great success throughout his coaching career—and has two sons who are now successful head coaches themselves. Though he's met many famous people, Thompson says his father is still the "finest" man he has ever met. When Thompson was growing up, his father clearly understood the importance of being there.

"Come on, Anna, I gotta go." Every weekday morning at five a.m., my father said those words to my mother on his way out the door. To my knowledge, we didn't have an alarm clock, but my father got up every morning at the same time to work as a laborer at the Standard Art Marble and Tile Company in Washington, D.C. My father worked hard his entire life, and for all of his hard work, he received a vinyl chair and no pension when he retired. So much for being rewarded for hard work and loyalty.

For ten years of my childhood we lived in public housing, but contrary to popular belief, all kids in public housing are not unloved and deserted by their parents. I always felt safe and loved. I knew my father loved me through his actions. I remember him patting me on the head, hugging me, and smiling at me. My father would go to work every day to support us. He would come home every night completely tired, but he never complained. He made all of us feel secure, both physically and emotionally, because of his work ethic and devotion to us as a family. It was almost amusing that even though I grew up in a low-income family, I thought I had everything that I could possibly want and need. The difference was that we were always taught what not to want!

My dad never took a vacation. Our family would go fifty-six miles down to southern Maryland once in a while, and that was considered a vacation. I have one vivid recollection of when I was a young boy and my father took me fishing. I had caught three fish that day and my dad had caught four. Well, when we got back home, my dad told everyone that I had caught four fish and that he had caught three. For some reason, that always stuck with me, and made a big impression on me. My dad was an honest man, with integrity. I distinctly remember that he had all of the keys to the doors where he worked. And I remember thinking that meant something important. Mostly that his employer trusted him and valued him, and that gave my father pride. Another memory is of my dad taking me to work with him after the Christmas party each year, and we were able to clean up and eat the leftovers. It was a real treat for me, and I always took a lot of goodies home to my sisters.

My father was a big sports enthusiast, but to my knowledge, he never played sports as a boy, because he had to work on a farm sunup to sundown. He would always tell me stories about great athletes, like Larry Doby, the second African-American to play major league baseball, and Joe Louis, the Brown Bomber prize-fighter. He would take me to see Doby every time the Cleveland Indians played in D.C. My love for sports came from my father's enthusiasm in how he told those stories. Looking back, I saw the sport itself, but my father saw black men finally placed in a positive light, knowing that it would serve as an inspiration to his young son.

When I first saw tears in my dad's eyes after he watched me play in a high school basketball game, it scared the hell out of me. I had never experienced this strong man crying. But as I later learned from my mom, those had been tears of joy from his being so proud of watching his only son play. Hearing those words put me on top of the world, because I wanted so much to please this man whom I had grown to love.

My dad always encouraged me and taught me the importance of staying out of trouble, and running from those who got in it.

Life could have treated him gentler, but he never complained, resented, denied, or stopped loving my mother, my sisters, and me. I always remember him treating my mother with the utmost respect. My father was not formally educated, he could not read or write, but he was one of the smartest and wisest men I ever knew. He understood and taught me the value of an education.

After graduating from college myself, working for a living, and trying to support my own family, it became even clearer to me how great a man my father was and the significance of how he had lived his life.

In my life, I've been fortunate enough to meet presidents, senators, congressmen, CEOs of major companies, cardinals of churches, heads of state from several countries, and some of the finest athletes and coaches this world has known. I've learned to respect them all and admired their accomplishments, but I've never met a man who accomplished so much with so little as my dad. And I have come to realize that nothing has more meaning to me than the honor of being named after the finest man I have ever met, my dad, John Robert Thompson.

When I think about how my views of fatherhood developed, how this urgent need to be there evolved, it's natural for me to go back to my own childhood. I was born thirty-three years ago in Harlem, but my parents moved the family to Tulsa, Oklahoma, when I was very young. My father worked as an engineer for American Airlines, and he got transferred. When I was in first grade, my parents got divorced and my father moved back to New York, leaving me, my little brother, and my mother in Tulsa. Tulsa was a good place to grow up, safe enough to allow kids plenty of freedom.

I have to be careful when talking about my father. While most of my friends truly had absentee fathers, that was definitely not the case with me. My father stayed closely involved in my life throughout my childhood, even though he was in New York, more than a thousand miles away from Tulsa. He didn't allow long gaps of time to pass without calling me and my brother, Julian, and he visited us often, sometimes as much as every other weekend (he could fly cheaply because of his job with American Airlines). But I must say, visiting is not the same as staying. Visiting is not being there. I could still relate to my friends who complained about not having a father in the house. My situation may not have been as bad as theirs, but seeing him once a month didn't give me the kind of connection I needed. I watch my son now as he watches me, how he tracks my every move. He's like a sponge, absorbing every bit of daddy detail he comes across. But I couldn't do that with my dad. There's just no substitution for contact.

When there are no daddy details there for the sponge to soak up, that sponge will soak up information from somewhere else— somewhere else that might be providing harmful, destructive details. That was definitely the case with **Malcolm Shabazz,** the grandson of Malcolm X. His story is a deeply sad illustration of the corrosive effects of fatherlessness. How ironic that we go to the family of one of the twentieth century's strongest symbols of manhood to find a child who was devastated by his father's absence.

In the days before I went to prison, when I was caught up in the streets, there were times when I would literally tell myself that it didn't really matter what I did, because my father wasn't around. I'd say, "F*ck it. I don't have a father." I'd actually make decisions based on that.

I grew up surrounded by women, very strong women. I rebelled against that in search of a male figure. I didn't even have any uncles. I'm not saying a woman can't do a good job in raising a son, but I believe a woman can't teach a boy how to be a man. When I was growing up, I can recall feeling bad in school whenever I saw other kids with their dads. I would be thinking, Man, I wish I had a dad! Ultimately that's what drove me to the streets. The guys on the corner were the closest thing I could see to a male role model. I gravitated toward the gangsters and the hustlers and that lifestyle. That represented strength to me.

From as early as I can remember, I felt like I was under a microscope, being the grandson of Malcolm X, the first male heir in his lineage. I wasn't afforded the luxury of making the same mistakes as my peers. If you invite someone to your house and offer them a meal and maybe they get sick and throw up all over the carpet, you'd clean it up and help them feel more comfortable. But with me, if I was walking down the street and spit on the sidewalk, everybody would say, "Hey, what the hell is wrong with him—he just spit on the sidewalk!" I'd say in some instances it could be a blessing, con-

necting me with other revolutionary-spirited individuals, but in other cases it would be . . . not necessarily a curse but definitely a disadvantage. When I was dealing with government officials and, after I went to prison, with the COs (corrections officers), there were people who harbored animosity toward me solely because of my lineage. The COs at Attica were a 100 percent white workforce, and many of them literally had tattoos on their neck or arms with black babies hanging from trees. They'd stand there with their sticks out and their veins popping from their neck, just dying for you to make a move. They would tell me, "Go ahead, boy, do something. I'm just begging for you to do something!" When we went out in the yard, they would tell us to go around the metal detectors so that brothers could bring weapons out there with them. The inmates would be out there killing each other; there was always a lot of bloodshed. That's how they kept control—divide and conquer. They'd tell us, "You could go out there and kill each other all you want—just don't touch one of us." You would think the brothers would know better, but they still would go out there stabbing and killing each other.

I was only seventeen when I went to prison. I got a sentence of three and a half years, but I was placed in maximum- and super-maximum-security prisons, even though you're supposed to have a minimum of ten years to go to these facilities. I spent my time around brothers who were never going home, who had life sentences or double life or who had just come down from death row.

The system wanted to break me, but what it did instead was make me stronger. When I went up there, a lot of the old-timers pulled me to the side and talked to me. I kept my ears open to them and learned a lot from the brothers behind the wall. I made a conscious effort not just to change my ways and actions, but to broaden my entire thought process. Of course, most of the men there also didn't grow up with their fathers. Prison is the type of place that will make you or break you. Most people leave worse off than when they

*went in, because the system is designed to indoctrinate, not reha-
bilitate.*

*When I was going through my transformation, I was aware that
my grandfather had gone through a similar process in prison. My
grandfather was the people's intellectual. The person who was a
drug dealer or drug addict or gangster could look at him and say,
"Wow, he's been in my shoes, and now look where he's at today."
With a lot of the work I do now, speaking at alternative high
schools, working with gang members, the Vice Lords, the Gangster
Disciples, people relate to me because I've been in the trenches. If
I hadn't gone through some of the things I went through, I wouldn't
have the credibility to do that.*

*But I often think about how I wouldn't have gone through what
I went through, prison and the group homes, if I had my father
around. Now that I have a daughter, I am more cautious about a
lot of things that I do, because I want to be around for her. She's
three now, but when she was born I was locked up for a parole vio-
lation. That took a toll on me, not being there for that. But having
her changed my life a great deal. I love her so much; she's so important to me, I couldn't imagine not being there for her. When I was
younger, I concluded that the only thing that could sever the relationship between a mother and her child probably was drugs. But
what about men? I don't see what it is that could make a man be
desensitized toward his children. Men need to be there for their
children. If they don't have the connection naturally, then they need
to be taught.*

This is a delicate topic for me, for all of us, because I understand
that there are going to be many, many fathers reading this who are
no longer living with their children because of the collapse of their
marriages or relationships with the mother. It happens—marriages
fall apart; relationships falter; love dissipates. And it would be won-

derful if I could say that these failed relationships don't have an impact on the children, as long as the father visits often and stays involved in their upbringing. Oh, if only that were the case! Our communities would be so much better off, wouldn't they? But as my childhood demonstrated, even when the father is committed to staying close to his children, once he leaves, everything changes for those children. Their view of the world changes. Their feelings of safety and security change. The bonds between father and child change.

Childhood is a mercurial time. Crises pop up in an instant, without warning, like a violent summer storm. Thousands of these little crises, strung together, make up the whole of a childhood. A father visiting every other weekend is going to miss most of that, those crucial moments when he would get to weigh in on punishment, or offer advice, or enforce discipline. That's the glue of a family life. If you miss those, you are ancillary to that family and those children. Nonessential. In our case, because my mother no longer had my father around, she became stricter with me and my brother than she probably would have been if they were still married and there was another adult voice in the house. Not to make any qualitative judgments about fathers versus mothers, but the male voice often has a different impact in the household—especially a household with boys. My mother had no backup; she didn't have the luxury of slacking off with us. As a result, I think we saw the strict side of her personality much more than the fun side. She didn't get to be as carefree with us as she might have been. I wonder how many of her smiles we missed out on.

This is not meant to imply that we should endure every bad relationship, no matter how painful, for the sake of the kids, but we should be well aware of the consequences when we decide to split. There's just no way to sugarcoat it.

My mother is a teacher—she taught high school for a long time, but now she teaches middle school—and with us she was often in teaching mode, giving a lesson, proving a point. When you're wrong, my mother's going to let you know about it. That's not to say that we never had great times with her. I have distinct memories of laughing and joking with her, going to the movies, having fun. But if my brother and I did something wrong, she would switch in an instant. We soon learned that we were in control of her demeanor—how she acted toward us was a direct result of our actions. Basically, she would be as nice and sweet as we would let her. But she never embarrassed us. The public never saw that really strict side of her. They saw a laughing, happy person who loves culture and politics—she will debate you in politics at the drop of a hat. Everybody would tell us, "Your mom is the sweetest lady." But when we messed up, she would lean over and tell us, "Just wait until we get home!"

I have a hard time describing my dad's personality. We didn't really see much of it. When he came to get us, we would go to fun places, like a bowling alley, the zoo, horseback riding. My brother and I would have a good time, but overall I remember my dad being serious most of the time. When I look back now as an adult, I wonder what would have been different if my dad were there in the house. How would I be a different person now? But I try not to spend too much time dwelling on such matters. I want to concentrate more on the things I have the ability to influence. It's like Niebuhr's "Serenity Prayer": "God grant me the serenity to accept the things I cannot change; courage to change the things I can; and wisdom to know the difference." Speaking to you now, on these pages, that's something I can change.

It was only when I became a dad that I understood how much a child could enrich my life. I'm not exaggerating when I say that fatherhood helped me get through one of the most difficult periods I've ever faced as an adult, when I had open-heart surgery at age twenty-nine to repair a leaky aortic valve. The heart problem had first been detected when I was in middle school. I didn't really think that much about it over the ensuing years, because I didn't think it was that big a deal. I figured maybe when I was old, eventually I might have to do something about it, but there was no way I thought that day would come at the age of twenty-nine. And I had been working really hard, feeling like I was in great shape, looking forward to a terrific season. I was a professional athlete in my twenties, at the height of my physical capabilities. But it was a precious lesson, not only for me but for anybody else out there who was following my story.

Tomorrow is never promised. We hear that often, but I had the lesson brought to me by special delivery, just to make sure I heard it. Who knows what would have happened to me if the doctors hadn't caught it? I think my whole medical adventure was especially scary for the people around me, such as my wife. But it was a fabulous time for my son, Malcolm! After my surgery, I couldn't go anywhere; I couldn't really do anything while I healed. So it was all about Malcolm, all the time. I couldn't imagine what it would have been like going through that without him and my family right there, offering their support. Malcolm, who was only two, and I really bonded during that year I had to take off from basketball. At first it was a little different for him. We usually do a lot of wrestling, but I couldn't wrestle with him at all. I couldn't pick him up and throw him on the bed; I couldn't do any of the things we usually do. I had to explain to him that Daddy had an "ouch" on his chest. But we both definitely enjoyed the time together. And just a couple months after my surgery, my daughter Imani was born, so I got to be there again to witness the birth of my second child, my precious little girl.

One of the beautiful gifts of fatherhood is that it teaches you selflessness. Children just don't allow you to be obsessively focused on self. This is especially beneficial to pro athletes, who are paid to be obsessively focused on self—and have a large coterie of people around us to help nurture the obsession. But when your kids are hungry and need someone to make them lunch, or when they need

help with a school project, they don't care how many points you
scored the night before or what your season average is for rebounds
per game. They just want help. And it is those little moments, such
as when you are working together on the class project or making a
mess together in the kitchen preparing dinner, that will come back
to you thirty years down the line. Those little moments all will be
woven together into a fine tapestry of parenthood. It won't be that
extra meeting with a client, or all those overtime hours you logged,
that will bring pleasure and substance to your later years. In her
wonderful book *A Short Guide to a Happy Life*, Anna Quindlen
wrote, "Life is made up of moments, small pieces of glittering mica
in a long stretch of gray cement. It would be wonderful if they came
to us unsummoned, but particularly in lives as busy as the ones most
of us lead now, that won't happen. We have to teach ourselves how
to make room for them, to love them, and to live, really live."

If you are not there, those missing moments will come back to
you, too. In ways painful and searing. Award-winning actor **Isaiah
Washington** has vivid memories of one of the most painful times
of his life, when all the years of his father's absence culminated in
shock and dismay as he heard words coming from the television set
that would change him forever.

> *I am thirteen years old and I am standing in the middle of Acres
> Home Funeral Home in Houston, Texas, staring down into the face
> of a dead man: me.*
>
> *Well, not quite me.*
>
> *This man's features are a little different from mine. His nose is
> wider. His cheekbones are higher. But his soulful eyes, big ears,
> and silky eyebrows are mine. His rich skin is the color of a Hershey
> bar. Just like mine. We even share the same name (with a different
> spelling): Isiah Washington. (Isiah Washington is on my birth cer-
> tificate, but I changed it to Isaiah Washington when I turned
> twenty-one.) The dead man is my father. Over the years he has*

been the biggest presence in my life, yet he's a stranger who means nothing to me. This is the first time I've ever seen him wearing a suit except in old pictures. In fact, this is the only time I even remember my mother and father being in the same room. Except for the phone calls telling me he was on the way, only to never show up, I've had almost no contact with him. I stand there looking at him, wanting to turn away, but I'm frozen. With the exception of my conception, this man has missed every single important moment in my life, including my birth, and yet, as many times as I've cursed his name, I have a difficult time mustering up any hate. We shared the same name.

That means something, right?

Every male role model in my life—my football coaches, my stepfather—I've held at an emotional arm's length. I'm respectful and obedient, of course, but not close. I've always felt that if I got too close to any male figure, I'd be betraying my father. I keep staring at him, because for the life of me, I can't figure out how I could love someone so much who obviously didn't love me. How can I have this deep attachment to someone who has never been there for me?

And why can't I move?

Strong, familiar fingers grip both of my shoulders. I know who it is without even turning around. "It's okay, Mickey," Mama says. "He's in a better place."

That's not much of an accomplishment. Because anywhere is better than this. And anything has to be better than leaving the world in the rushed manner that he did. Two slugs to the chest. Point-blank range. He was long dead by the time the police and paramedics arrived. The sirens were just for show. He caught two not from hanging out on the street, or getting into it with a cop. He was shot by his common-law wife.

No one told me about it. I was home, watching TV, when I

heard the news. It was a typical Saturday afternoon. The Beverly Hillbillies *had just gone off, and the news came on. "In local news, earlier today, there was a fatal shooting on West Little York Street. Thirty-seven-year-old Isiah Washington was found dead outside his home, the victim of a gunshot wound following a domestic dispute with this woman. . . ." I did a double take.*

Was that my name I just heard on TV?

I knew they had to be talking about my father. How many Isiah Washingtons could there be in Houston? Later on that night, my mother told me that my father's girlfriend shot him. Apparently, he went upside her head for the last time. My mother knew that violent side of his personality all too well.

"I love you, but I can't take any more of these whuppins," my mother had told him. She said this while she packed her bags to move back to her mother (Muh Dear) and father (Pa-Pa)'s house with me and my sister, Savannah. "There's gonna be a woman out there who's not gonna take this kind of abuse from you."

As usual, Mama was right.

I looked down at my father one last time. Right near the casket were roses. And just like that, a memory came back of when I was four years old and my mother and father got into a fight. They were outside, and he pushed her into a rosebush. I remember the small cuts my mother had after that. I looked closely at the bush and saw all the thorns. Roses were supposed to be beautiful, but the only thing I could see were the thorns.

And here lay my father. But I could never see the bloom of what our relationship was supposed to be as father and son, the good times, the happy times. When I looked at his face, as I was search-ing for just one good memory of this man, all I could remember were the thorns in our relationship. He looked so much like me, but at the same time nothing like me at all. I tried to remember the good times we had, but all that really came to mind was the smell of whiskey on his breath and the waft of fresh cigarette smoke that was his personal cologne.

"I love you, Daddy," I said. The tears came fast, and profusely. I still don't know where they came from, only that I can still taste the salt. When I leaned down to kiss his cheek, it was fleshy, swollen, and ice cold. The taste reminded me of the time I picked a nickel off the living room floor as a toddler and put it in my mouth—that same metallic, sulfuric taste.

I sat back down next to my mother in the front row. While I tuned out the eulogy the preacher was giving and stared at the casket, my own mortality felt real to me for the very first time in my young life. Right then, right there, I made a few promises to myself, promises that since then have run through my mind every single day. For one, I promised myself that if I ever became a father, I would always be a part of my children's lives. They'd see me every day, and I'd be the one teaching them how to shoot a free throw, how to tie their shoes, how to comb their hair, how to look a man in the eye when you shake his hand, how not to back down from a fight, all of the things my mother and grandmother taught me. But even more than that, as I envisioned my father's last few moments on earth, the blood spurting from his chest, the smoking gun, how hard it must have been to breathe as his chest filled with bile and blood, the thoughts he must have had as he helplessly watched his life slip away from him, I considered how horrible that must have been. I made a second promise—when the time came for me to die, it was never going to be like that.

I thought about the sound of Mama and Muh Dear's voices at night when they washed the dishes together after supper. When they thought Savannah and I were watching TV or asleep, they loved to gossip about what was going on in our small, all-black section of northeast Houston, called Studewood. There was always news of something happening, and they had more breaking news than Wolf

Blitzer: who was sneaking out of whose bedroom window, who died, who got pregnant, who wore the loudest suit or biggest Sunday hat, whose kids just graduated—to college, military, or the state penitentiary. The worst thing they could say about any of the sinners— which they always said with the most damning, conspiratorial whispers—was that they were simply "triflin'-ass Negroes." To be a triflin'-ass Negro was spiritual death. The ninth circle of hell. People who committed violent crimes were held in better judgment than triflin'-ass Negroes.

They didn't even have to use the label about my father. No one ever said it. Not to my face. But they didn't have to. I took one more look at the casket. I promised myself that if anyone ever said my name on the evening news, it would be for scoring a touchdown for the Houston Oilers. I was never going to live—or die—like a triflin'-ass Negro. No way. I decided then that my name was going to mean something to the world. . . .

Something great.

There have been entire heart-wrenching books written about the issues Washington raises, such as *Whatever Happened to Daddy's Little Girl?* by Jonetta Rose Barras. We cannot forget that it is the journey that is the joy of fatherhood. Those little moments you get with your children are the reward for a well-lived life. That's what you should treasure. Don't miss those in a rush to get somewhere. If those little people are in your life, you have already gotten there. They are going to give you more unadulterated bliss than anything you could buy, any high-priced gadget or big empty house. But to get the bliss, you got to be there.

Sometimes making a point by way of poetry can be even more powerful than with prose. Certainly in the right hands, a poem can speak volumes. Author and spoken-word artist **Taalam Acey** is one of those poets who can wield his words like a scalpel, and in the following poem, which he calls "Far from the Tree," he eloquently paints a picture of the difficulties faced by kids who don't know their fathers.

You reap what you sow
And just like us some trees have seeds that are gender specific
For instance
You can't just plant an apple tree seed in the dirt and expect
it to work because there's male and female
And the proper union has to be cultivated
And just like them
Johnny can't just roam these city streets spreading his apple seeds and
hoping that they make it
And just because he learned how to convince lonely women to get naked
Then con them out of using a condom and losing
the same way he found them
It only means that his seeds are going to have a hard time trying to live
And John
I know in your mind you think you're big
But your physical form would have to be deaf dumb and blind to never
mind the fact that an Oedipus Rex often wrecks city streets
And sometimes
Estranged children catch up with deadbeats
Because you reap what you sow
And in the best-case scenario
They come back donning big names like Keyshia
Cole and Lebron James
But if she can't sing
Or he ain't got game
There's nobody in the community to help her with her homework
Or him with his book report to cultivate their brain
They just might resort to a life of crime

And in such cases
Instead of coming back donning big names
they come back donning big .45s and 9s
And then you're liable to find that the prime reason for the destruction of
black civilization is the fact that black fathers are becoming extinct
And my father's father barely knew how to locate his son
but he damn sure knew how to find a drink
And if you were looking for my father?
The best place to start was wherever I wasn't
Now, it didn't mean that I didn't have a dad
It simply means that my dad's name was Mom
And she worked overtime
Trying to find the kind of life support
Called child support
While he thought it was a good idea to lay down
Apparently he felt a diametric opposite way about staying around
And handling his business
But then you reap what you sow
And who knows
Maybe I could've been a lawyer or a dentist
But instead I branched out into a Conan the Destroyer type menace
But that was back when I was a sapling
But I've grown a lot since then
But I still spent some unnecessary nights in jail cells
before it was finished
Now raise your hand if you're not surprised
In fact, why don't you raise your hand if your father was not
quite a man in your eyes
And I met my father like five times since I been an adult,
and each time I look into his eyes I fail to recognize the type of
resemblance that my children recognize between them and I
Which is a shame, because their great-grandfather, their grandfather,
and I all gave them that last name but apparently only one of

us cared enough about their children to put them first
Them other cats must have been like yo
I'mma plant my seeds in the earth because I can
But if you don't remember anything else that
I said tonight remember this
If you can't expect your children to consider yourself a father
Then you must be absolutely out of your mind if you ever expect
anyone else in this world to ever consider you a man

CHAPTER TWO

HAPPY FEELINGS: FINDING JOY WITH YOUR CHILDREN

There I was, my long six-foot-ten-inch frame crouched in my daughter Imani's closet, wedged in between the frilly Sunday dresses, the tutus from her ballet class, all the bright and colorful garments of a lively three-year-old girl. At that moment, I was Daddy the Monster Slayer, and my job was to chase all the monsters and scary things far from Imani's bedroom so that she could go back to sleep. I jumped from the closet with a growl and started swinging wildly, hitting the invisible beasts with powerful right hooks and left uppercuts while Imani giggled and squirmed on the bed. Once again, Daddy the Monster Slayer had come to her rescue!

After I tucked her in and walked down the hallway back to my bed, the delightful, stirring sound of her giggles still fluttered in my head. It's a sound I always want to hold close to my heart. To me, that is the sound of fatherhood.

In many ways, bringing joy to our children is our reason for being. It is the force that makes our sky blue, that fills up the empty places in our hearts, that pushes us out of bed in the morning. But too often, we can lose sight of that basic fact, adrift in the tangled weeds of adult worries and responsibilities. If we aren't called to task, we can allow years to go by without ever emerging from those weeds. One morning we wake up and our children are grown and distant; we have missed the best years of fatherhood, years we will never get back.

As fathers, we have to recognize that while being there is a prerequisite for good parenthood, it's not always enough. We have to make concerted and continuous efforts to truly find happiness with our children. Joy isn't something that time will automatically bring to your doorstep, like missing teeth and puberty. No, we have to make careful plans to create joy, to nurture it, protect it.

Believe me, I know it's not always easy. For most of us, our lives almost seem to be programmed to pull us away from our children as often as possible, or to throw such a steady stream of worry and distraction at us that we can't fight off our nightly transformation into the sour Grinch. As a professional basketball player, I spend a great deal of time on the road, so I can't help but be away from my children much more than I would like. Sometimes when we return home from a road trip, I might not walk through my front door until one or two a.m., greeted only by the sound of chirping crickets. I look at the clock, those hands stuck in the lonely chasm of predawn, and I know that in a few short hours, no matter what time I finally manage to fall asleep, there is one thing I can be certain of: Come seven a.m., I will be awakened by my children bounding into my room and jumping on the bed, showing me how excited they are that I'm back home. I might have been deep into a delicious slumber, trying to restore my energy so that I'd soon be able to sprint around a basketball court. But none of that matters to my son and my daughter as they burst through our bedroom door. Daddy's home and they must see him. If it is a school day for Malcolm, he can't walk out the door without a little Daddy time. Though my first reaction may sometimes be exasperation, I can't get mad when the kiddie parade comes. I know they're just eager to see me, to jump on top of me, to fill me in on the many details of their little lives. At least now I've gotten them to the point where they sometimes let me go back to sleep. Sometimes.

When I talk to older fathers, the thing I hear most often is the need for me to take a step back and realize how precious and meaningful these moments will become in the whole arc of my life. They remind me that one day my children may grow into surly adolescents or distant teens, and then they will be off to college, out of the house, no longer an everyday presence in my life. In other words, whatever I do, make sure I don't take any of these moments for granted. Even the annoying, exasperating ones. These are words I always try to hold close, never letting them stray too far from my conscious thoughts. They are words that move me to action on those occasions when I have pushed away my children because they approached me at the wrong time. These are moments every parent can identify with—you are immersed deep in a project or chore (or just some general state of anxiety), paying bills, cooking dinner, finishing up paperwork from the office. Something that demands your undivided attention. And here comes the little one, wanting to play. Or read a book with you. Or show you the picture he just created. Or tell you a joke she made up herself. Without thinking, your first reaction is dismissal. "No, not now!" A quick brush-off. You watch him walk away, his slumped shoulders and heavy sigh displaying his disappointment. If enough of these dismissals build up, they become a bitter tower of rejection for your kid. Next thing you know, he stops coming to you, in order to shield himself from further disappointment. The next time she draws a picture, she'll just keep her satisfaction to herself. Potential moments of joy for you, gone forever.

Like everyone else, I have those moments when I let the brush-off fall from my lips. But lately I've been trying to catch it before it's out there. If I don't grab it in time, what I have been trying to do more and more is go find Malcolm and Imani and, basically, ask them for a do-over. I am greeted with a smile that spreads across Malcolm's face as I take the sixty seconds he was seeking to watch him do some new karate move, or Imani tells me a joke she has told me a million times. Her favorite joke: "Why did the bee get married?" She pauses dramatically, as if this moment is fraught with suspense, then proudly says, "Because he found his honey," and laughs hysterically. When these things happen, I am the one who experiences the jolt of pleasure—pleasure that I almost missed out on. It makes me feel horrible when I disappoint my kids. Maybe it's something left over from my childhood, when I had to battle disappointment because my own father missed so many important moments. Or maybe it's not even that deep—perhaps it's just something built into the DNA of parenthood.

Most of the time, our children aren't even looking for us to become Richard Pryor or Eddie Murphy and entertain them with an extended bit of silliness or stand-up comedy. They just want to be with us, as I discussed in the previous chapter. But they know that tucked within those moments of together time, there is always the possibility of joy—or fun, as they would describe it. I am reminded of this whenever I am about to leave my house to run an errand and I hear the *tap-tap-tap* of Malcolm's little footsteps coming in my direction, or I see him rushing to get his coat. "Daddy, can I come with you?" he asks breathlessly. In the back of my mind I am considering how much easier it would be to buy the milk and orange juice or negotiate the aisles of Target without having to keep my eye on my rambunctious, curious little boy. Little boys can do some quick and serious damage at Target. Sometimes, with the sound of crashing lightbulbs or broken flowerpots playing in my head, I might give him a little push back. "But I'm just going to the store, Malcolm." Then I'll see the shoulders start to slump and I'll pinch myself. Would it kill me to get out of my self-indulgence for a second and let my little man tag along? Easy answer: no.

Recently I got my own little surprise when I succumbed to

Malcolm's bubbly enthusiasm. One of my teammates was having a birthday party for his kid at Pump It Up, one of those places filled with inflatable slides, inflatable castles, and obstacle courses for little kids to jump themselves into a stupor. I was tired and didn't feel like going to the party, but I knew Malcolm and I had to go and represent for the Thomas family. But one thing I definitely didn't feel like doing was climbing my two hundred and sixty pounds into an inflatable castle to bounce around. But Malcolm really wanted me to jump with him, and he begged me to crawl inside that thing. With some reluctance—and more than a little difficulty—I squeezed into the inflatable contraption with him . . . and I actually had fun. The look on his face watching his rather large dad bounce up and down was something I'll never forget. It was another reminder that sometimes we need to sacrifice our own comfort, or our rest, or our unpleasant mood, and allow ourselves to step into their joy. Once I do that, I find quickly that getting rest becomes a little less important. After all, if you're so worried about rest, you can always get your behind to sleep earlier!

I once heard Kevin Garnett talk about how different he is at home than on the court, where he can sometimes be a bundle of extreme emotions. We see him screaming out in frustration on the court, or pounding his chest in exultation. But when he gets home, he's just Dad. I know exactly what he's talking about. Even though the successes and failures of pro athletes are laid out for everyone to see every night, this same principle applies to every working person who comes home after a difficult or emotional day at work. The kids simply do not care. Nor should they. We are sometimes so consumed with our problems—and admittedly these problems can often be quite consuming—that we can't see anything else. Not even that desperate little kid in front of us. They just want us to kick it with them, to show them that they are as important to us as the career, or the promotion, or the paycheck. It may even be tempting to point to the paycheck as evidence that we do love them—you know the old cliché: "The reason that I drag myself into work every day and work so hard is for the benefit of my children." But it probably doesn't look like that from their perspective if we never demonstrate our affection for them with our actions. All they see is the sour Grinch who shows them nothing more than the fact that he doesn't want them around. I will talk more about the importance of fathers showing love and affection in the next chapter, but it's all wrapped up in their joy.

For my friend **Chris Paul**, a superstar guard with the Los Angeles Clippers (formerly with the New Orleans Hornets), time spent with his little boy is all about the fun and joy. That's why it pains Chris so much to be away from his little boy when the team is on the road—something with which all of us traveling dads can definitely identify. In the following piece, Chris talks about how he tries as much as he can to be his son's primary caregiver when he's home.

I've already had so many fun times with my son, and he's only a year and a half. His name is Christopher Emanuel Paul II. Growing up, I was fortunate enough to have a mom and dad always there for me in everything I've done. But playing in the NBA, it's kind of a given that I will miss some things. I feel I was fortunate that I was there for his birth. It was in the summer, May 24, 2009, and we were not in the play-offs. I took pictures then and I'm still taking pictures of him all the time. Since I've been in the league, I've always treated my teammates' kids like they were my own. I just love kids. Now to have my own son is the best thing ever. When I'm home, I try to do everything with him. I take him to school. I pick him up from school. His first word was "Dada"; it made his mom mad.

His mom and I have been together since my freshman year of college. It's funny how our relationship has grown. When I first came into the league, I couldn't wait to go on the road. I wanted to see the world. Now I hate road trips. I can't stand leaving my family. As soon as I get into the room on the road, I get on Skype. My son will kiss the computer; he'll run up and give me five on the computer. But it's bittersweet—it's great I get the opportunity to see him, but it's tough that I'm not there. I just always want to be there. I know when he gets older there will be things that I will miss, like games that he's playing in. That's one of things you love to hate about the NBA.

He already has a hoop, and when you tell him to shoot, he'll do the hand motion like he's following through. He will go up to the hoop and dunk it. He knows the chants at our Hornets games. He goes to school here in New Orleans, and his teachers have been talking to us about him developing more words. In school, anytime he saw a basketball or any ball, he'd say, "Dada." But his teachers want him to say "ball," not "Dada." So when I got back from a road trip last week, he was saying "ball" now. Ball. Ball.

As far as him playing ball himself, I think about it all the time. The best thing I could do is go from what I saw with my dad. My dad was always my coach when I was growing up. You could take a lot of good things from watching him. At end of the day, I play in the NBA, so my son will be around basketball all the time. But I never want to force it on him. I want him to enjoy what he wants to enjoy. I tell people all the time that I think I want him to have a baseball or a golf club in his hands, for the longevity.

I'm so glad I was there to see his first step. Those are things I don't take for granted. We were actually in the passport office, a week before his first birthday. His mother, my mom, and I had just been saying that he needed to start walking, because we couldn't be carrying him around at his first birthday party. So there we were, waiting at the passport office. He was standing and holding on to my knee. The lady who works in the office said, "Come here," and don't you know that little joker took off walking! He took five or six *steps. We were hot. We were happy but mad, since we had been trying all this time to get him to walk. Now we can't even get him to hold our hand. He wants to walk and run everywhere.*

I wrote a children's book called Long Shot: Never Too Small to Dream Big *that came out just around the time that he was born. It's crazy now to read the book to him, because he's looking through it and looking at all the pictures of a book that I wrote. It's surreal.*

NBA players get stereotyped that we just make our wives do everything with the kids. But I'm so against that. When I'm home, I'm going to pick him up from school. I put him to sleep, take him in the bathroom and bathe him. Those things are priceless. Even though we have it tough with the traveling, a lot of times our wives and significant others are somewhat overlooked. It's so tough to watch a small child every single day, especially if you have more than one. When we go on the road, we can go in our room and shut the door, and it's just us. Sometimes our significant others need that personal alone time, too. When I'm home, I try to give her that. When we get home from the road and have a day off, I always tell her, "Little Chris is staying out of school today. I got a day off."

But she fights it. "No, he has to go to school," she says.

I beg her. Please.

For a lot of part-time fathers, their time with their kids often gets tied up in the issue of child support. Sometimes this is the idea of the mom, who decides that the father can't see the kids unless he has some child support money in his hand. But I know that sometimes it can be the dads who are a rare presence in the lives of their kids because they are embarrassed by the child support arrears. While this situation is common, it is tragic. Because that kid doesn't care about these adult matters like child support and arrears—all he wants is time with his daddy. The fights over money, while understandable, can quickly pull the focus away from the person this was all supposed to be about—the child. This may sound a little naive to some, since the real world is a complicated place, especially when we factor in relationship dramas and hurt feelings. But that's precisely the point: We make all of this way too complicated when it comes to children. Let that child experience some joyful moments with her dad on a regular basis and the world will look like a significantly brighter place to her.

It doesn't take long for me to notice how clingy my children get when they don't get enough time with me. It's as if their emotional well-being requires a certain amount of Daddy time to maintain a state of equilibrium. So when I return from a lengthy trip, they crave as much contact as they can get. Under such circumstances, it would be cruel for me to push them away if they haven't gotten enough time with me. I am blessed to have a wife who can give me constant reminders of the need to cherish every second with my children while they are young. And I hope that I can be responsible for passing it along to other men who are in similar positions—men who may be tempted to put other concerns ahead of the kids.

Speaking of other concerns, let me take a moment to mention something that seems to be growing into an ever-larger problem in American society—cell phones. Those dastardly minicomputers that we all carry around with us have taken the form of a deadly virus in our families and relationships, sucking all the joy out of the room. The more time that we spend with them around our children and significant others, the weaker our bonds become. I have taken to actually turning my phone off when I go into the kids' rooms for our nightly bedtime ritual. The ritual consists of me telling Anansi the Spider stories—just like my grandmother used to tell me when I was little. I will even use my grandmother's West Indian dialect when doing the characters. When I'm finished, they have to tell me the moral of the story. Then they say their prayers and I sit with them for a few minutes until they are ready to go to sleep. This is their special time with Daddy, and I just can't have a phone getting in the way. Whatever or whoever is on the phone can wait until our ritual is over. My children need to know that they are important enough to get my undivided time, more important than the world that is waiting for me inside the phone. Because we aren't fooling anybody when we try to do both at once—scroll through the e-mails but look up at the kid every few seconds when he's trying to tell you a story. You think that kid doesn't know that he's competing with something? I know how distracting it can be when I'm trying to talk to my wife or to a teammate or colleague and they are looking down at their phone while I'm talking. I can imagine that it must be quite disheartening for a little person to experience that. When I was little, I eagerly awaited the time when my mother would put aside the class papers she was grading and put all her focus on me and my brother, Julian. We didn't have cell phones back then; I can't imagine how disappointing it would have been if Mom proceeded to put her paperwork down and then pick up her phone when she was supposed to be playing with us. I might have been tempted to do exactly what Malcolm started doing to me a couple of years ago when I was spending too much time immersed in phone world. My phone kept disappearing on me, and I had no idea what was going on. I would scour the house, to no avail. Then when I'd get the house phone and call my cell phone, I would find it in odd places, places that had Malcolm written all over them—under his toy chest, under his bed. He was only three at the time. I kept asking myself, *Why is my phone under his bed?* Then one day it dawned on me—he was hiding the phone from me because I was spending too much time on it. I wasn't bringing that special Daddy joy into his life when my eyes were riveted on the little phone screen. The phone was his competition, and, in his own three-year-old way, he was burying the competition! I must say, I was impressed by the initiative he demonstrated at such a tender age. And I was a little embarrassed that I had driven my little man into taking such drastic action.

This whole issue of joyful time with the kids can be even more challenging for a professional athlete. Our schedules are very regimented, sometimes down to the minute. And when we are home, that is when we are supposed to get rest. Basically it's considered part of our job. If we fly back home to Atlanta after playing in Utah and I hit the house at two a.m., I still will likely have practice the next morning. So when they come into the room at seven to say, "Hi," that is cutting severely into my rest time before practice. What I usually do is try to take a nap after practice before they get home from school, but I know that I am often not operating with the amount of sleep I need. Surely it's the same for many parents out there with young children—we spend the first decade of our children's lives in a state of perpetual sleep deprivation. It's funny, because you can usually tell which players have young kids—they're the ones who are sleeping on the plane or the bus or whatever mode of transportation we're taking to our next destination. We look forward to the road trips; that's when we get to catch up on the shut-eye. When I was a young player on the Washington Wizards, I used to wonder why the older guys were asleep all the time. We'd be on the plane playing cards, watching movies, having a good time, and you'd look back at the older guys and they'd be in deep snore. Knocked out. I would be thinking, *Man, what is* wrong *with y'all?* All they seemed to care about was grabbing some food and then grabbing some sleep. But now I understand. It was all about the kids. Now I'm one of those guys, with three little ones at home. When I hit the house, there's no guarantee that I'm going to be able to find rest anytime soon. So I have to get it whenever I can. If you ever run into me on a plane, I'll be the guy whose snores are as loud as the jet engine.

Pro athletes can exert a lot of control over our surroundings, but the one thing we can't control is our kids. And that's okay. These years when our children are young won't be given back to us. So sometimes that means we have to sacrifice things like rest and sleep in order to maximize kid time, to allow them to think of you with a smile. We don't want to be so focused on the job that we forget about the things that are most important. You don't want to be the guy listening to his teenage son explain how he became a juvenile delinquent and, when the kid says he didn't get enough time with his father during those formative years, your response is, "But I averaged ten rebounds a game!" Sure, accomplishments are nice, and your kids love to brag about you to their friends, but I'm certain most of them would trade the Daddy accomplishments in a heartbeat if they could be replaced with meaningful and consistent Daddy face time, with Daddy joy. In the documentary *Listen Up*, about the life of the legendary Quincy Jones, his oldest daughter, Jolie, was reflecting on the fateful decision that Quincy made when she was young to leave his wife, Jeri, and Jolie behind while he went to Hollywood to pursue a career in scoring films. Of course it turned out to be a great decision for his career—the man has won twenty-seven Grammys!—but as for the wife and child . . . not so much. Jolie said, "You can't do a career like he's done and still be the perfect father." What she was saying was that in order to become the legendary producer, Quincy made some painful sacrifices. And she was one of them.

One thing I don't want to do is give the impression that spending time with my children is a chore. The truth is quite the opposite. Nothing is more infectious than the joy of children. It's as if they are programmed for fun; they have an internal GPS that allows them to find fun whenever it's within a hundred-foot radius. Bring your child to the park and watch him sweep his gaze across the fields and trees and animals; when he spots something that might qualify as "fun," he hones in like a hound on the scent of a rabbit. In the blink of an eye, he's off! And they are incredibly creative in finding their fun, locating plenty where it doesn't seem like there's any. I bet my kids could find a carnival in an abandoned building. That's why Christmas morning can be so hilarious when you have little ones— they can find many more moments of joy with the box or the wrapping paper than the $79 toy that was wrapped inside. When I call my wife and she's in the car with the kids or out at Chuck E. Cheese or somewhere like that, you can hear the kids in the background, squealing, laughing, having the time of their lives. Whenever I step into their space, I quickly find myself laughing too. And I try not to hold back. When my daughter Imani invites me to have a tea party with her, I'm going all in. I will slip the scarf around my neck or wear whatever frilly thing she tells me to wear, and I will somehow squat my frame into her miniature chair. Imani will be thrilled to no end. My God, that look on her face! I know this is an image that will stay with her forever—I know the image of her face will always stay with me.

This joy that our children can bring to us fathers is an emotion so strong that at times it can seem otherworldly. Veteran actor **Taye Diggs** told me he is still in heaven over the birth of his son, Walker. In the following piece, he talks about how much joy Walker has brought to him.

When you have a child—and I can't speak for everyone, but definitely for myself—and when your first child is a son, it's a little extra-special. Experiencing the father-son dynamic is a feeling I have trouble putting into words—it's almost indescribable.

My son, Walker, is starting to do everything now. He's starting to talk. His communication skills are really impressive—and I'm not just saying that because he's my son. They really are impressive. We put a little basketball in his hands and he's dunking on his little hoop. Every day I come home from work he has learned something new. He is exactly how I have fantasized that he would be. Growing up and watching other people's children, I always envisioned my son being attracted to sports and athletics—and as soon as he could grip the ball, he was throwing it around. As soon as he could bend his knees or stand up, even when he was holding on to something for support, he was dancing and feeling the rhythm of the music. Whenever there is anything even remotely rhythmical around him, he stops what he's doing and starts to dance. And his smile . . . Whenever he smiles, it's as if I am being blessed; as if an angel is actually blessing me. It's humbling. It makes me feel small and humble and grateful and things I never expected to feel.

I attempt to rock him to sleep sometimes, but of course his mama has a special effect that I don't have. He relates me to play-time. My wife tells me not to get him all excited and energized right before he is about to hit the hay, but I can't help it. Especially if I haven't seen him all day, I just have to get a little time and see that smile, because no matter what has happened throughout the course of my day, his smile makes everything better. It calms my spirit and my soul.

Sometimes I just stare at him while he is asleep and I think about all of the things I want to teach him. I tend to overthink things. Sometimes I have to take everything a day at a time and trust my support system around me and let everything come as it is supposed to. I have to tell myself that or else I will get overwhelmed. There is so much that I've learned that I have benefited from; there's so much that I had to learn on my own; there is so much I'm learning now. You want what's impossible for your children. You want them to have a perfect life; grow up to be a perfect person; for people to be perfect to him; and for him to make a perfect imprint in this world. And of course that is impossible. I want to show him the perfect love that exists between a husband and wife. I want to be the perfect role model and example for him. We strive to get as close to perfection in every aspect that we can, but that's when I slow myself down and just say to myself, One day at a time.

I just turned forty a couple of days ago, and at my age you figure that you have felt most of the emotions that you are going to feel in life. You've experienced death, love, heartbreak, etc. But when your child is born, there is no possible way to be prepared. My body actually freaked out a little bit. It's a love that is almost violent and heartbreaking, because you can't imagine loving anything else this much. You can be stuck in a moment of joy, but then at the same time it's kind of tinged with this ridiculous fear, because you love this child so much that you don't want anything bad to ever happen to him. So that freaked me out.

At the childbirth I was next to my wife's face, helping her breathe and relax. She did a completely natural childbirth. And after I saw the complete miracle of birth, I simply told my wife that I will be in her debt for the rest of my life. Watching her undergo that process changes your entire level of respect for women. That was a proud moment for me, and a feeling of joy that my woman had accomplished this feat. She climbed this mountain of childbirth and produced a miracle whose name is Walker Nathaniel Diggs.

I'm not even sure my daughter Imani really hears monsters in her closet anymore. Perhaps she did when she was younger, but I think the reason she summons me now to slay the monsters is because she just wants to have Daddy in her room, hiding in her closet, jumping around in front of her. I'm her protector, and she enjoys the feeling of putting me to work. You can tell when your kids are really scared. I see that glint in my daughter's eye now; it's a giveaway that what's going on is a bit of Daddy manipulation. But it's some Daddy manipulation that I will always volunteer for. I want her to think of me as her protector, so these early sessions with the monsters perhaps are training for later on, when she really needs me. Once, Malcolm came into our room and woke me up to say that there was a monster outside his window. I turned over and told him to go back to sleep. "No, there's really a monster outside my window!" he said. I could tell right away that the little guy was actually scared. There was no manipulation going on here. When I went to investigate, I saw that there was actually a deer outside his window, eating leaves or something. He had reason to be scared. If I heard something moving around outside my window, I wouldn't have been too happy about it either.

Sometimes when I take Malcolm to the park or to a basketball court somewhere and I'm encouraging him and giving him pointers, I can see another little boy or two watching us. There's a certain look on their faces that is painful to see, because I know that look so well. It's the envy of a boy who doesn't have a father in the house to bring him to the park. I know it so well because it's a look that used to be on my face when I was a little boy seeing some other kid playing with his father. When I spot it on another kid when I'm out with Malcolm, it cuts me to the quick. But I try to shake it off so that I can focus on my son. It is amazing how much our children crave our encouragement and praise. As soon as I compliment Malcolm on a shot, his whole body language changes. His chest puffs out a little bit more; he gets this magical smile on his face. This is the epitome of bringing him joy. It's so easy; it doesn't cost me a thing. But its worth is priceless. Parents have a power that is unequaled by anything else in a child's life. I hurt for the kids who don't know that.

I have distinct memories of my mother playing with me and Julian when we were little. She would be tired after a long day at school, she'd have a ton of things to do, but she'd still manage to set aside time for us. She would go outside in the backyard with us and play catch, grabbing a glove and tossing a ball back and forth. Or she would watch us while we showed her a new move we had mastered on the basketball court. I would love to sit down at the piano and show her a new song I had learned how to play. It tickled me to see the smile spread across her face. My mother has always been extremely musical, so there would always be music playing in our house in Tulsa—jazz, reggae, gospel. And sometimes my mother would have us dance with her in the living room. I can still remember all of us—me, her, and Julian—doing the electric slide together. I'm dating myself a bit, but I was really into break dancing when I was little. So I was always real anxious to show her some new move I had mastered, spinning on my back or doing something I had seen

Ozone and Turbo do in the movie *Breakin'*. The memories will always live inside of me. It's decades later, but I guess I still love to hear her praise and approval. When I have some great news to report in my life, it's not going to be long before I get on the phone to my mom. I guess it's a parent thing.

Talk about wonderful memories—this next piece by veteran ESPN broadcaster **Stuart Scott** is a moving tribute to some of Stuart's most loving memories with his two daughters. Every time I read this piece, I can virtually feel the emotion coming off the page—the joy Stuart gets from his children and from the fact that he is still here to enjoy every day with them despite his health challenges. After reading this, I won't ever look at Stuart Scott the same way when I see him behind that desk on ESPN. My connection to him is so much deeper just knowing he is capable of expressing such powerful emotion.

I have two daughters, Taelor, age seventeen, and Sydni, age twelve, and I can tell you I've had a million happy times with them. When they're young, they love you up and down. Every time you walk in the door, they yell, they scream, they sprint to you. As they get older that kind of subsides. A lot of times, you feel kind of bad about it. You walk in and you get, "Hey, how are ya?" You're thinking, Why don't you run up and hug me anymore? So it makes the times when they do that real special.

Some of the best times we have, the three of us together, are when we're just being silly and stupid. They like the TV show Glee. I'll put the Glee CD on in the car, and we're screaming and singing at the top of our lungs, rolling down the street. When we get to a stoplight, my youngest and I keep singing. My oldest daughter will reach over and turn the volume down and tell us to stop singing. My youngest and I are like, "No, we're gonna sing."

Everyone says this and it sounds like a cliché, but it really isn't: There's nothing like being a father with daughters. One of the cool-

est things my girls and I do every year is a daddy-daughter vacation. We've been doing this for seven or eight years. My best friend from college, he's also got a daughter named Sidney, who is two months older than mine. So it's usually me and him and our three girls. My brother has a daughter eight months older than my oldest, and they came with us last summer to New York. We've done L.A., Aspen, Florida a couple of times. We go for a week and it's a blast. Last year in New York, we went to the zoo for a day, we went to Broadway shows, and we went to a Yankee game. None of the girls cared much about going to the baseball game, but it happened to be the game where A-Rod hit his six hundredth home run. None of them are baseball fans, but they understood it was a piece of history they got to see live. My oldest daughter put on her Facebook page that "I saw history today." She could care less about baseball, but that was cool.

For me, a lot of the happy times are the simplest things in the world. They sit on your heart. My youngest daughter is a big soccer player; her U11 team won the state cup championship. Last week at soccer practice, she got hit in the chest with the ball and then she sprained her Achilles tendon. We're walking off the field. She doesn't grab my hand nearly as much as she used to. But we're walking and she's limping and she grabs my hand and puts her head on my shoulder as we're walking to the car. That was the best feeling I had all week. It was quiet; it was subtle. She's getting to be that age where, like her sister, she doesn't want as much affection, but it was like, I need to lean on you right now, Dad, and I'm glad you're here. I was blown away by it. They both know I'm an emotional sap, one of those superemotional guys.

I tell people sometimes that although I write for a living, I still have never been able to find words to describe the feeling of them, having them, loving them—I can't describe it. It's the only thing in my life that every moment I am aware, conscious, and cognizant that I am a father; they are the two most important things to me on the face of the earth. Loving your children is a feeling; it's an action; it's a verb. Literally it's emotions you feel can knock you over. I know that sounds crazy.

I'm battling cancer now for the second time. Three years ago I had it; I beat it. I promised them three years ago and I promised them this time that our life will not change. I'm still gonna work, still gonna work out. We're still gonna live our life and we're gonna have a positive attitude. I have chemo every other week. The weeks of chemo are rough; off weeks are better. I call them bye weeks. On a Tuesday recently, I blasted a workout that day. I killed it. I was doing this P90X exercise routine and I felt better that day than any day since before the surgery. I told this to my oldest daughter. On her Facebook page, she wrote, "Dad felt his strongest today since surgery. He had his best workout. Dad said, Cancer, in your face." She told me about it the next day. Once you have a daughter who is sixteen years old, her life is her life, and it seems like you're not as much a part of it—even though you know you are and you know she counts on you. For her to put that on her Facebook page . . . I had to sit down when she told me that. It knocked me over. It was amazing.

One night my youngest daughter was sick. She knew I wasn't feeling great that day. It was a couple of months after my surgery this time. In the middle of the night I hear her coughing. She's in her bathroom sitting on the floor, kinda crying a little bit. She said, "I can't breathe." Her nose was stopped up. She said she couldn't lie down and breathe and sleep. I said, "Why didn't you wake me up?" She said, "Because I knew you weren't feeling well." I lost it. I sat down on the floor of the bathroom with her. I said, "You al-ways wake me up when you're not feeling well. I'm going to sit here on this floor with you all night, if it takes all night." I said, "I'm not going to sleep until you go to sleep. If you want me to sit here, then we will sit up here together." We sat there a half hour. I gave her some medicine. When she said she was ready to go back to bed, she went back in her room. I said, "You want me to go back to my room or you want me to grab a pillow and lie here on the floor until you go to sleep?" She said, "Dad, grab a pillow and lie on the floor next to my bed until I go to sleep." I said, "Done. I'll do it." The whole time, I knew I had a busy day ahead of me and I had to get up at six to take them to school. But you don't care at all; you don't care a tiny bit. You just do it, and you enjoy doing it. If somebody had said, "Here's a million dollars cash, tax-free, if you just put her in bed and go back to your room," I would have said, "I don't want the money. I'm going to sit up with her until she's ready to go to sleep." You do it every time. You won't do that for anybody else in the world.

This connection is serious. With men who have kids who don't have that connection, part of the problem is, some men were never taught that kind of connection is good. They were taught either that's the mother's role, that's not cool, or they have to be the tough guy. It's almost like it's embedded in them—I'm losing my manhood if I get silly-sweet emotional. Man, it's the opposite. You're more of a man when you show your daughters everything. The funny thing is, your kids know you better in some ways than you want them to know you. My daughters know that when it comes to them and expressing my love for them and sentimental things, I'm stupidly emotional. But they also know that when it comes to protecting them, I can be an idiot. There are times they've said, "I wouldn't want anybody to do anything to us, because I'd be scared of what you'd do to them."

In my business, when you do things and you have a public name, you get used to people, fans, who don't realize they're being rude, coming up and talking to you. They don't mean it the wrong way, but they might be interrupting a conversation you're having, and they don't say, "Excuse me." On the surface it seems like the rudest thing in the world. It happens when I'm with the girls fairly regularly. I will always turn to the person and say, "You've got to wait." Then I'll turn back to my daughters and I won't rush them through whatever conversation we're having. I won't say, "Hurry up." I will finish talking to them and have that person stand there and wait. The biggest reason I do it is I want to let them know, when you have my time and attention, somebody can't come up and take it. Even though they say, "It's okay, Dad; go talk to them," I don't want to do that. I want them to know somebody can't take my attention away from them just because.

I appreciate Etan giving me the opportunity to talk about this. I'm glad he's doing this to show men, especially black men, that this is what it's about. More than fame, more than money, our life more than anything is about being a father.

I am trying to form the kind of vivid, joyful memories that Stuart writes about with my kids now. For Malcolm, it's all about the karate. My little man is obsessed with this show called *Avatar: The Last Airbender*, although by the time you're reading this, I'm sure he will be on to a new obsession. But for now it's *Avatar* and karate. When the show comes on, there's a whole fighting sequence that Malcolm has memorized. He wants me to stand up and do the moves with him, so I have to do it. He looks so intense when he's doing his moves, like he knows he's engaged in a life-or-death battle with the forces of evil. And as soon as it's finished, we can sit down and watch the show. Imani's favorite shows are *Rugrats*, *The Backyardigans*, *My Little Pony*, and *Little Bill*. One *Rugrats* episode featured Chuckie, a character on the show, successfully using the potty. This thrilled Imani, because she had recently learned to do the same thing. She kept saying, "I went to the potty like Chuckie!" And what a great day it was when she learned how to use the potty.

We made a big deal out of it in the house, dancing around and singing the "Pee-pee in the Potty" song. She was so proud of herself. It was a fun day that will always stay in my head. I can vividly picture all of it.

I got another example last year of the power of positive reinforcement with Malcolm. This time it happened on the soccer field. Now, let me say first of all that I'm no soccer player. By now we all know what I do for a living. Kicking the ball is nowhere in my job description. But I try to do the best I can now that my son is taking to the sport, so I'll get out there and kick the ball around with his team. We had a bit of an issue when Malcolm went to the initial tryouts. When the kids were all gathered together, the other parents began to protest that Malcolm was too big to play with their children. I told them that he was the same age as everybody else and that he was just as clueless as the other kids. He was just big for his age. But they wouldn't hear it. So I brought him over to the older group, where the kids were about his size. Because most of them had played before, they were doing all kinds of tricks with the ball that Malcolm had never seen before. They looked really advanced. I could tell that he was intimidated. He said, "I don't think I can do it." So I took him over to the side, where we could ponder our next move. I began to show him how to kick the ball with the side of his foot and how to stop it with his toe. I kept telling him, "Good, Malcolm!" As I'm encouraging him, I could see him begin to fill with confidence, like it's being pumped inside of him. Soon, he was ready. He marched right over there and played with the big kids, and he did fine. It was so simple, yet so powerful. I gave him a little confidence and boom! He's ready. That's some serious stuff. My kids are young, so I know these incidents will only get more intense as they get older.

Speaking of kids getting older, smooth R & B crooner **Will Downing** has seen his children grow up and, in the case of his firstborn, have a child of his own. So Will has seen every stage of fatherhood—the good, the bad, and the ugly. But throughout it all, the entire experience has still been immensely joyful.

Parenting has given me the most gratifying moments I've had in my life. But there's also a great deal of stress. When I first became a parent I had a full head of wavy hair—now I'm bald! When your kids are small, you're their hero. They want to be around you twenty-four hours a day; they have a thousand questions; in their minds you can do anything. You are the smartest guy on the planet. But somehow you go from sugar to s#*t. You start as a hero, but the years go by, and a hero to them becomes, well . . . just a sandwich. If you have little ones, be prepared. It's coming—you won't be exempt. Because eventually they hit the teenage years. When they're young, they want to sit with you for hours to watch TV or a movie, but now they want nothing to do with you. When you go to the mall, they want you to walk two, three, four steps behind them and act like you don't know them. Before, they wanted to talk to you all the time; you couldn't shut them up. Now they got nothing for you. They come in the house and you ask them, "Hey, what's going on?" "Nothing." "Want to go to a movie?" "Nah." They have no words. But when their friends call, they have diarrhea of the mouth; they can't stop talking.

You try to teach them, but at some point kids are going to do what they're going to do. They hit a certain age and they think they are adults. I have a nineteen-year-old and she now has so many tattoos, she looks like a billboard. I try to tell her, "I think you're making a big mistake. When you're going for job interviews, you're going to have to cover all that stuff up." You just have to keep advising them until they get it. You see things about to happen and you warn them, but . . . they do it anyway. You wonder at times, "Are they ever gonna get it? Are they listening?" You talk with them and they look at you as if you're speaking a foreign language. But then one day it happens. They do something that you've been trying to get them to understand and it's a feeling like no other. Accomplishment! My oldest serves proudly in the U.S. Navy; my second-oldest is in school pursuing a career in medicine; and my youngest is following in my footsteps in entertainment.

I had my oldest son when I was only nineteen years old. It was the biggest wake-up call I ever had in my life. I had a nothing job— a job that paid me enough to go out on the weekends. That was my life. All that changed the moment when my girlfriend came home and said, "I'm pregnant." Those few minutes of pleasure you might have had turn into a lifetime of responsibility. Everything changes. You're not partying the way you used to; you're not coming and going; any extra money you had before—all of that is gone. You aren't going anywhere by yourself. Everything you do now has to be calculated based on this new arrival you have in your life forever.

But it actually worked out well for me. It made me focus on my career. I sat down and said to myself, What do you want to do; how will you get there? I wasn't qualified to do anything other than sing. In a warped way, my son and I grew up together. I wasn't an old man who couldn't participate in his life. I could teach him to play ball; as he got older we started listening to music together and found out we had similar tastes.

It worked out for me, but don't get it twisted: I was scared to death. Fortunately I had good family support—a mom, dad, and siblings who all helped me raise that first child together. We were all responsible for making him who he is today. Now I'm a grandfather—he's twenty-five and has a child of his own. He's seeing exactly what I went through. He called me three weeks ago to tell me the baby was here. He said, "I understand the reason you were the way you were. I get it now; I totally get it." After a lifetime of responsibility and giving up a portion of my life with him, it all paid off with that one line.

To spend as much fun time with my son as possible, I've figured out a way to incorporate Malcolm into my off-season workouts. This really gives him a thrill, because he feels like he's helping me with my work. It's the ultimate Take Your Kids to Work Day. Malcolm's job will be to get a basketball and place it somewhere on the court. From the half-court line, I run to the ball and either shoot it or do a move from the spot where I picked it up. Malcolm will then retrieve the ball and place it somewhere else while I go back to half-court and do it again. When we've done this for a while, he will go take a swig from his water bottle and towel off, imitating me.

Though my son is crazy about sports, the one thing I will not do is push him into playing. I will not be Joe Jackson, berating and scolding and beating my kids to success. I trained at a basketball camp down in Sarasota, Florida, at a place called IMG, and there I met a lot of young kids who were at the tennis camp. Some of them were as young as seven, working out as hard as professional athletes. I asked them if they even liked tennis anymore; they said, "No, we hate it, we just do it because our parents want us to!" I said, "That's terrible!" That certainly won't be Malcolm or my daughters. Malcolm finds so much joy in playing sports right now, it would be horrible to take all that pleasure away from him by turning it into a chore.

With Imani, it's all about ballet. When she learns a new move and she wants to show me, she'll run and put on the whole outfit first, tutu and all. With Imani, everything has to be just right. So in full costume, tutu, pink tights, she'll show me her little pirouette, something they did in class, her face proud and beaming. Watching her, my heart is full.

I even have a ritual with Sierra, the baby. When she is upset and we're having difficulty getting her to sleep, I will place her on my chest. For some reason, when she feels the vibration of my chest, rising and falling, it will calm her down and eventually lull her into a slumber. Those are precious, delicious moments for me—the world is quiet, tuned out, everything focused on me and the delicate little creature perched on my chest. I can hear her soft breaths when she is finally knocked out, sweet whispers as melodic as a harp, slowly sending me along with her into the warm, contented arms of sleep.

In the following poem, called "Dear Father," **J. Ivy** explores the pain, heartache, and eventual forgiveness of his father. In the end, J. Ivy recalls a joyful time that takes him to the place he wants to be.

These words are being written and spoken because my heart and soul
    feel broken
I laugh to keep from crying but I still haven't healed after all of my
    years of my goofiness and joking
You got me open
Hoping this ill feeling will pass
Won't last
I'll wear a mask
So my peeps won't ask for the truth
Truthfully speaking the truth hurts
But I'm beyond hurtin'
I'm in pain
And when I was a shorty I thought you left because I wouldn't behave
Later on in life I found out that it was the cane
As well as other thangs
And with all the scars
I learned it was hard
And I learned to forgive and forgave

I forgave you despite the fight for tears
For all the years lost
Wondering if I was loved
Sometimes all I needed was a call and a hug
I mean, I understand that people break up and don't make up

And some relationships don't last forever but
Why weren't we together?
Ma could've found a new man but where was I gonna find a new dad?
Looking back I wish I would've begged and pleaded my case
Because I felt like I didn't matter like I was deleted and erased
I would cry still cry so much that I would get headaches
I would try to get you off of my mind but I can't get you off of my face
I see you every time I see me
And I can't do nothin' but ask God to bless me
Because my love is amputated
My life is complicated
My family became dysfunctional

I remember
I remember how you pushed Ma and she broke her ankle
And I was sitting there thinking
How could you do this to such a beautiful angel?
I remember Ma waking us up in the middle of the night saying
Ssshhhhhhh
Jimmy put some clothes in the jewels bag
We're going over to Grandma's
And if your father comes to your school don't tell him where we'll be
I remember spending Christmas at Grandma's playing with my
     Stretch Armstrong, Thinking man, this ain't my house
How did Santa Claus find me?
I remember your stinky feet.
I remember all the pepper you would put in those ghetto meals,
that you would fix for us to eat.
I remember listening to you on the radio . . . "WVON,"
Before I would go to school.
I remember those cars and planes you would make,
And all the kids on the block thought that my dad was so cool.
I remember when you ran down the car,

And I was thinking, "Damn, Dad's fast!"
I remember how you would curl your mustache.
I remember . . . I remember the past.
I remember the good and the bad.
But the little boy in me still wants his daddy badly
I feel like a scared little boy afraid to become a man when
*   I think I'm ready*
All I ever wanted to do was to make you and Ma proud,
And I wonder if you are; I wonder if you know.
I wonder if you know that God gave me a Gift.
I wonder if you know about the Spirits that I Lift.
I wonder if you know that I touch People with my Words.
I wonder if you know that I inspire action with my Verbs!
I wonder if you know that your Baby Boy did a show,
that aired for millions to see on HBO,
And that hard-ass New York crowd that I didn't even know,
Actually gave me a standin' O!!
I know you know! I know you're proud!
Cause I'm a be the best just like you wanted to be.
Watch and see.
And just in case you can't, I'm a scream it so loud that
*   I shake the clouds,*
And move 'em out the way of my Sunshine.
'Cause that's what you are, Dad,
You are my Sunshine!
James Ivy Richardson, Sr. . . . Do you hear me!
You are my Sunshine!
That's why I forgave you!
My Love for you is still the same.
It may have gone through a transformation,
But it never really changed,
So I swear on my Mama and on my Name,
I'm going to stop this rain!

Conquer this pain!
Make sure that you did not die in vain!
And when I get to Heaven . . .
When I get to Heaven,
I'm going to jump in your arms,
We're going to kick back, like when I was little,
And watch the Bears game!
I love you Dad

CHAPTER THREE

STRONGER THAN PRIDE: SHOWING LOVE TO YOUR CHILDREN

Daddy love. It is undoubtedly one of the world's most powerful forces, a phenomenon as profound as the beams of the sun, as transformational as the rains that enable life. When I began thinking about this book on fathers, the prevalence and destructiveness of anger was a propelling force, but the power of love was always its counterpoint. They are the twin poles of parenthood, the two sides of the same coin. Where there is no love, there surely will be anger. When there is no anger, love is abundant.

From the moment we are old enough to distinguish between mother and father, our most pervasive instinct after feeding our hunger is craving their love. Mother love becomes the most reliable element in our lives, the comforting presence that can heal all wounds. Whenever we look up, it is there—so much so that it might even be taken for granted. Father love, because of its impermanence, its fleeting, flitting movements, becomes our obsession, the assurance that we're always seeking, the approval that we need to help us define who we are. When it is missing, the loss is devastating.

Music has always played an important role in my life, something that often has helped me to work out confusing or over-whelming feelings. This subject is no different. Immediately I think about a song that blew me away from the first moment I heard it—Beyoncé's "Daddy." It still gives me chills every time I hear it. When I listen to those lyrics, I think about my daughters, Imani and Sierra. I was even moved to write the lyrics down. When Beyoncé sings, "I want my unborn son to be like my daddy; I want my husband to be like my daddy," I am so deeply moved by the love dripping from those words. It just stops me in my tracks and makes me say, "Wow. That's how I want my daughters to think about me, to look at me, to view me."

She goes on to say that her father has given her so much security throughout her life that she doesn't even have the words to describe the gratitude she feels, knowing he will always be there to protect her through her mistakes, disappointments, and pain. Now, that is the kind of relationship I want with my daughters. It's all spelled out for me in this song. Beyoncé hit the nail right on the head with her description of that special relationship between father and daughter. She talks about the confidence and security that her father's love has given her, and I can't overemphasize this point, how important it is to me: If we fathers do our job correctly, we actually create a shield for our daughters, almost like bodily armor that they can use whenever they might be halted by fear, whenever they might wonder if they have the stuff that might be needed to achieve their loftiest goals.

I have little girls, so I haven't gone through all the difficulty of the teenage years and come out on the other side of that. But I listen to this song and I know what I want. I want little Imani and little Sierra to grow up one day and say these words about me. Beyoncé says, "Even if my man broke my heart today; no matter how much pain I'm in I will be okay." Beyoncé tells us that her father has given her a strength that stretches all the way into her adulthood, an insulation from hurt, because she will always have the unconditional love of her father out there wrapping her in its embrace, no matter what drama some dude might bring her way. I just love hearing that! So as I set about to fathering my girls over the coming decades, I will have these words playing in the back of my mind, like a powerful soundtrack to my fatherhood.

Having daughters can definitely bolster your dedication to your kids, because as a man you've seen so many cases of girls and women who didn't have father love. We all remember those girls in high school and college whom the guys would point to and say, "She has daddy issues." What that meant was that she was so clingy and needy, so desperately yearning for affection from males, that guys knew they could say anything and do anything to her. She was down for whatever. So she ends up giving her most prized possession to cats to get the kind of love and connection from a man that she craves. How horrible that must be as a father, to have your daughter run to another man to get the love she needed from you. That is devastating to even imagine.

NBA star **Derek Fisher** received a great deal of praise during the 2007 Western Conference semifinals when he decided to skip a play-off game to be by his daughter's side as she underwent surgery for eye cancer. It was a decision that got a great deal of media attention and, in many ways, has become one of the defining moments of Fisher's stellar career—during which he has won an amazing five championships and served as president of the NBA Players Association. In the following piece, Fisher talks about growing up with his father's strong sense of discipline and how his love for his children will always trump a basketball game.

When I was growing up, my relationship with my father was very solid. He was an extremely strong presence in my life. An ex-military man, he was there with us every day, strict and methodical, smart and savvy; he was the boss in our house. We had rules that we had to abide by in order to live under his roof, but behind that tough exterior was a man who truly loved us. He wanted the best for his children, and he would not fail us.

His father, my grandfather, passed away when my father was very young, so he made sure that he gave me the things that he missed growing up. I know for a fact that without the lessons that my father taught me—discipline, hard work, persistence—I wouldn't be the man that I am today.

My parents were married until I left high school, and it was after that that they announced they were going to officially separate. They had decided to stay together as long as they had for the good of our family. They felt strongly that staying together created a stable environment for our family, and even though they had known they would be separating long before the announcement, they sacrificed for me and my siblings.

It was a life lesson for me that I realized many years later. Sometimes you need to do what is best not just for you, but the bigger picture, and especially make those sacrifices when family is involved.

I've learned through my parents, but now in my own experience, and particularly in marriage, that sacrifice is a key component to achieving success. You can no longer be selfish; you must consider what is best for the ones you care about as well. My father chose to put aside feelings he had about his marriage and do what he thought would be best to benefit the kids. And in our situation, he felt it was best to remain in the home, because it was what our family needed. Regardless of the separation, my father always made it clear that he was there for us. I could rely on him, depend on him, and lean on him. That was and still is invaluable.

Now that I have children of my own, I see that being a father is truly the most difficult yet rewarding job any man can have. Nothing prepares you for the challenges, the emotions, and the rewards of being a father. No matter what you think you know, have read, or have spoken to other men about, you really don't know. So I do the *absolute best I can with the support of my family, the lessons learned from my father, and I continue to learn every day and strive to do better than the day before.*

I've also learned that my children come first. Even with the career I have chosen, my children and their needs are the top priority. Basketball is for a moment, but my family will last forever, and that is what I truly cherish. I have been blessed more than words can express. Seeing my children's faces light up when I come home, or taking them to the park or the swimming pool are precious moments that can never be replaced. Just to hear them call my name, "Daddy," it just warms my heart.

I represent to them what my father represented to me, and to be able to play that role in their lives is a special feeling. It's a gift that I am thankful for.

Just like Derek, my feelings for my children will always outweigh everything else in my life. While I talked about the Beyoncé song and my daughters, I need to add a word or two about loving my boy, Malcolm. For me, my thoughts about Malcolm hit so close to home, because I can so easily put myself in his position and remember how I felt about my father's love when I was a boy. I go out of my way to tell him all the time that I love him, because I didn't get that from my father. I am affectionate with him, because I didn't get that from my father. My relationship with my dad was much more casual. He was a guy I saw once or twice a month and spent some time hanging out with. When I started getting older, I realized this was not the way it was supposed to be. And that's when the anger rushed in.

I will go into more detail about anger in a later chapter, but it's so clear to me that the anger so many men feel is actually predicated on an absence of love from their fathers. It morphs and grows and evolves, but the bud first bursts open when they have to figure out how to handle that painful yearning for their dad. Many guys never really figure out how to handle it without hurting themselves and everyone around them.

I talked in the first chapter about the father's need to just be there for his kid, and that nothing can replace his presence, but the one thing that can come close is his love. Father love is something that can stay with you long after you are out of your father's house. It can provide the child with an emotional warm blanket when the father isn't around. So for those fathers out there who no longer have the benefit of living with their children because of a splintered relationship with the children's mother, I would urge you to go overboard with the love. Shower them with as much of it as you can. When you feel like you've given them enough, give them a little more. What you are doing is equipping them with an abundant supply that can sustain them when you aren't around. When they're having a rough day, when they are in need of the strong shoulder you would have provided if you were in the house, your love will be something they can wallow in, splash all over themselves, to instantly lift them up. That's why daily phone calls are important when you are an absentee dad—your voice on the other end of the line serves as a daily reminder of how much you love them, how much you support them, how much you are willing to protect them. But they can have short memories when they are young; you have to keep doing it, even if the only thing you get on the other end of the line is a lot of silence and breathing. Your voice will be a soothing balm—even if they have nothing to say in return.

The wages of parenting are played out in the many split-second decisions we have to make regarding our children and our lives. Sometimes we make decisions that we immediately wish we could get back—decisions that we know will have long-term consequences that won't be good for us, nor for our child. In the following essay, rapper **Talib Kweli** eloquently discusses his love and pride for his children, but he also talks about a fateful decision he made when he put his career ahead of his child—a decision he still regrets.

When my son was two years old and my wife was pregnant with my daughter, I got a memorable lesson in prioritizing. I was doing a show in Baltimore with Mos Def, promoting the Black Star album, and I had been debating with myself whether I should go to the show, because of how far along my wife was with the pregnancy. I decided to do the show, and right as I was going onstage, she was going into labor. So I did my part, left the show a little early, hopped in a Baltimore cab and said, "Take me to Brooklyn." The cabdriver looked at me like I was crazy, because Brooklyn was nearly two hundred miles away, but he took me. Unfortunately I missed the birth. That hurt me. It was a lesson in prioritizing for me, because, in the grand scheme of things, that show was nowhere near as important as the birth of my daughter. To this day, I wish that I had made a different decision. I wrote a song with Mos Def called "Joy" that was a tribute to my daughter for missing that moment.

I am thankful to my father, Perry Greene, for showing me how to convey the message of love to my kids. When my parents were together, and even after they split up, when I was just entering my teenage years, my pops was always very good at saying, "Son, I love you." Of course, I didn't recognize the power of those words coming from my father until I grew much older, but I did recognize at a young age that a lot of the other kids whose parents weren't around or who just simply didn't get that from their fathers would pay attention or notice when my father was affectionate with me. My father showing me that love affected me in such a positive way. He was focused on independence and strength and knowledge. He would tell me that he loved me and respected me. That was really big for me growing up. My father treated me like a person and not like a second-class citizen or someone who was beneath him. He treated me like I mattered. I didn't grow up in a household where I was expected to be seen and not heard. My father expressed a love to me that manifested itself by my being treated with respect and knowing I was important and my feelings were important. I knew without a doubt that my parents loved and respected me, so I felt no need to rebel against them. That is the relationship I want to have with my children. I want them to know that no matter what mistakes they make, no matter if they choose to become a rapper, ballplayer, singer, doctor, lawyer, scientist, teacher, or whatever their hearts desire, I want them to know that their daddy will always love them, respect them, and have their back.

My son is fourteen now, and he's really into music. He is part of the Internet generation that can just Google anything they want. We didn't have that as little kids. He is so into hip-hop, and I like to think that is because of me. At around eight or nine, he started to Google KRS-One and Rakim, and really started almost studying their lyrics. He was actually starstruck when he met KRS. You would imagine someone his age being starstruck from meeting Lil Wayne, Drake, Snoop, or some of the other people who are the most popular. He knew them, and gave them their respect, but he admired KRS-One and Rakim. He raps now and even gave me one of his classmates' demo tapes. I have to say that the kid is pretty good. I couldn't be more proud of my son. He's also really into basketball. He Googles Kobe and Lebron and is just infatuated with the entire sport. I didn't have anything to do with that—my sport growing up was baseball—but I enjoy taking an interest in whatever he is interested in. It is just as much a blessing for him to be a part of my life as it is for me to be a part of his.

My daughter right now is eleven, and I try to have her around positive women. There is enough negativity that kids are constantly being bombarded with; I want her to pick up on examples of great women to emulate. She also loves music; right now she is infatuated with Willow Smith. It's almost as if she is trying to catch up to her with singing and dancing and acting, and it is truly a joy to see her passion. Now, I know that she will be getting older soon and approaching her teenage years. And like every father on earth, I worry about those teenage years, because I want to protect her. And of course every father, including myself, thinks that he has the most beautiful daughter in the world. So I am trying to make sure that she knows the nature of human beings, that she is well-read, and prepared for society, for boys, for everything that she is going to be introduced to as she gets older. I want to make sure she has the right mind frame, and she doesn't put herself into just any situation. And as any father, I have had scenarios played out in my head, like what would happen if . . . But I pray and pray that it will never come to that, and prepare her, make sure she knows how much her daddy loves her so that she knows she doesn't have to seek love from any man, that she knows she has a man in her father who will always be there for her. I really think that is important with the development of girls.

All of this goes back to my father, because that is the love that he showed me growing up. If I could do half as good a job with my kids as he did with his, I will be more than successful.

Talib Kweli's words are so powerful in that every father will have regrets. We will all have things that we wish we could take back and do differently, but the key is to learn from our mistakes and the mistakes of others.

There was some controversy last year in the professional basketball ranks when ESPN released a documentary about the impact of the University of Michigan's "Fab Five" basketball team of 1991. Those five guys—Chris Webber, Juwan Howard, Jalen Rose, Jimmy King, and Ray Jackson—changed the basketball landscape when they hit the court with their long, baggy shorts, black socks, black shoes, and bald heads. Young black kids across America imitated their style and swagger, while much of the mainstream found them to be arrogant and a bit scary. In the film, Jalen Rose opens up on his feelings about the Duke team at the time. He said he hated **Grant Hill** because he was so jealous of him, with his loving family and successful, distinguished, wealthy parents. He said he thought

Duke was a team of "Uncle Toms" because they only recruited middle-class black kids, not poor kids like him. Jalen caught a lot of flak for his comments, though he explained that they were his feelings a long time ago, when he was an immature seventeen-year-old, and it's clearly not the way he feels now. But it was Grant's response to Jalen that really touched me. He talked about how much his father, Calvin Hill, a Yale graduate and former NFL star himself, loved and supported Grant when he was growing up. You feel his appreciation for his father and the way he was raised, how his father has always been there for him. When I saw that, even all these years later, it still pained me that I couldn't say those things about my own childhood and my relationship with my father. But I bet my son will be able to say those things about me one day. That much I promise. In the following piece, I got Grant to expound on his love and respect for his dad. When I read it for the first time, it sent shivers down my spine. Growing up, I don't think I could have named five guys who would speak about their fathers the way Grant does.

When I think about my dad, Calvin Hill, unconditional love and support are the first things that come to my mind. He has so much personal integrity in the way that he's lived his life; he's always been the perfect role model.

From a genetic standpoint, in my mannerisms and things of that nature, I obviously got a lot from him. But now that I'm an adult with my own children, I'm getting even more from him: how to interact with my children, how to deal with adversity, how to be a role model myself. I now realize how fortunate and blessed I have been over the years to have him there. When I was younger, I thought everybody had that in their lives. He would tell me there's six inches between a pat on the back and a pat on the butt—and a parent has to do both. But the key is constant contact. Whether you're praising or disciplining, you're involved; you're there. He drove me to practice; he corrected my homework; he respected my mother; he was interested in my friends and the things we were in-volved with at different stages of my childhood. He was always in contact. Even now, as an adult, even though obviously you cut the umbilical cord at some point, he's still there for me. I'm thirty-nine, but I still lean on him and still look up to him. When I was younger, there was the fear of getting in trouble and being disciplined if I wasn't conducting myself in a certain way, if I wasn't respecting my peers, if I wasn't taking the high road, if I wasn't doing the right thing. But even now, as an adult, one of the things that's helped me stay grounded is the fear of disappointing my parents. He's still teaching me, encouraging me, and holding me accountable. Nothing's changed—just our ages.

Part of parental love is being able to balance the constant praise and instilling of confidence in your child with teaching them right from wrong. You have to be able to tell them "No" and discipline them when necessary. I might have thought my parents were tough when I was younger, but I certainly have appreciation, admiration, and respect for their approach now.

It was huge for me to see my father be a good husband to my mother. Somewhere I read that the best way to love kids is to love and respect their mother. My parents have been married for forty-two years. My mom has been successful in business; she has a very dominating personality. Watching the way he's treated her over the years, how he respected her and how he never mistreated her—to her face or when she wasn't around—the way he's loved her, has all helped me immensely in understanding the importance of the marriage bond, the strength that comes from that, and the effect it has on kids. I know I'm the first man my daughters are ever going to love. That is a huge responsibility—it is up to me to set the standard, to be an example of the type of man they should seek when it comes time for them to find a man. That's important to me—once I get my mind past the teenage dating years that are coming! I want my daughters to find somebody who lives up to the standard—and

*my standard is my father, their grandfather. If they can find some-
body who treats them as my father treats my mom, I'd be more than
pleased.*

*Having children is an interesting experience for athletes. Some-
times as athletes we live sort of a selfish existence. Everything re-
volves around us, our season, our schedule. Those who are around
us have to make sacrifices—our families, our wives. Obviously my
wife and I have a great relationship, but when you have kids you
experience this amazing thing called unconditional love. When my
first daughter was born, I never thought I could love someone or
something as much as I loved her. All of a sudden you realize how
selfish you've been. Nothing, even loving yourself, could compare to
that kind of love. When my second daughter was born five years
later, by then I had gotten to know my now nine-year-old daughter
and I had this great bond and relationship with her. I was worried.
I couldn't imagine having to share that love. I'm an only child, so I
wasn't used to the family dynamic of multiple children and all of
that. But after she was born, I certainly learned what it was all
about.*

*In the sports world and even in business, people who are suc-
cessful get consumed with their legacy, leaving their mark, doing
something that folks will remember. But I think without a doubt the
most important thing you can do for your legacy is your children. If
I can turn out people who respect other people, live honorably, and
do what's right in life, I can look back and be proud. That's my
biggest challenge, my biggest hope. Parenting is the hardest thing
I've ever done. You're constantly second-guessing yourself, constantly
aware of the responsibilities at hand. But it's also the most important thing and the most fulfilling thing I've ever done.*

That's how I want Malcolm to view me. I want him to speak of
me with that level of pride and admiration. I want him to lean on
me for support, even when he is Grant Hill's age of thirty-nine years

old. I want to be the perfect illustration for him of what a father should be so that he patterns himself after me the way Grant Hill patterned himself after his father.

Like most people, I enjoy seeing fathers being affectionate with their children. I think it's something you see these days much more than you did with previous generations. Only in the last few decades has public affection from fathers toward their daughters and their sons been something that is widely accepted and prevalent. No longer is it deemed unmanly to give it and for the son to receive it. All I can say is, It's about time! But although it's more common now, I think most of us are still a bit startled when we see it. It moves us, reaches down and touches us, because it is not the customary way that we are used to seeing strong male figures. We grow up craving the love of our father, but then society steps in and totally confuses the picture, telling us that we aren't supposed to want it and telling the father that he's not supposed to give it. So there we stand, two solitary figures, gazing at each other across the divide, unsure of how much what we are feeling in our hearts for each other can actually be expressed, shown, admitted. It's ridiculous. But I am pleased that this seems to be changing. It reminds me of a scene in the movie *300*. King Leonidas, played by Gerard Butler, is preparing to go to battle against Persian "god king" Xerxes, and he is being seen off by his wife. We hear a voice-over from his character, saying that he wishes he could tell his wife how much he loves her, how much he'll miss her. But he can't, because he's a warrior, and warriors aren't supposed to show emotion. It might be a bit extreme, but it always struck me as a clear example of the prison that we sometimes get trapped in by our male stereotypes.

I sometimes joke with my wife that as my kids are growing up, I'm going to be like the over-the-top parents of Ben Stiller's character in the movie *Meet the Fockers*. You remember that scene, where Stiller is embarrassed because his parents, played by Dustin Hoffman and Barbra Streisand, are still proudly displaying his "ninth-place" sports ribbons? It's a funny sight, intended to ridicule the overprotective, smothering parents who would reward their child for coming in ninth place. But it's also a statement about how much his parents cherish him and adore everything he did as a child. Even if he wasn't the world's greatest athlete, they wanted him to feel supported by them. I am going to be proud of everything my children do—even if they come in ninth place! When I was little, my mother used to tell me and my brother that whatever we wanted to become when we grew up—doctor, lawyer, teacher, carpenter, or Indian chief—she wanted us to be the best we could be and she'd be proud of us. I don't know why she threw Indian chief in there, but I think she was just trying to cover the entire spectrum. Getting that from your parents is so important. The world is going to deliver some serious blows—we need to know that somebody out there has our back. That's how it's going to go down with my kids. I don't want Malcolm to think he has to play basketball because I play basketball. The same with my daughters. Right now Malcolm is into guitar and soccer. So if he decides he wants to be a soccer-playing guitarist, or a guitar-playing soccer player, I'll be okay with that. With Imani, it's all about ballet—and I'll always be right there, cheering her on.

Tennis legend **Andre Agassi**, married to another tennis legend, Steffi Graf, ought to know a thing or two about the pitfalls of pushing your child into the sport that made you famous. As he explains in the following essay, Agassi believes strongly in letting his children find their own passions. Agassi also isn't shy about showing his children as much love as he can muster. In this essay, it's interesting to contrast the old-school way that Andre's dad showed love for his children and the way that Agassi shows it now—a perfect illustration of the much-needed societal evolution I describe above.

Like many first-generation immigrants, my father showed his love in an old-school way. It was more physical than verbal. He chal-

lenged us to evolve, which didn't always feel like love at the time, but now I know that it really was pure love. Old-school parenting usually involved pushing from behind rather than inspiring from in front. We didn't end conversations with, "I love you." The love and protection were tangible, but lived out quietly. His love compelled him to be very demanding of his children, which made me wish at the time that he would go love something else for a while. Looking back, my feelings were similar to a quote from Fiddler on the Roof: *"I know we're your chosen people, but could you choose someone else for a while?"*

My wife, Stefanie, and I have broken the chain of that old-school environment in our home with our children, who are ten and eight. Our affection is physical, it is verbal, and it is nonstop. The default setting is fun and laughter. If a child can feel the safety and consistency of a positive environment, then it gives a parent far more leverage when there needs to be discipline. When our children misbehave, many times nothing more than a look of displeasure gets them back on track. They are so in tune with our emotions, and so dependent on our approval, that when it is interrupted by their actions, they can self-correct in order to right the relationship.

If you could physically monitor or measure a child's heart rate or stress levels when he is on the receiving end of some tangible sign of affection, you would see a demonstrable change. When we carry out the ritual of walking our children to bed at night, we say to them, "Good night, God bless you; I love you." Then we read to them and stick around until they start to doze. You can see in their eyes, the comfort they feel from that loving, consistent action. They rely on it, and they mentally let go of the day and its troubles. They change physical gears as a response to our attention.

I think we demonstrate our love for them by learning more than we teach. This sentiment plays out every day, many times a day. You have to be present, not just physically, but really present for them. Children know when you're phoning it in, so the answer is to interact, to be responsive, and to be inquisitive. *When we interact with our children, our outside world comes to a stop and they experience everything we have to give and everything we are as adults. To me, that is true affection. It may be a verbal cue, it may be a hug, it may be interacting with a book or toy, but all of it is a demonstration of affection in action.*

When you have two parents and two children, the division of labor has certain consequences. If I tend to spend bulk time with my son, Jaden, for instance, at baseball doubleheaders and practices, I can sometimes notice an imbalance the next time I see my daughter, Jaz. She may seem needier and longing for more of my personal time and attention the next day. The same is true with Jaden as well when I spend time with Jaz. We always seek to negotiate the right balance of time and attention so that all the relationships in the home stay healthy.

The satisfaction of a well-played match, or even a whole career in which you won a lot more than you lost, is, at its heart, self-centered. Not to say selfish, because many people will benefit from your success, but it is self-focused. Therefore the joy you feel is contained and temporary. The joy of seeing your children develop their personality, their values—that brings you joy that is limitless. I think that is where our greatest experiences on earth take place: outside of ourselves, giving of ourselves, contributing to the success of others. When that person is your own flesh and blood, I think the appropriate word would be "indescribable." What I often tell people without children is this: I promise you, once you have children you will forget a lot of what you used to care about. Parenting is so intense, you will wonder, What did I used to do with this part of my brain I'm using now? I was once asked the question, When was the last time you did something for the first time? With children, that happens every day, and it's beautiful. Watching children discover some truth or watching them see the beach for the first time, makes you see it through their eyes, as if for the first time. I can say I see the world differently as I rediscover it with my children.

Several years ago I had a real heart-in-my-throat moment with my son. We were in the backyard doing one of our favorite things, jumping on the trampoline together. He was about four at the time, and having the time of his life. I did all the typical circus moves, throwing him up in the air, and getting him to jump higher. After a while we both collapsed in laughter and fell to the surface, catching our breath. He stopped and his expression froze as if he was struck by something profound, as if he had a life-changing realization. I was so curious to see what he might say next, what truth he had discovered. Then he simply said, "I always wanted a daddy like you." That's it, lights out, cue the music, I'm done emotionally. How can a child make a dad feel so loved?

My son, Jaden, has an interest in, and a talent for, baseball. My greatest joy comes from knowing that he chose it, and is self-motivated to improve and grow. Some disciplines can be imposed from outside, but we also need to recognize that each soul has its own code, and our role as parents is to maximize a child's options until he identifies his life's passions. Once we as parents see something resonate with our children, then our responsibility is to maximize their ability to pursue it, and to support and inspire them. For me this happens at every level, from verbal encouragement, to rides to the ballpark, to playing catcher to his pitching in the backyard. It would be heartbreaking, as a parent, to feel that your child had abilities, talent, and a desire to experience success, and that you failed to deliver the access for your child to connect with that passion.

A discussion of paternal love wouldn't be complete if I didn't talk about discipline. At first it may strike you as bizarre that discipline would make an appearance in this chapter, but any parent knows how crucial discipline becomes in the day-to-day performance of our parental duties and the daily demonstrations of our love. From the time they first get mobile, our children quickly make us realize that perhaps our biggest job will be to get them out of childhood alive and in one piece, as they seem on a daily basis to be overcome with the self-destructive crazies. When he thinks, *Hmm, what would happen if I jump off the banister and try to land on the dining room table?* Immediately after that thought needs to be another voice in his head—his mother's or father's voice—saying, *Boy, you know good and well that's a crazy idea!* And, of course, when they get older and start driving, or maybe move away from home when they go to college, and you aren't there to observe them twenty-four/seven anymore, yours still needs to be the voice in their head, telling them, *Slow down. . . . Don't try to drive after you've been drinking. . . . You know you need to study tonight—the party can wait.*

When I was little, my mother had a whole procedure, like a ritual she went through when she gave us a spanking. There was always a lesson that she was trying to impart. The ritual was passed down from her mother and her mother's mother. My grandmother, whom we called Ning, was "old-school" from Grenada—way stricter than my mother ever was. And my great-grandmother was even worse—we couldn't even sit on the furniture in her apartment; we had to sit on the floor! The way my mother's ritual went, the physical spanking was just the beginning. After that, there would be "the talk." I had to verbalize what I did wrong and then what I should have done differently. Then would come the reinforcement of love—she would tell us she was disciplining us because she loves us, which was not something you wanted to hear right after you got spanked. There was a memorable incident during my childhood when I got disciplined by my grandmother. My grandparents loved to tell this story. It all started at the Boys and Girls Club in Harlem. One of the counselors was teasing me about my accent. My accent was hard to peg when I was younger—in Oklahoma they thought I sounded like I was from New York, but in New York they thought I sounded country. At any rate, I didn't like being teased about it. As a matter of fact, I didn't like being teased about anything. So we got into an altercation and I took a swing at him. I could tell the counselor was shocked. He was thinking, *Whoa, this young cat actually swung on me!* I got sent home—to my grandmother. When West Indians get upset, their accents can get thicker, so Ning's accent was real thick that day. She spanked me, but then she started teaching me afterward. She told me that I have to respect people who are in positions of authority. She worked at the Spofford Correctional Facility in the Bronx and she saw a lot of bad kids come through there. She used to tell me stories about Mike Tyson, whom she remembered coming through Spofford and wanting to fight anyone who would tease him about his unusually high voice. She said that was a big problem with the kids at Spofford: They didn't respect authority. I remember her hugging and kissing me at the end of it. It was about much more than the spanking. And it was effective. I learned a serious lesson that day—and I did feel her love, even after she had just finished spanking me.

Now that I have kids of my own, I have tried to incorporate that ritual into my child-rearing style. It's something I hate to do, but it's something I know I have to do. Because you can't let them run wild—you have to check them on things. It's a vital part of raising kids. Kids will try to get away with whatever you allow them to get away with. If I let Malcolm run crazy, talk disrespectful, throw tantrums, and not listen to the teachers, he will do it. You have to set the rules. And it has to be grounded in love. Discipline doesn't mean just inflicting physical punishment. That's not what it's about at all. Parents who don't believe in spankings still have to use something to get the kid's attention, something that will make the child understand that what he did was wrong and that the parent means business. I guess my old-school spanking-teaching method must be effective, because I actually heard Malcolm, at age five, explain to his little sister, who was three and going through the rebellious stage, how the process works. He said, "You have to understand that Daddy and Mommy love us, so they have to discipline us. If they let us do whatever we wanted, we would grow up to be bad." Smart kid.

I think discipline feels different to a kid when it comes from the father. Naturally I'm not saying that a mother can't be the disciplinarian, because my mom did it for me and my brother with surgical skill. But I think the voice of impending doom is perhaps taken more seriously by the child when it comes from Dad. I don't have any scientific data to back this up, but I can bring you a whole lot of anecdotal evidence.

Former basketball great **Allan Houston** has six kids in his house, so he says he has had to try just about every method of discipline in the book, because no one method is going to work on every child. Parents have to be flexible, willing to try whatever does the job. But healthy doses of both parental love and a love of God are always present in the Houston household, as he explains in the following essay.

Because I had such a strong family background myself, I realize how significant my role is in the lives of my children. I have five girls and one boy—yes, we're rolling deep in the Houston household! I feel like my wife and I are literally shaping six beings to send into this world to be who they are going to be and, God willing, be productive children of God. I feel that in our role as parents, our kids are not really ours, but rather they are gifts from God. And it is our responsibility to first usher them into their own personal relationships with God and then train them and equip them to be the men and women in Christ they should grow to be. That's why it is a huge responsibility and at the same time a huge blessing. We have the role of monitoring their lives and helping them be the best that they can be. We are the ones who help them realize what their purpose is, and for each child it could be something completely different, but the main thing is that we raise them to grow up to be good people.

This outlook came from the examples my wife and I saw grow-ing up. We grew up in Louisville, Kentucky, and with my genera-tion, especially when you grow up in the South, going to church—and not just going, but having church be a major part of your life—is just part of the culture. So I saw strong family units. We would travel together, and since my father was coaching at the University of Louisville we would make our vacations part of the trips when the team would go on Christmas tournaments or play in tournaments during the summer. We would always make sure that we were to-gether, spending time as a family. Even when I was in high school and I was playing in summer camps, we would make those vaca-tions. So that strong family bond is something that I saw growing up. We never saw my parents fight or argue. I can't even remember one time. Now, being a realist, I'm sure they had a disagreement or two, but they never let us see it. They had something of a united front. They made sure that we saw them as a unit, on the same team. Ultimately, what I saw from my parents was unconditional love. I saw how it was supposed to be. My parents were really de-manding of us—how we studied, how we spoke to adults, our be-havior, our overall respect for life. And I think that, coupled with the spiritual aspect, the unity and the discipline, really laid the foundation for my entire life.

I am eager to pass this on to my kids. My wife got her master's in education, so what I've found is that the things we learned grow-ing up, not only could we try to apply them, but we found out that we could start instilling these principles at an early age. For exam-ple, when your kids are as young as one or two years old, they are very aware of saying, "No," when they speak to people. One thing that we do is we don't allow them to say certain things or respond in certain ways, even as young as two. And the reason I'm so eager to teach them is because I understand how important our role is in who they are going to be. Now, they're going to have their own personality and their own purpose, but the way they go about it is going to be on us. I think the biggest compliment you can ever get as a parent is if your child is well behaved, respectful, and hardworking, because to me that's a reflection of you. It takes a lot of energy and a lot of time. My wife and I put so much into them, but that's what it takes. It's like, if a coach lets you slide with a couple things and doesn't hold you accountable, then he's not really helping you. In the same way, as parents we can't let them get away with things, so we have to set rules. Even if it's something that seems small, like going to bed on time, doing their homework diligently, speaking to adults the right way, these little things add up. Yes, this takes a lot of work, and sometimes it is easier to just let things slide, because you don't have the energy to deal with it, but it's your legacy. And to me, legacy isn't how many points you score; it's what you are leaving behind.

My dad never forced basketball on me. He was a coach and I was around it all the time, and I saw my dad in action coaching his players, teaching them, getting on them, challenging them, encouraging them, but he never forced it on me. I'm trying to take that approach with my son. He is also around basketball a lot, he's around the team, he goes to practices and games, but I am not forcing it on him. But he does love the game and I can see it. I try to make it fun for him. I don't want to take the joy for basketball away from him because I am drilling him too hard. I have seen that happen with kids before. They have parents who want them to succeed so much that they become drill sergeants and take all of the fun away. I don't want to be like that, so I make it fun for him.

As far as disciplining the kids, some of my kids we had to spank, but some didn't respond to spankings. Some responded better if they had something taken away from them, like their favorite toy, or couldn't go outside and play, or had to be in isolation. We have so many kids that we have seen different methods work differently. If you say you are going to be punished if a certain action occurs, as a parent you have to follow through with the punishment, or else the threat doesn't mean anything. If you are constantly saying, "You're gonna get it," and the child never actually gets it but just keeps being warned, then eventually the child is going to figure out that it's just a bluff. I think that discipline is very important—not just the physical spanking, but how we do it. You explain to them with love. For example, if my son and my daughter fight, I'm not going to just go punch him in the chest, and let that be the end of it. If I have to snatch him up, or light him up, I then have to explain why he can't hit his sister like that. How he can't hit girls like that. Translating it into why he can't hit women. It's a lesson that is learned. Much more than the physical part, communication is really key.

Showing love and affection toward your wife or significant other in front of your kids is also an essential aspect of fathering. I think this one has consequences that extend far beyond that quick hug or kiss with the kids watching. It can have a profound effect on the way your children view the form and mechanics of a successful loving relationship. In this day and age, that is crucial—and in short supply.

I don't ever recall seeing my parents showing affection toward each other when I was a kid. Granted, I was only about six when they got divorced. But I do remember the arguing. That clearly sticks out in my mind. Before I got married, I even had a conversation about it with my mom, when we were discussing my anger. I pulled up specific arguments from my childhood and she looked at me with this shocked expression. She was amazed that I could remember such specific details. I went through my entire childhood not really knowing what a healthy, supportive, loving relationship between a husband and a wife looked like.

When Nichole and I decided to get married, I was intent on giving my children a model of everyday love, with its affection, arguments, and compromises, growing and changing and supporting each other. I love to watch Malcolm's and Imani's faces when Nichole and I are showing each other affection. Sometimes when Nichole and I are hugging or when we kiss, Nichole will say, "Look at your daughter over there." And I'll see Imani wearing this huge grin. I think that's so important for little girls, to see a man treating a woman the right way. They need to always have this as a frame of reference, so they know what it looks like when the fellas start coming their way. And it's just as crucial for a son to see the correct male relationship behavior modeled in front of him on an everyday basis.

Any married couple will tell you that throughout the course of a marriage, there are going to be disagreements. There are going to be arguments. That's just reality. But I am cognizant of me and Nichole not arguing in front of the kids because of how the images of my parents arguing have been permanently etched into my memory. I don't want that same thing to happen to Malcolm, Imani, or Sierra. What I saw in my childhood also makes me more protective and appreciative of a woman, just because I grew up watching a woman do it all by herself.

As a society, we would all benefit by seeing more examples of men showing love to those around them. Right now it's all so sexualized, to the point where too many of our young people see that as the only way that men and women are supposed to interact, by having sex. But if we surrounded our kids from an early age with more examples of loving relationships, of fathers showering their kids with affection, men and women loving each other and fighting and making up and bringing a full range of passion and vitality to their partnership, I think our world would be a very different place. A better place.

When it comes to expressing the pain, the longing, the bitterness of the missing love that comes from having an absent father, no one brings more to the table than a skilled poet. So in closing, let us be led by the powerful words of **Black Ice**, in this poem called "Lone Soldier."

My father always told me that I'd understand when I got older
This internal hurt of a lone soldier so
Held firmly in my right arm with her head on my shoulder
because that's the way she likes me to hold her
That's what I told her
Speaking about my daughter in order to save face because just
before the embrace and all the I love yous and I miss yous she
clearly let me know that she had issues talkin' about "Daddy
where you been?"
And just then my mind began sinking back
Thinking back to those Saturday seldom show up days
Those seem like my father don't wanna bother helping me grow
up days
So sick of not seeing my dad I wanna throw up days
Those my mom said you shouldn't come nowhere near where we
resided because she decided to blow up days
Well anyways
Her eyes were always able to pull the disguise off of any lies
I might try to use to summarize the situation
You see it's funny the way it's second nature
The way I put these words to paper
But couldn't figure out a simple explanation to offer my
baby girl
Don't like having to admit that tomorrow is just a maybe girl
And the famous ask your mom and see what she say
But the ball's in her court so we got to play how she play
But hey
I tell my fat girl not to fret
Cuz all this dirty will come out in life's wash and we haven't
finished filling up yet
See when two parents are not in conjunction
A dysfunctional child is inevitable
See Mommy's not on time with Daddy

And Daddy's not on time with Mommy
So the child grows up off schedule

CHORUS

Baby girl life will be all right in a minute
And you cannot prepare for what's in it
But you will learn as you grow older
That I'm a lone soldier
And if you ever need to reach for me
You know exactly where I'm gonna be
Just know I love you and your daddy's
A lone soldier

And it's incredible because he always told me that I would
  understand when I got older
Why he used to call himself the lone soldier
And one night when she called crying and I couldn't get to
  her to hold her
Even though it wasn't some game $#!*
I felt like it was some lame $#!* I told her
Just because I couldn't be right there
After a nightmare
Because of a fight between me and her mother
You see she's six and can't conceive
How I can leave
And still tell her I love her so
Her inquisitive little mind forces her to question
And my rationale begs me to not reply
See I know she won't see why
We have to live in different places
Or how come her and her little brother don't see each other's
  faces on a consistent basis

And it hurts when I have to lay down the hand of discipline
Knowing that I'll just get to spend a short segment of time with her
So imagine how I feel when I have to hit her and
don't get it twisted sometimes I %^&@ up and don't get her
Because my ego won't let her mother call me a babysitter
But for my baby girl I swallow my pride and show through
See for kids
It ain't nothing I won't go through
Lone soldier

CHORUS

Baby girl life will be all right in a minute
And you cannot prepare for what's in it
But you will learn as you grow older
That I'm a lone soldier
And if you ever need to reach for me
You know exactly where I'm gonna be
Just know I love you and your daddy's
A lone soldier

CHAPTER FOUR

YOU'VE GOT A FRIEND: USING ELDERS TO DELIVER HONESTY AND WISDOM TO YOUR CHILDREN

In every child's life, there comes a time when we desperately need the wisdom of elders. I will remain thankful that I've always had men around me who could fill that critical role in my life. In the day-to-day absence of a father figure, I realize now that I went out seeking those figures. Lucky for me, the men I found turned out to be enormously positive influences on my life. There were plenty of guys around me who weren't so lucky—our communities are littered with the broken lives of men who, in seeking father figures, became captured by the outstretched tentacles of drug dealers and gangbangers who could only offer them paths to short-term glory and long-term misery.

There was a pastor, Reverend M. C. Potter, whom I latched onto in my early years. One of the things that stood out most about Reverend Potter was his mellow personality. He coached the AAU team sponsored by his church, Antioch Baptist Church, and he was even mellow when he preached. He never raised his voice; his approach to coaching and to preaching was to say things that would make you think. I clicked with him from the beginning. I probably asked him a million questions in the years that I played for him, from fourth grade all the way through high school. I asked him a lot of questions about religion, because I went to a Catholic school called Monte Cassino for several years and I didn't understand a lot of the customs in the Catholic church. We'd sit down and have these long conversations. On the court, he had a way of pushing me that wasn't belittling. He was demanding and a great motivator, ideal qualities in a coach. Some coaches are screamers and yellers; they berate you and belittle you, like the Bobby Knight style, using embarrassment. But Reverend Potter would manage to make you feel bad if you didn't do your best, without resorting to the verbal abuse. He knew how to use encouragement to bring out the best in everybody. Positive reinforcement was his primary tool; when we did something well, we would look over at him and he would clap his hands three times. That was high praise from him. Three quick claps. *Pow-pow-pow.* Over the years, as I got better, other teams would approach me to play for them, but I would refuse. I had no interest in leaving Reverend Potter.

In middle school, basketball began to emerge as a major factor in my life. I remember being surrounded by players who were a lot better than me. I was tall, but that certainly didn't automatically make me one of the best players. Height had very little correlation to skill in those early years. (My dad is six-four and my mom is six feet tall, so I was always one of the tallest kids in the class. My wife, Nichole, is also a six-footer, so I think my son, Malcolm, is going to be the same way. I don't really notice how tall he is until I see him next to kids his age.) I had to work hard. These were the years when I was faced with a million little decisions about the way I was going to be, the direction I was going to take. Many of the guys I played with, some of them much better players than me, made bad decisions and took ill-fated paths. I know now that many of them were looking for replacements for their fathers. They found replacements in gangs, or in older guys who led them down the wrong paths, toward drugs and crime. I am so fortunate that Reverend Potter was there for me. And I'm sure it wasn't by accident; I think my mother consciously brought me to his church and encouraged our bond.

The prisons are filled with guys who were looking for father figures and made the wrong choice, maybe picked an OG (original gangsta) in a gang. That's a big part of the intrigue of gangs. It was never an interest of mine, but I could see the attraction of the brotherhood. Suddenly you have people you can go to for advice, people to listen to, who will tell you stories in the same way that I got stories from Reverend Potter. Most gang members don't join the gang because they want to do malicious things: kill, maim, and hurt people. They see a form of brotherhood that they've never gotten; they see the OG as a father they never had, someone to take them under his wing, show them how to make money. Of course, it's a horrible thing that they're being taught, and the benefits are all short-term gains that will almost definitely not have a happy ending. When I talk to them, I'm always asking, "Why would you even try that? How could you think this plan would work? Look at all the people who came before you—they're all dead or in jail. That doesn't seem to me to be a good plan." But all they see is somebody who has their back. Just like kids in college look to fraternities and sororities. The same concept. It's just so negative in the gang, while the college kids are doing positive things—well, at least most of the time.

My grandfather Fred Bodger (Grandpa Freddy) was another man who had a huge impact on me. I got the chance to spend quality time with him when I would go to his apartment in Harlem for the summers. He served in the Korean War (Korean Conflict—he always corrected me) as a paratrooper for the 173rd brigade. His proper title was CSM (Commander Sergeant Major) Fred Bodger. My grandfather was a longtime Yankees fan, so we would sit and watch entire baseball games on the big television in the corner of the bedroom he shared with my grandmother. Now, I don't mean to put down my professional colleagues who happen to be baseball players, but when I was little I thought baseball was really boring. When I watched it with my grandfather, however, it was fun. We would also watch the Knicks and wrestling and have conversations about the past, politics, sports, history—you name it. When I began to do a lot of reading, I'd ask him questions about different people, like Malcolm X, Bob Marley, Huey P. Newton. He remembered when Malcolm used to speak on the street corner on 125th Street; he'd tell me stories about it. He talked a lot about Kareem Abdul-Jabbar and Wilt Chamberlain. He broke down for me why he didn't like the Harlem Globetrotters and respected and admired the Harlem Rens. He would equate the Globetrotters with the degrading minstrel-show characters. Whenever he would speak on the Globetrotters, he would use a particular quote from the great Bill Russell: "I refuse to allow you to reduce me to a clown used to entertain your circus." I was so proud to be able to tell him that I was part of a documentary that Kareem produced called *On the Shoulders of Giants*, that told the story of the Harlem Rens. I remember him telling me how beautiful a place Harlem was before Frank Lucas and Nicky Barnes came along flooding the community with drugs. We would talk about the Harlem Renaissance and the amazing culture that it birthed. We would debate about politics and sports. He was not a fan of Mayor Rudolph Giuliani at all and would voice his opinions whenever he got the chance. He was also very critical of the Knicks (as most New Yorkers were), and they were my favorite team growing up, so every time the Knicks played, you can bet we were in his room cheering and debating. He taught me so much growing up, and without him I would have been another lost youth without a constant male figure in his life. He was constantly guiding me through life, and preparing me for the future the way a father is supposed to do.

My grandfather knew that the level of basketball I was playing in Tulsa was different from the ball they played in New York City, so he was keen on making sure I was tested on the New York courts. He'd take me to the park and watch me play against the older guys. I learned so much by watching him. He'd be on the sidelines talking to me during the games. If I made a good move and he saw that some guy was getting upset, he'd tell me to ease up a bit. Guys in the city don't react well when they get embarrassed. He would talk to me about recognizing situations and being aware of what was going on around me, which was something I definitely didn't do at the time. He took me to the Rucker, a famous park in Harlem, and I was blown away by how good the players were. They were playing a different game on a different plane than I was used to. My grandfather was always trying to make me better, looking for the best competition for me to play against. The Rucker was a real proving ground for me.

There's one afternoon I can remember clearly, when I was getting my butt kicked on the court. I was in maybe the sixth grade and I was playing against older guys, as I often did because of my height. On this day, with my grandfather watching, I kept getting my shot blocked; I was being totally outplayed. When we were walking back home, I was depressed about playing badly. I was walking with my head down. My grandfather noticed and started talking to me about not giving up, about trying harder the next time. He was so matter-of-fact about it. He said, "Are you going to give up or are you going to do better the next time?" He would make it sound so absurd to take the other route, to give up. That's how he would approach it. I said, "No, I'm not going to quit." That philosophy has stuck with me throughout my life. He would tell me of the many challenges our people faced throughout history, and he would always stress, "But we never gave up; we never quit." I was so blessed to have him in my life growing up.

Many successful people can similarly point to a special person who came along and rescued them when they were headed down the wrong path. In the following essay, **Representative Elijah**

Cummings, whose Maryland district includes the city of Baltimore, shares a dramatic story about his difficult early days in special
education, and the man who came along at just the right moment
to show him how to get out. Cummings also offers a moving tale
about the wisdom and sensitivity of his own father, who wasn't formally educated but was one of the smartest men Cummings says he's
ever met.

*The power of a man in a boy's life is amazing. There's something
about that respect, that level of discipline, knowing that this man is
stronger than me and wiser than me. Women who are raising boys will
attempt to have some type of strong male figures around him, whether
a cousin, uncle, grandfather, pastor, coach, teacher, etc., because they
see the necessity for their son to be around positive men. Nothing
against the women who are doing and have done a phenomenal job,
but they will tell you there has to be some type of positive male presence. When you do not have this, it opens the door for the boy to grow
up without a certain level of guidance, direction, or purpose.*

*Having positive men around young men is immensely impor-
tant to their growth. We spend so much time concentrating on negative role models, because those are the people who are constantly
being shown, and young people pay attention. I have seen Etan
involved here in the Maryland community, especially when he was
with the Wizards. It is important that older brothers understand
and do not take on the philosophy of Charles Barkley in saying that
he is not a role model, because that simply isn't true. You are a role
model. And I understand his point was that your teacher, parents,
etc., should be your role models, but the reality is that you as an
athlete in the public eye are in fact a role model, because kids are
watching. They have their eyes on your every move.*

*But more than that, young people need to know that we give a
damn. They need to know that we care about their future. When the*

basketball players and the football players do their programs here, those programs are important, because they let kids know that someone gives a damn about them. And like it or not, they are all role models. If I was the NBA and I was really serious about having a tremendous effect on our youth, I would expand the little cute commercials about the NBA Cares campaign. Now, nothing against those commercials—I think they are nice; they make you feel warm and fuzzy inside. Showing the different players doing things in the community to show the importance of caring, I get that and I'm not knocking it. What I am saying is that I would expand it to say, "Yes, the NBA cares, but we need you. We need you to go out and mentor some young kids, because you can affect their entire lives and put them on the right path so that they can grow up to be the best that they can be." I would add, "We in the NBA care about our community, and we have our own mentoring programs, but we can't do it all; we need you to help our children." And show black players, white players, Spanish players, Asian, all mentoring all types of kids, while emphasizing to the cameras that we need you to make a difference. That would be my commercial.

I have a program called the Elijah Cummings Youth Program in Israel. This program has taught me so much about young people. We send inner-city kids on an all-expenses-paid trip to Israel, where they will meet and interact with Ethiopians, Jews, Palestinians, Egyptians, kids from all different backgrounds, cultures, dealing with all types of issues. Their lodging is a college dormitory type of setup, so they are in close quarters, and after this trip they realize that the world is bigger than them. They become appreciative that they are not dealing with the issues that these other kids are dealing with, and I don't have to go into the issues that I am talking about; everyone is well aware of the complexity of what has been going on in the Middle East. I have seen the toughest little knuckleheads from the roughest sections of Baltimore break down in tears after hearing of the issues of other kids in different parts of the world. It's not just the mentoring—and believe me, that is an important aspect of their development—but it's exposing them to as much as we possibly can.

I always had my father in my life. He only had a second-grade education, but is one of the smartest men I have ever met in the lessons he taught me. I remember one Christmas, it was the worst and the best Christmas I had ever had. My father was laid off from Davison Chemical Company, and I'll never forget it. We came down Christmas morning and there was nothing under the Christmas tree. My father reached behind his back and gave each of us a toothbrush. He said, "I want you to keep this toothbrush, and I know that you all were expecting presents, and I wanted you to have presents, but Daddy just couldn't afford it." And he had tears in his eyes; I remember seeing them building in his eyes. They didn't fall but they were definitely building, because Christmas meant a lot to him. And he looked at us and said, "Let me tell you something, and you're not going to understand it now, but you'll understand it by and by. My presence in your life is present enough." And what he said is true. Without him I would not be the man I am today. The presence he had in my life is what I owe everything to.

And as strong a presence of a father I had, I, too, was influenced by strong men in my life. I could name five off the top of my head, but I will talk about one person in particular. I was in special education from the time I was in kindergarten to half of the sixth grade. And the kids would call me everything short of a child of God. I was in school level 121 in Baltimore, and a man by the name of Mr. Hollis Posey came to my school. Something told me that this man would understand me. I told him that I felt like a caged bird, that I could achieve higher than a special ed student, and I didn't want to be in special ed anymore. He encouraged me, and said he believed that I could do the regular work. So he gave me regular books and told me to go study and he would tutor me and guide me, and after about a month or two he'd test me and see if I tested well enough to qualify as a regular student. Well, I worked and studied diligently, because I was determined not to be in special ed; he was there encouraging me and telling me that I could do it. See, back in those days, once you were in special ed, there really wasn't much of a way to get out. You were just kind of stuck. So the odds were definitely stacked against me, but he told me that he believed in me. And you know what? After about two and a half months I took the test, and I did better than simply pass; I scored— and I remember my exact scores—an 85 in math and a 92 in reading. He told me to keep reading. Every time I had a chance, I read everything I could get my hands on. That opened the door for me to be successful in life, because, before then, I was trapped in the confines of special ed. I definitely wouldn't have ended up being a Congressman. The fact that he believed in me pushed me to break through that barrier. That is the power that having a mentor and a positive male role model in your life can have. And I had a father, so imagine how important and advantageous it can be for someone who doesn't.

After high school, I left the comfort of Tulsa and found myself on the campus of Syracuse University. Very quickly I thought I had made a grave mistake. I was eighteen years old, away from home for the first time, and I was miserable. Once it started snowing after Halloween, it didn't stop all year. It was gloomy, cold, and it seemed like I was sneezing and sniffling for the entire year. I remember thinking that maybe I was just allergic to Syracuse. I suffered from a severe case of homesickness. And things quickly went further downhill when I stepped onto the basketball court with head coach Jim Boeheim. In practice at times it seemed like I couldn't do anything right. He would be yelling at me so much that I could not believe this was the same person who sat in my living room with me and my mom and persuaded me to come to this school. The same guy who offered me the world. But that's often the way it goes with freshmen. Syracuse had just been in the NCAA championship game the year before, led by forward John Wallace and center Otis Hill. They eventually lost to Kentucky in the championship game. But when I got there, Otis Hill was still the starting center, making me the low man on the totem pole. I was coming from being the man at Booker T. Washington High School, winning back-to-back Oklahoma state championships and losing just one game my senior year. Now I was a lowly freshman getting reamed out by the coach all the time. I was not happy. This was not the way I had planned that first year.

In fact, I was ready to transfer. To find my way to some kinder voices, I called up my boys and told them I wanted out. A lot of people from my high school were at the University of Oklahoma. I can remember my thinking at the time: *Oklahoma is a good school. They recruited me when I was coming out; everybody was mad when I didn't go there anyway. Man, I'm out of here!* I had a conversation with one of my boys, Zee. I told him I didn't like Syracuse. "He's disrespecting me," I said. I remember saying to him that Boeheim had better watch out before he got "Sprewelled." (A reference to the infamous incident when Latrell Sprewell choked his coach P. J. Carlesimo during a practice of the Golden State Warriors.) My boy Zee gave me great advice—though I didn't want to hear it. He said, "You'll be fine up there. Stop being a big baby and tough it out. You're not gonna Sprewell anyone; you're smarter than that." He told me that Otis was going to be leaving after this year, and that I always dreamed about playing in the Big East and had been talking about it since we met. It's good to have homeboys who will tell you what you need to hear when you need to hear it.

But then came Coach Louis Orr. Like my grandfather and Reverend Potter, he was another elder who came to my rescue. It was like I was handed from one to the next to the next. Coach Orr took me under his wing and began to talk to me. All the time. Sometimes he would take me to church with him and talk to me. We'd go in the gym and do drills and he'd talk to me. The man could talk for hours. He would tell me stories about guys who let their frustrations get the best of them. He was a constant voice in my ear, telling me not to give up, to stay focused. He was trying to tell me that things wouldn't always be this way; I wouldn't always be the low man on the totem pole. When I got my chance in the spotlight, I needed to be ready. And when the success came, how would I handle it? Would I continue to work, remembering this time when I was frustrated and not getting any playing time, ready to transfer to another school, or would I sit back and rest on my laurels? He would preach that to me all the time. "Otis is a senior; he's leaving next year. It's right there for you. But how will you handle it?" I didn't know what he was talking about; I really couldn't see that far. I could only see what was right in front of me.

A big issue for me in those years was getting upset when I perceived something to be unfair. I would do something wrong, Coach Boeheim would yell at me, and I'd be like, "Hey, wait a minute, I saw Otis do the same thing and he didn't get yelled at. That's not fair!"

But then I'd hear Coach Orr in my ear. "Who said everything has to be fair? Where did you hear that? Life isn't fair." Then he'd go into a bigger life lesson, telling me about guys who didn't make it because of situations that were thoroughly unfair. He would talk my ear off until he got his point across. He had the same methods of motivation as my grandfather and Reverend Potter. They all could really get on me, but I'd never get offended.

I've thought a lot about what happened at Syracuse between me and Coach Boeheim. I truly believe that some of the friction was caused by the approach he took. I got offended very quickly with male authority figures coming at me a certain way, doing a lot of yelling. Was that the result of not growing up with a male authority figure in my house? Possibly. Or, maybe I just was not used to grown men in my face, hollering at me. Growing up, whenever I encountered someone who operated that way, I usually did not react well. That method, whether I was being more sensitive than I should have been or not, was counterproductive. I did not do well when approached with a lack of respect. I needed to feel a connection with the authority figure, a sense that he cared about me and my fate, and wasn't trying to simply exert his power over me. I never got offended with my grandfather, Reverend Potter, or Coach Orr because I knew they were doing it out of love and not maliciousness.

Track star **John Carlos** and his partner, Tommie Smith, are iconic figures in the African-American community and beyond for the principled stand they took at the 1968 Mexico City Olympics. When they stood on that medal stand and thrust their fists in the air in the Black Power salute, people around the world were infused with an overwhelming pride and respect for these two men. That one act made them major players in the history of the civil rights movement. I'm not old enough to have seen it firsthand, but I've certainly seen that footage over and over throughout my lifetime. Each time it sends a shiver down my spine. Mr. Carlos says the stand he took that day in Mexico wouldn't have been possible without the lessons he got from his father—the ultimate elder who was eager to share his wisdom. In the following essay, Mr. Carlos shows exactly how his father exerted his powerful influence over the young Carlos.

I was fortunate growing up—I had a mom and a dad in my household. However, I was surrounded by a lot of kids who weren't as fortunate. A lot of them didn't have a father in their homes to guide them like I did. Not to say that all of their lives turned out negatively, but I can honestly say that a lot of them struggled by not having a father in their households.

I cannot say enough about my father. In fact, I wish I could take a mold of my father and make other fathers like him. He taught me everything: to respect the rights of others as well as your own rights; to have honor and respect and pride and dignity; to share with your friends and the people close to you. We would bring people over to our house if they didn't have any food at their house. He was really big on the community helping each other to survive, and always instilled in me that a strong community can stand any negative force that comes its way. My father was my biggest influence; I wanted to be just like him. He had a strong character and was a very prideful man. And not prideful in a bad way, but had pride in how he carried himself, and he instilled that same sense of pride in me and my brothers and sisters. He taught me to think. To examine situations, analyze situations that I became involved in. He was very courageous. He taught me about my culture and my history so that I saw myself as part of a tradition much bigger than myself. He also taught me to be steadfast and courageous in what I believe in.

My father owned a candy shop right on Lenox Avenue that was also a shoe shine in the back. I saw my father work hard and take pride in his work and at the same time help his community every chance he got. He taught me the importance of being a man, and what he called "the order of life." He taught me the responsibility of having jobs, the necessity of actually leading your household. Not in a chauvinistic, domineering capacity, but in a providing-for capacity—clothes, food, and a roof over their heads. He would say, "If you don't provide that for your family, how can you call yourself a man?" He taught me about the responsibility of educating your children, teaching them life lessons. He put everything in perspective, as far as what role you had as a man. He would speak about being the captain of your ship, and how important it is to make decisions that will affect the entire family when it's time to make those decisions. My father would teach me lessons of life by using people from the past as examples. He told me so much about them that I felt as if I actually knew them.

The courage that I had to take the public stance we took in

1968 at the Olympics was directly instilled in me by my father from the time I was a little kid running around on Lenox Avenue. He would use someone like Jackie Robinson. I would go to the YMCA on 135th Street and Lenox and watch videos of him when he first broke the color barrier in major league baseball. My father used these videos to show us the sacrifices that Jackie Robinson had to make and what he had to endure. He made us have a clear understanding that Robinson wasn't just concerned about Robinson, but rather about all the young people who would follow in his footsteps. He showed us how, when they put him on the field and they called him every racial slur that they have ever invented, he had to have tolerance and not retaliate. He taught me how it wasn't a symbol of weakness but rather an example of strength to be able to have the self-discipline not to stoop to another man's level because you see the big picture. And when Jackie Robinson one day walked into my father's shop to have his shoes shined, I felt connected to him, because I knew what he was about as a man, and that had a tremendous influence on me. I got the chance to meet a lot of the people whom my father would tell me about, because his shop was right at 626 Lenox Avenue, next to the Savoy Ballroom, and anyone who knows anything about Harlem in that time period knows that the Savoy Ballroom was the happenin' spot.

He spoke to me a lot about Paul Robeson. He would talk about how dignified an individual he was. And about how proud he was as a black man. How he was not one to take the backseat on the bus. He explained to us how he was not only a world-class athlete, but he was highly educated and a Rhodes scholar. He was teaching me that his athletic gifts were only a small piece of who this person was as a whole.

After I returned home from the '68 Olympics, my father was reading a newspaper, the New York Times, *and he asked me why I was doing all these bad things. I didn't know what he was talking about, so he showed me an article that was attempting to not only criminalize but tear to shreds the character, name, and reputation of various people—Harry Edwards, H. Rap Brown, Stokely Carmichael, myself, and a few other brothers who had taken various stances in different areas and causes. I had to bring back the messages and examples that he taught me growing up, kind of like the student teaching the teacher in saying, "Remember how you taught me about all of those great people in the past and showed me how they were persecuted? You showed me what they did to Robeson after he stood up for his people. Well, that's what's happening to me. You know me; you may not know H. Rap Brown and Carmichael, but you know me, and you know you did not raise me to do any of those things that paper is saying." He vowed to me that he would never let anyone hurt me. He said, "Don't worry about anything, son. I got your back."*

"I got your back." What an important message to hear from your father—or, if not your father, from another influential elder in your life. When I was growing up in Tulsa, there was a group of police officers known as the Black Cops Coalition. They were all big, burly men who looked like they spent much of their lives in the weight room. These men would keep a close eye on us. If they saw us acting out in public, they would get on us real hard. In other words, they had our backs. One of them in particular, Marvin Blades, would stay on us constantly. Somehow we knew they were doing it out of love, so we would listen to them. I still talk to them now when I go back to Tulsa. It says a lot about the power of having police officers patrolling a neighborhood who are actually from the neighborhood. We knew they were trying to teach us right from wrong and show us the consequences of our actions. Marvin Blades went to the AAU teams, the churches, wherever he could find young boys, and he would hold seminars for us. I remember my mother bringing me to some of them. He'd show us footage of different gang members, how they lived and how they died. There'd be horrific pictures of dead bodies with their chests blown open at age nineteen. Very graphic stuff that could turn your stomach. And he'd ask us, "So, is this what you want your future to be?"

When you were out in the street, possibly on the verge of messing up, you didn't want to run into Marvin Blades and one of the Black Cops Coalition. Just imagine, these were cops who knew your parents. Elders with the ultimate influence. Whatever they told us to do, we did. And we never got offended.

At Syracuse, sometimes Coach Boeheim would actually use Coach Orr as a surrogate and tell him to get on me about something. I guess maybe he saw that his own interactions with me weren't so fruitful. Coach Orr wasn't even the coach assigned to work with me; he worked with the forwards, while I was a center who worked with a different assistant coach. But I was Orr's guy.

Now that I've spent more than a decade in the NBA, I have a more nuanced, perhaps more generous perspective on Coach Jim Boeheim. He treats his players at Syracuse like they are already professionals, like they are adults. If you want to work hard, you can. But he's not going to be monitoring you every second like a lot of coaches. Your practice habits, the manner and degree you choose to push yourself, he leaves that up to you, but once you step on the court, he expects results. Some guys handle it well; some guys don't.

I think the key to dealing with young men who grew up without fathers is developing trust. If you sense that the person truly wants you to do your best, and wants the best for you, then you learn to trust him. As I said before, if you have trust that the person in authority is acting out of love, then he can be as strict and disciplined as he wants because he has your respect. That's the way Coach John Thompson was at Georgetown. I've spoken to quite a few players who played for him, and they all said Coach Thompson would get on you like you wouldn't believe. But he had their respect, because they knew he was doing it out of love. He always wanted the best for them, whether it was in school or generally to be great men.

Without Coach Orr, I don't think I would have made it through Syracuse. There would have been some kind of conflict, or something would have happened that first year and it just wouldn't have worked. Because I didn't have that connection with Coach Boeheim. Every time he said something to me, I would immediately take offense. I'd be thinking, *You're not going to be yelling at me like that.* It was almost like he was challenging my manhood—something that I would pick up on right away. That's why I connect on so many levels with the young guys in prison. Instinctively I understand the mentality they have. We hear young cats talking about that word, "respect," all the time; I think a lot of older adults don't understand how important that is to a young man. Once someone feels disrespected, all bets are off—all clear thinking, all inhibition just goes out the window. All you're thinking about is, *This person disrespected me.* So when I go into the prisons, I tell them stories about me; I tell them stories about Coach Boeheim, all the times when I felt disrespected. I tell them about encounters I had with the police when their intention was to disrespect me, but I had to somehow find some self-control. We all have heard of instances where players in the NBA have had conflicts with their coach—in the famous Sprewell case, even choking the coach. I'm not saying it's the right thing to do, but I understand it. Guys fly off the handle and make a really bad decision. If you took the influential elders—my grandfather, Reverend Potter, and Coach Orr—out of the equation for me, I might have been one of those guys making a terrible, fateful decision, dooming the rest of my life. I can name twenty or twenty-five guys off the top of my head, both in Tulsa and in Harlem, who should have made the NBA before me, but one bad decision along the way ended it all for them. One split second, something happens, you feel disrespected and you react without even thinking. Next thing you know, you're sitting up in a prison somewhere, wondering where your life went. Most of these guys aren't bad people; they're just guys who made the wrong choices—and who probably didn't have the kinds of elders that I had to talk them through it, to give them a much-needed dose of common sense.

Mumia Abu-Jamal had long been described as probably the most famous death row inmate in the world. (His sentence was recently reduced from a death sentence to life in prison.) He has seen the inner workings of the prison system for three decades. In this piece, he describes a prison phenomenon he calls "father hunger"—the desperation he has seen among men behind bars to have a wise elder in their lives.

In prisons throughout the nation, sullen men, sentenced to some of the most isolated existences imaginable, draw on the bitter well of memory in search of a father that too many of them have never known. That heart-aching, soul-searching sense of loss colors their lives, and often poisons their relationships with other men. In one of my books, I called this phenomenon "father hunger," to describe the acute sense of hurt, want, and betrayal that comes from not knowing or interacting with one's father, and the sometimes freighted search for a replacement.

Years ago, while at a prison in central Pennsylvania, another man and I met a somewhat younger man, who had a distinctly standoffish and strained relationship with every one of the older men. He talked nastily to men of his cohort, until an older man let him know that this was unacceptable. It dawned on us that we were men who would be his father's age, and when he looked at us, he saw (and, more important, felt) the figure of his hated and detested father. In psychology, this would be called projection, or negative transference. None of us knew his father, and he didn't know any of us prior to his incarceration. But the intense feelings surging within him often spilled out when he met men who, perhaps uncon-

sciously, reminded him of the hated, absent father. Perhaps he didn't know who his father was, and felt that in this group, one of these older dudes could be him. Perhaps one of us was. It was like a fever in the brain that sent him into rages for years.

Another example shows me how deep it lives in the consciousness. I met a younger man from North Philadelphia, which was once the biggest black community in Pennsylvania. He was bright, extroverted, and aggressive. But he had no idea of black (local or national) history beyond the safe, sedate stories that millions of black kids are taught in public schools. I loaned him a copy of Revolutionary Suicide by Huey P. Newton (the cofounder of the Black Panther Party). The very next day he almost exploded with excitement and exclaimed, "Y'all brothas are rollin' like that!" He requested—no, demanded—more books, and went through them like a hurricane. He read Huey, Eldridge Cleaver, Malcolm X, Frantz Fanon, Assata Shakur, and demanded more. He read and read and read. And he grew. One day, while we were in the law library, he stopped calling me "Old-head" and began calling me "Papa." I thought it was a reference to the late Eldridge Cleaver, former minister of information of the Black Panther Party, and a prison writer. He explained it wasn't that, but "as far as I'm concerned, you're my papa." I was dumbfounded and extremely uncomfortable. I responded to him, "Dude, I ain't your pop, man. You got a father. It ain't right for you to call another man that." He replied, "That chump [except he didn't say chump] didn't teach me none of the stuff you did! You taught me! Not him! He should've did it but he didn't. . . . He's nothing but a coward!" I told him that he shouldn't talk that way about his father, and he almost went off. "F&$k that dude!" he snarled. He added that he shouldn't have to learn the things he did after coming to prison.

He was right—his father should have taught him. And since I was doing the teaching, I was Papa to him. And that was that. For too many young black men, Mom is both mother and father. And

though they teach valuable life lessons (mothers are the first teachers),
there are some things that only men can teach.

It is so supremely important for young men to feel like there's a
man out there who has them covered. If it's not Dad, then they have
to find somebody else. Young men are on a constant quest to find
that. My mother talks to me all the time about her students, how
some of the teachers complain to her that they could never get away
with talking to the kids the way my mother does. She's real tough
on the kids. The other teachers tell her, "If I said that to them,
they'd blow up on me." But she responds, "You don't have their
respect. They don't know you're on their side and have their best
interests at heart." When I was in school, I could tell right away if
a teacher had my best interest at heart. It doesn't take much for a
kid to know a person doesn't respect him or is not on his side. Now,
I wasn't one to get upset over stuff like somebody stepping on
my sneakers. That wasn't me. My big problem was dealing with
authority figures. To learn how to bite your tongue and not react
when somebody in a position of authority is disrespecting you is a
tough lesson for young people to learn. I think adults need to be
more sensitive to that, to try to understand how major this is for
young people. This is one of the places where a well-respected elder
can make a big difference. When I talk to young people in the prisons, I tell them that I know they probably were even right to get
offended sometimes, but they still have to learn self-control. More
than anything, self-control is a way of protecting yourself, of not
allowing somebody else's actions or words to get you in a situation
you can't get out of. Sometimes when I think back to those college
days, I wonder what would have happened to me if, instead of an
elder like Coach Orr in my ear, I had some knucklehead or bad
influence who was telling me to react in negative, unhelpful ways,
advising me that what I should do was punch my coach in the face
for talking to me that way. I know what would have happened—I

wouldn't be where I am now. But that's the situation so many young people are in—they have somebody whispering in their ear, but that person is telling them all the wrong things. Everybody gets in these situations, when they have someone who doesn't respect them up in their face. I know I've made my share of bad choices. Speaking from experience, it definitely helps to have the guidance of a wise mentor or elder along that journey.

During the summer after my freshman year, I worked out with Coach Orr all the time while I took a few extra classes toward my major, which was business. I came to Syracuse kind of skinny, so I knew I needed to hit the weights after battling Otis Hill in practice every day and playing against the tough guys in the Big East. After banging with players like Jahidi White at Georgetown, Jason Lawson at Villanova, Danya Abrams at Boston College, Adonal Foyle at Colgate, etc., I knew I needed to hit the weight room. I lifted with the football players and worked hard that summer. It paid off; I had a great sophomore season. Right away, Coach Orr's lessons from the previous year became clearer. He was always asking me, "When you find some success, how will you react to it?" Now he constantly worked to keep me humble—just like my mom did before I got to college. I could have a great game with twenty points, thirteen rebounds, six blocks (for you non–basketball fans, this is about as good as it gets for a big man), and he'd still be in my ear: "That was good, but you did this wrong; you missed this; you forgot this. Alonzo Mourning and Derrick Coleman [two of my favorite players at the time] wouldn't have done it wrong." He had me working on shooting a hook with my left hand in addition to my right. After I was able to shoot with both hands, it made it even more difficult for opposing centers to guard me in the post. Now, my right hand was working just fine, but Coach Orr wanted more.

Coach Orr's point was that I should never settle, never just rest on my laurels. Often in the sports world, guys get comfortable when they get a little success. It's human nature. But Coach Orr was having none of that. It was a great message for me to hear at that age. It's something that has stayed with me over the years. It was especially important to hear that at Syracuse, because it was a place where you could rest on your laurels if that's what you wanted to do. I'm sure it's not just Syracuse—a lot of schools, teams, companies I'm sure operate the same way.

After my junior year of college, I started thinking about coming out early and entering the NBA draft. I had just had a great season; I was chosen as the Big East Defensive Player of the Year, and the draft projections had me being chosen somewhere between eighteen and twenty-four, meaning I'd be one of the first two dozen players drafted. Of course, these were just predictions—guesses, really. They could be wrong. But if they were right, being a first-round draft choice between eighteen and twenty-four would mean a lot of money. I was torn. I thought, *The whole purpose of college is to get a good job, right?* I had a very good job being waved right in front of my face, so why stay in school? But then there was Coach Orr talking in my ear. He was telling me, "You could do more. Do you want to settle for being chosen in the twenties, or do want to push for more? Don't you want your degree, considering all the work you put into your studies?" I listened to Coach Orr and I stayed. I'm glad I did. I had another great season my senior year—I was chosen again as the Big East Defensive Player of the Year, the only player besides Allen Iverson ever to win the honor two years in a row—and I moved up in the draft. Ultimately I was chosen twelfth.

When I got to the NBA I eventually found my way onto the roster of the Washington Wizards, coached by former NBA star Doug Collins. Collins was another coach with a style that I didn't particularly enjoy. Early on in my tenure there, Coach Collins called me into his office. He looked at me and said he didn't think I would make it in the NBA past my rookie season. In that moment, a thousand different responses flashed through my mind. But somehow I was able to find some self-control. It was a horrible thing for him to say to me—to this day, I'm not sure exactly what he thought he might accomplish by saying that.

Fortunately for me, by this time I had managed to find another elder to mentor me, Pastor John Jenkins of First Baptist Church in Maryland. I had visited several churches before I made my way to First Baptist, but after I watched Pastor Jenkins in action and then met him, I knew I had found a new home. He felt very genuine, someone that I'd have an easy time talking to. I leaned heavily on Pastor Jenkins during that time, especially after that meeting with Coach Collins. Pastor Jenkins asked me how I was going to respond. Was I going to choke him, punch him in the face—or go out on the court and prove him wrong? Well, obviously I didn't put my hands on my coach. But I did go to work on the hardwood. I progressed and improved so much that Wizards management eventually offered me a long-term contract. After I signed the contract, I sat down and wrote a poem called "Haters" that I sent to Coach Collins. I wanted him to know his words didn't stop me. You might ask whether the things he said to me were his own form of motivation, some clever scheme to get me to work harder. I can't say for sure. But time has passed and I don't hold any grudges toward him. I saw him last year during the playoffs and we exchanged pleasantries; I asked about his wife and kids; he remembered Nichole and asked how she was doing. Everything was peaceful. However, I have to admit, every time I see him, I take great pleasure in knowing that I proved him wrong. That is one of the best feelings in the world. There will always be haters out there—taking their words and flipping them around as a form of motivation is a much better response than punching them in the face!

What I appreciated most about Pastor Jenkins's approach was his honesty. Too many pastors try to portray themselves as perfect, holier-than-thou. That is such an immediate turnoff for me. But Pastor Jenkins was quick to let you know he was still on the same journey as everybody else. I would go to him all the time during my years with the Wizards, and when I handled something the wrong way, he was not shy about telling me. He would tell me a story about how he also made the wrong choices when he was in a similar situation. But he'd also be quick to tell me he didn't have all the answers. It felt very human. That's always worked better for me.

Too many young people have yes-men around them, homeboys who won't tell them the truth. You see it all over the NBA. I feel fortunate that I've always had a group of friends who are honest with one another. Now that I'm an elder on the team, I try to be as honest as possible when young players come to me with questions. I'll tell them, "Man, that was a terrible decision you made. You really thought that was going to work?"

That's the kind of relationship I hope to have with my son, Malcolm. When he comes to me with questions and problems, I want to be able to tell him about my mistakes, about the things I struggled with. I think young men need that. Unfortunately, so many young men are growing up without that, so they spend way too many years in a desperate search to find it somewhere. Anywhere. Because everybody needs that voice. Too many young people find it in the wrong places. Dangerous places. That's messed up, but that's where we are right now.

As I discussed earlier, my grandpa Freddy was a monumental figure in my life, providing me with an essential male role model at a time when I needed one badly. He also played the same role in the childhood of my brother, **Julian Thomas**. In closing this chapter, I am featuring a poem written by my brother that describes exactly what our grandfather meant to us.

For Grandpa Freddy

What is the measure of the life of a man?
Is it medals and ribbons, placards with gold nameplates,

A closet full of memories and the neckties to match,
Elegant, faded like the lingering sun at dusk.

Is it measured in laughter and shared remembrances,
The telling and retelling of neighborhood lore
Handed down like winter pants to younger siblings,
Or a secret family recipe for the perfect batch of collards.

Is it calculated with accomplished feats and heroics,
The scores of courageous acts in a youth who saw
Barriers broken down by a black airborne division
As a paratrooper in war-torn Korea.

My grandfather was a man of strong opinions
And broad perspective,
Strong hands, and a strong mind.
An avid student of history,
He spoke of wartime conflicts
With the ease and grace of a college professor,
Clarity without condemnation.

A Harlem tenement sits vacant and still,
Yet still I can hear laughter and shouts outside my window,
Young people set loose to run free in El Barrio
The rumble of the street with its bustle and its song.

And still I can hear Grandpa,
The resonating chuckle dissecting the latest blunder by Giuliani,
Or the lingering derision that follows every time the Yankees lose,
Again, and again . . .

My grandfather was a man of conviction,
His presence a calm and tranquil gust of soothing air,

And his words, though at times sparse,
Would set my mind to undulate,
Like a smooth stone into a still pond.
I never saw him angry.

You measure a man by the people who love him,
By the wisdom he left behind,
The legacy of a life lived with honor and dignity
And without regret.

You measure a tree
By its fruit.

CHAPTER FIVE

THE ROOTS OF A TREE: REACHING BACK INTO HISTORY TO LIFT UP YOUR CHILDREN

After their presence, their joy, their love, and their wisdom, the final gift that fathers should present to their children is the gift of history. I think this is an area that is too often left ignored and forgotten these days. Too many parents think it is the job of the schools to teach their children about history. But the schools can't teach history the way a parent can. I'm a living testament to that fact. I don't even want to think about what kind of person I would have turned out to be without the years of history lessons my mother provided me and my brother. She approached the assignment with a vengeance, buying books, talking to us, showing us movies and documentaries, slowly but surely building a base of knowledge that would give us a confidence and sense of self that would serve us extremely well out in the real world. She started very early, because you can't really begin this stuff too early, and every year she would add on to our knowledge, stacking more blocks onto the foundation until the desire to know more had been internalized by us. After that, she could just watch as we set off on our own quests to learn as much as we could about our history and our people.

No matter who you are or where you're from, we all need a connection with our ancestors. The power of knowing that you descend from a long line of mighty or successful or brilliant or resourceful people is incalculable. It certainly was in my case. My mother figured out how to use history as a motivational tool. She inundated us with books about important African-American figures in our past, from Matthew Henson and Nat Turner to Dr. Martin Luther King (besides the typical "I Have a Dream" speech that schools solely focus on) and Denmark Vesey. She saw that she had a willing pupil in me, so she kept it coming. I knew that my friends were not getting this stuff, because it wasn't something we were taught in school. At one memorable point, my mother turned her attention to my name. Etan was derived from the Egyptian king Akhenaton. He was the husband of Nefertiti and the father of King Tut, and he is credited with ushering in a wave of artistic freedom and invention and trying to change the Egyptian religion from the worshiping of many gods to the worship of one god, the sun god, Aton Ra. His name means "servant of Aton." My mother had much admiration for what he stood for and she fell in love with his name. But she changed the spelling because my father's name is Antone and they didn't want it to look like I was a junior. Having a connection to this historic figure was a big deal for me; it put me in an entirely different frame of mind. It's unusual in the black community to have any kind of connection to our culture through our names, because our last names were often the names of our slave masters. Most other cultures have names that speak of their origins, even if they are removed from their homelands—Chinese, Spanish, Irish, Jewish, etc. They all have names reflective of their culture. But with us, the line stops at slavery. All we have are slave names, as is my last name, Thomas. I think that's perhaps why we have tried to fashion our own culture with what some may consider "unusual names." I feel that we have the power and the ability to, as

Michael Eric Dyson states, "create the meanings of our own names and fulfill our own destinies the best we can."

For some reason, black elitists become embarrassed at names their white colleagues, friends, acquaintances, etc., can't pronounce. I have seen black people just about hold their heads in shame when a white person struggles to pronounce a name they are not used to hearing. My question is this: Why shouldn't black people have African names? How peculiar would it be for a Japanese person to have a Muslim name? Or an Italian person to have a Swahili name? But we as black people feel ashamed to have African names? How backward is that? Who is it that taught us to be ashamed of ourselves, and why would we still feel ashamed today? The only explanation I can come up with is because many of us do not know enough about where we come from and therefore we are ashamed of anything that is associated with where we come from.

For me, having a meaningful name gave me a sense of belonging to something bigger than myself. That's some powerful stuff. We gave my son Aton as a middle name, so that he can have that same connection. His first name is Malcolm, after Malcolm X. I can't wait to teach him all about Malcolm X, who had such a huge influence on me. He already knows who he was named after; he's seen pictures of Malcolm. But at age five, he's not ready yet for the autobiography. I still have a few more years for that. My middle daughter's name is Imani, which means "faith" in Swahili. A few years ago I took a DNA test to see where in Africa my origins lie. I discovered the country where my ancestors originated was Sierra Leone, specifically the Temne tribe. The Temne were a major source for the slave trade in the sixteenth, seventeenth, and eighteenth centuries. In honor of this information, I named my third child Sierra when she was born in the summer of 2010. I think it's so important for African-Americans to do this DNA test, so that we're not wandering around thinking our history started at the end of slavery.

Tito Puente Jr. wears his father's name with pride. He has carried the torch and nurtured the musical legacy left by his father while exuding a pride in his Hispanic heritage that is locked in his soul. In this piece, he talks about how continuing the traditions, the principles and ideals of his father have become his destiny.

My father, Ernesto Anthony Puente Jr., better known as Tito Puente, taught me from a very young age to be proud of my Hispanic heritage and culture. My father was a busy man. Being a world-renowned phenomenon and credited as "the King of Latin Music" keeps your schedule pretty busy. My father had a career for over fifty years touring around the world bringing the gift of music to the masses. He played in almost two hundred places a year. In all of that, he still found time to be a devoted father, a great provider, and a teacher. He, along with my mother, Margaret, gave me the foundation that helped me become the man I am today. One thing he always made sure of was that I had pride in my heritage.

I am Puerto Rican, born and raised in New York City. My son, who, continuing the tradition, I named after me, as well as my daughter, Miranda, are very young right now. They are mostly into playgrounds and cartoons and having fun. But I know that I want them to also have tremendous pride in their culture and their heritage the same way I do. I hope that they keep the spirit of their grandfather alive in whatever they choose to do. This is my job. I can't wait for the schools to teach them about their culture. The way for them to learn about their heritage is for me as their parent to teach them about it from an early age. I will be able to guide them and teach them their history and their culture more as they get older, but it starts now, while they're young. They are royalty in my eyes, and I cherish them. I want them to have pride in themselves and to become strong men and women as they grow older and to take pride in whatever they do. I am going to teach them all about their beautiful Puerto Rican heritage.

My grandparents were both born in Puerto Rico. My father was very proud of being Puerto Rican and from New York. He was a Nuyorican, which described people from New York and Puerto Rico. He had an appreciation of his heritage that was passed to me. We've learned a lot as musicians, being from New York and in particular Spanish Harlem in New York. An area called El Barrio. Harlem was the center of where the music industry evolved. It was where the greatest musicians of our time came from. My father played at the Apollo Theater and was partly responsible for helping to bring the two cultures together through music. My father was raised around Duke Ellington, Count Basie, Ella Fitzgerald, Jelly Roll Morton, Fats Waller, and all of the greats who came out of the Harlem Renaissance, and he gravitated toward the jazz music that was invented in the 1920s. Those traditions took on a fusion, so to speak, and my father created Latin jazz in the forties, and the Afro-Cuban and Caribbean sounds, like mambo and cha-cha.

Myself, I am a little more modern in my music, because I have more of the 1970s, 1980s feel, when hip-hop music was invented out of New York City, but the appreciation I have for what my father created is what has driven me to continue nurturing the musical legacy.

The Puerto Rican pride and overall Hispanic pride that we have is something that I directly learned from my father. He was an ambassador of Latin music. He made that a priority. He held his head high and was proud to play Afro-Cuban music that came directly from Africa and Cuba. He was the only Puerto Rican who presented that in a Latin jazz sound. It's almost as if you have to be born and raised in New York to understand the level of Puerto Rican pride that runs through our veins. It is something that is put on display. It's not hidden or done behind closed doors, but I was always taught to have tremendous pride outwardly. Every year, around the second week of June, we have what is called the Puerto Rican Day Parade. Three or four million people line the parade route, and another nine million people watch on television, all to celebrate the pride of our heritage. You'll see Puerto Rican flags and hear music and see celebrities such as Jimmy Smits, Ricky Martin, Jennifer Lopez, Marc Anthony, and many more, all showing the world that we are proud of our roots. For us to be able to translate Puerto Rican achievements into a visible demonstration of the intricate dynamics of the Puerto Rican community as a whole in an effort to further achieve Hispanic unification is beyond special. The celebration then becomes a way to promote not only cultural awareness, but education, leadership, and community engagement among all Spanish-speaking people. For us to be able to say on a big stage that we are Latino, we are unified, and we are proud is a direct continuation of my father's passion. That's what he was able to show through his music, and for me to be able to continue that tradition has become my destiny.

Having the pride that Tito Puente Jr. was speaking of in where you come from is crucial in one's development. I saw another result of my mother's teaching when I took a trip to Africa with the NBA Players Association a few years ago. My mother had given me many lessons about Africa—its beauty, its development, its cities, its people. She talked about it; we read about it; we watched films about it. I had that pride because my mother made sure of it. That's why I was so excited before the trip, because I was finally going to get a chance to see it in person. When I got to Kenya, I was struck by how often I heard the other players say that it looked totally different from what they expected. I remember Metta World Peace (formerly Ron Artest) kept saying that he didn't know about this side of Africa. They had grown up with so many negative images of the continent, about how backward and uncivilized it was, that they were shocked when they saw the real thing. We were in Nairobi and it looked like any big city in the United States. We got there in the middle of the winter season, and we weren't prepared for the cold. Of course, when you think of Africa, you think of unbearable heat. But that's just more misinformation and brainwashing. In fact it was cold and rainy. It reminded me of Seattle. I was all the way unprepared, because I brought all summer clothes. When we got there, I couldn't help but think of Malcolm X's quote, "You can't hate the roots of a tree without hating the whole tree; you can't hate your origin and not end up hating yourself." If the only information we have of our place of origin is negative, it's almost impossible to have pride in yourself. That's why it's so crucial for fathers and mothers to take an active role in educating their children about their roots. You certainly can't leave it to the schools to teach black children about Africa. You have to teach them truth, and start as early as possible with it—because kids start developing their self-identity at a very early age. You want to get there before all those negative images start flooding in from the outside world. After seeing Africa firsthand on our trip, Metta World Peace (formerly Ron Artest) returned to build and equip an HIV testing clinic for the Ray of Hope Clinic in Nairobi, and made an additional donation to pay for the lab technicians' salaries for 2009. He now had a connection that he never had before.

Chicago Bulls star **Joakim Noah** has a fascinating personal history—a history that he has been fortunate enough to learn thoroughly since he was a child. Being of mixed race might be a source of confusion or frustration for some, but that's certainly not the case with Joakim. In this piece, he talks about the importance of learning about his multiple roots, and his strong connection to both Africa and Europe.

Let me start out by saying that I come from a very different background. My mother is a white, blond-haired, green-eyed Swedish lady who comes from a farm country in Sweden where there are no black people. My father, however, who is French and West African, is black, with dreads, and is from Cameroon. When I was very young they divorced, but growing up I was always in the position to enjoy both cultures and compare them to one another. I would be able to go visit my mom's parents in Sweden, then go to Cameroon and see my grandfather. I lived in France, since I had family living there as well.

The athletic genes must run in my family, since my father was a professional athlete himself. He was a tennis player (Yannick Noah) who was discovered by Arthur Ashe. As a kid growing up in Africa he would play tennis with wooden paddles. Ashe was doing a tour in Africa for kids and he came across my father, who was ten at the time. He thought my father had a great deal of talent, exceptional hand-eye coordination, and saw something in him. Ashe called his agent, a man by the name of Donald Dell, and said, "I really like this kid; I want to help him out." Two years later, at the age of twelve, my father decided to leave Cameroon, essentially sacrificing his childhood so that he could go to boarding school to become a tennis player. On the same wooden paddle that my dad had grown up playing tennis on, Arthur signed, "See you at Wimbledon." Eventually, my father's hard work and self-sacrifice paid off, since he became the best junior player in France and, at the age of sixteen, ended up playing doubles with Arthur Ashe at Wimbledon. This story is part of my heritage, something I will never forget.

I consider myself a very fortunate, blessed individual, because growing up I was able to go back to Africa. My trips to Cameroon always put my life, the world, everything in perspective for me. Personally, I believe that every black child in America should have a chance to go to Africa once in his or her lifetime, just as Muslims are encouraged to go to Mecca once in their lifetimes. In fact, black kids in the Caribbean and South America too. I partly grew up in Africa, and some of my closest friends are from there. What I love about Cameroon, my country, is that although it is very poor, the people there are some of the happiest, funniest people you will ever meet. While the country is extremely corrupt—the only people who make it out of poverty are the athletes and politicians—unlike other corrupt societies, Cameroon is near the equator. This means that a person can just throw a couple of seeds in the ground, and practically anything will grow, so no one goes hungry. This may be a poverty-stricken country; however, the individuals living there do not let it affect them. Cameroon was colonized by the French, so everybody speaks French, and just like the people who colonized their country, the people of Cameroon love to eat good food, drink good wine, and have a good time. The country has some spectacular cities and top-notch restaurants. Eventually, I want to bring some of my team-mates there so that they can check it out. I want them to personally experience what I try to describe to them. Every time I go there I have a great time, but when I go there and then come back to the United States, I remember how fortunate I am for the things I have in my life.

After I was born, I lived in France for ten years. I moved to the States when I was twelve, and New York City became my new home. Being that my father was a very successful tennis player (and a successful musician after his tennis career ended), we lived in a brownstone. However, because I played basketball, most of my friends were kids from the projects. It opened my eyes to a world that I would not have been able to see if not for basketball, because I was able to witness how they lived and how they were growing up in a different lifestyle from my own. I realized pretty quickly that these kids did not know anything about their roots, though. Whenever I would talk about Africa to them, they would sound surprised by everything I was saying. The way Africa was presented to them was so wrong. So when I would talk about going there and visiting cities, and the parties, and the clubs, that would all be unheard-of to them.

It was as if Africa could not have any of those things. It was just really sad how ignorant they were about their roots, yet I knew they were not the only ones.

When I received my first check from the NBA, I did not spend it on fancy cars or expensive jewelry. Instead, I just wanted to travel and bring some of my friends to the places I have seen. I brought my one best friend from Harlem and my other best friend from Brooklyn to Hawaii with me, because I wanted them to see something different and new. I did not want to spend my money in a club—even though I have to admit I do that sometimes—I wanted to show my friends that there is more to life than flashing what you have. I have family who live in Hawaii, so while there we visited them and listened to the elders, my grandfather in particular, who has just passed away. Listening to them allowed me to recollect where my family comes from while also learning life lessons that I will always remember. My family lives all throughout the world, it seems, so I always make an effort to visit all the places they live, although some places love me better than others. This past summer I made a trip to Sweden. When I walked around over there, this place where there is nothing but white farmers, they were like, "Who the hell is that?" Afterward, though, I went straight to Cameroon, where I am practically seen as white. They know who I am, though, because my father is probably the most well-known figure in Cameroon, so I get a lot of love. Being able to travel to these places, and surround myself with the elders in my family, has always kept me grounded and made me feel like I knew where I was from, even when I am in America and none of my family is here with me.

When I attended the University of Florida, I decided to minor in African-American studies, because I felt it was important to know as much as I could about the African diasporas, the spread of black people throughout the world. As a child, whether I was with my dad or my mom, I remember waking up and hearing Bob Marley play-

ing in the house. I knew all of the lyrics to his songs before I even knew what they meant. So in college, I was happy to be able to study the history of the Rastafarians, the people who rebelled against the slave owners in Jamaica, and Marcus Garvey's thought processes of repatriation. School was always kind of tough for me, but once I found something I was interested in learning, I loved it.

When you are biracial like me, it can feel like everything bothers you. If a black person says something bad about whites you feel affected, and when a white person says something about blacks you feel affected. Everybody, even in Africa and Europe, tries to put you in a box. Yet I am from all these places, so I cannot really be put in a box. I am very comfortable with who I am. People think biracial people do not feel like they belong anywhere and that they always have to defend themselves because there is a lot of ignorance out there, but at the same time, a lot of biracial people are pretty comfortable with who they are. Look at Barack Obama. Obama looks pretty comfortable in his own skin. We cannot forget about Bob Marley, who also looked comfortable in his own skin. People are quick to say, "Wait, those are all black leaders," but to me they are people who have been raised with love. Obama went to school in Hawaii, he had a white mother and an African father, and he traveled back to Africa, Europe, and other places—growing up he saw a lot of cultures and had a lot of experiences. I think that is something that is missing with a lot of black people in America. The first thing we do when we get money is want to show it, instead of thinking, Let me travel, see the world, check out my heritage, and see my roots in Africa. That is really, really important. It amazes me that Africa still has all these negative connotations here in America. It should not be like that. We still have a lot to learn and see.

Noah was disturbed when he realized how little children in this country learn about Africa—and how everything they learn is negative and wrong. My mother made sure the same thing didn't happen to me and my brother. One of her most memorable lessons was on the history of the "n-word." To teach it, she used the story of Emmett Till. She told me how fourteen-year-old Emmett was mutilated and killed—brutally beaten, with his eye gouged out, shot through the head, and dumped in a river with a seventy-pound weight tied around his neck—all because he had supposedly whistled at a white woman. My mother said the "n-word" may have been the last word Emmett heard yelled at him before he was killed. She said, "So why would you ever want to trivialize that word by throwing it around with your friends? After what our ancestors went through, are you going to disrespect them by using that word?" My God, that was such a potent picture she had drawn for me. From that moment on, I never looked at that word the same way again, and I would immediately check someone if they addressed me in that manner. This was early middle school when this happened, but I was old enough to develop an understanding of that word's history and power that was very different from my peers'. I'm a big fan of hip-hop, and unfortunately that word has become as common as a drumbeat in hip-hop culture. I don't know if we'll ever be able to totally purge the word from the culture, but if more kids were given as detailed and dramatic an accounting of that word's history as I was, I have no doubt that it would be a lot less common. Tell a child about the horrible things that were done to this fourteen-year-old boy just because of his skin color, the pain and bone-chilling fear that he must have felt coursing through his veins as that ugly word rattled around in his brain, a word intended to make him feel the virulent hatred of his attackers. It makes me shudder all over again just thinking about it. Never again could I take that word lightly.

As I've mentioned before, my mother's family hails from St. Croix of the U.S. Virgin Islands, and Grenada, a small island in the southeast Caribbean, north of Venezuela and Trinidad. From an early age, I took a great deal of pride in my West Indian heritage. I got a thrill when I took a trip back there with my grandmother about three years after I graduated from Syracuse. She brought me to places she remembered from when she was a little girl. She showed me the school her mother attended, the church her mother went to, the town they lived in. Walking on the same land that my great-grandmother walked on was an amazing feeling for me. I felt such a powerful connection to the place. And I loved to see the pride and happiness on my grandmother's face as she showed me these sites. My grandparents had always inundated me with West Indian culture from a young age. My grandmother would tell me about Bob Marley, Marcus Garvey, and many West Indian heroes. I loved West Indian food and Caribbean music from as early as I can remember. Once you start learning about your heritage, that's what happens—you soak up everything and always want more and more. It was a blessing for me to have had a link to an actual place. Unfortunately, this is something that so many African-Americans don't have. I can't overemphasize the value of this information, knowing that there was a land where my people sank their hands into the soil, where they drank deeply of the water, breathed the air. Whenever I wanted, I could travel there and do the same things that my people had done there two hundred years ago. That land, those people, are now such an integral part of who I am, I can't even imagine not knowing anything about my history and culture. I would encourage anyone out there who doesn't know any of their history to go to the elders in the family and find out as much as you can. You might be surprised by how the information transforms you, frees you, empowers you. That's why family reunions have become so important in the black community—we feel a desperate need to reach out to family, to hold on to family, to find out more, to establish as many connections as we can.

There are not many figures in black history as influential as the late Bob Marley. I am so pleased that one of his sons, **Damian Marley**, agreed to delve into the influence his father has had not only on young Damian, but on an entire country and the world. In this piece, we can clearly feel the pride Damian has in his father and his heritage.

My father has had a great influence on my life, but mine is a unique case, because Bob Marley is one of the biggest influences on the entire planet. He was a spiritual father for a lot of people. I was very young when my father passed away—age two, almost three. So I don't have a lot of hands-on memories to share with people. I couldn't tell you what time he used to come home every night or anything like that. But I think it's a great testament to what a great spirit he is, my not knowing him personally but being like him in a lot of ways because of the energy and the legacy he left here for the world.

My father guided a lot of people to see Rastafari, which definitely influences my life on a day-to-day basis. He has been my gateway to that, influencing how I eat, how I think, how I talk, how I dress, my hair, everything. When you look now at the modern world, you see a lot of dreadlocks all over the place. But when the Rasta movement started, you might be abused by the police in Jamaica for having dreadlocks. For a lot of people now it's a style, but it still comes from my father's influence as one of the first persons with dreadlocks who exposed it to the world.

If you look at my family, over 50 percent of us are in the music business. That's because of our looking up to our father. That tells you what kind of person he was. When you have children and they want to emulate you and walk in your footsteps, it says a lot about the kind of role model you are. We are a living testament to what a great father he was.

I was born and grew up in Jamaica—I'm definitely Jamaican to the bone, in terms of the customs and culture and choices I make. Bob Marley is the identity of the culture, the country, the music. But he was a man from my understanding who was very adamant about his children coming together. I have brothers and sisters who have different moms, but he would try to bring us to one central location so that we would know each other. He was passionate about his kids; he really cared about them. Even now, we're all still together as a family. Now that we've grown and he's no longer here in the flesh, we live very close to each other and are involved in each other's careers. That's because of him.

Before I move on, I must say that I was also privileged to have a great stepfather growing up. My mother got married to a man named Tom Finson when I was about three. He cared for me as if I were his own. I can remember many nights when I was doing homework and he was sitting right there with me, correcting me if I got something wrong. He is one of Jamaica's top criminal lawyers; he has a very brilliant mind. He has been a father to me throughout my life. My biological father has been a social icon for the world, but I was blessed to have a day-to-day role model growing up. I was blessed by the angels, because a lot of people don't get half of that.

Everyone wants to be a man, and that's what a father teaches you: how to be a man. It's not always about material things—it's about how you carry yourself, being true to your word, living up to what is expected of a man. What's going on now in Jamaica . . . the violence has become a monster of its own. You have people waking up every morning being aggressive and looking for a fight, a fight for no reason. There are a lot of young fathers who have passed away due to this violence. More so than people not wanting to be fathers, you find that a lot of children's fathers have died. We actually have a gang in Jamaica called the Fatherless Crew. All of their fathers were murdered when they were very young; now they have grown up to be gangsters themselves.

I had a son last year and I'm looking forward to teaching him about my father. But it will happen in a natural, organic way. He will start asking about certain things and he will learn. My mother says when a child is born, that child has the capacity to be anything.

People then start telling them what they can't do and that stops them. But my perspective on children is, let them experience life and learn themselves, and you will find you can learn from them, too.

In Grenada, I tried to research my family history on my mother's side, seeing how far back I could trace ancestors. Not surprisingly, I hit a roadblock when I got to the slavery period. I wanted to see if it was possible to get my family's original name, the one my mother's ancestors had when they landed on Grenada from Africa. The name was the final piece, those magical letters that remain a tragic mystery to most every African-American on the planet. I found out that much of the erasures of history were done by Catholic missionaries on the island. I learned a lot about the island's history during my quest, but I wasn't able to get close to a family name.

When Hurricane Ivan hit Grenada in 2004, by some estimates destroying or damaging as many as 90 percent of the homes on this island of a hundred and ten thousand people, I knew I had to do something. I went down there and helped rebuild. I met with Prime Minister Keith Mitchell, donated money, and did everything I could to help. I spoke at different schools, encouraging the young people to keep their heads up, and telling them that they had someone in the States who cared about them. I told them how proud I was to have a connection to a place of such strength. I told them that in them I saw people who could conquer anything, even one of the worst hurricanes the country had ever seen. Even though I wasn't born there and had never lived there, I still felt like this was my home and I had a responsibility to the place. The people of Grenada were so appreciative and so embracing of me. One person introduced me to a crowd as a "son of Grenada." That was special to me beyond words.

In Tulsa, Oklahoma, where I grew up, it seemed like there was black history greeting us at every turn. I think the adults in Tulsa felt as if that were part of their job, to tell the children about Tulsa's roots. One of the city's most famous black historical markers was Black Wall Street, the name given to the black community of Greenwood. During the oil boom of the 1910s, this area flourished along with the rest of Tulsa, boasting thriving businesses, lawyers, doctors, and real estate agents, and many black multimillionaires all up and down Greenwood Avenue. It was a self-sustaining black community at a time when such a thing was virtually unheard-of. They didn't have to go across the railroad tracks (to the white side of town) for anything. They didn't need anybody else. For a community of black folks where most of the elders actually had been born as slaves, this probably felt like a gift from the heavens.

But it all ended tragically in 1921 with one of the most despicable acts of racial violence in the country's history. A white community that had grown jealous and resentful of the thriving black community, a throng spurred on by the alleged assault of a white woman by a black man, amassed and descended on Greenwood. They proceeded to burn it to the ground, torching thirty-five square blocks of homes and businesses. The whites even held the firemen at gunpoint so that they couldn't put out the flames. When it was over, more than six hundred black businesses were destroyed, about $1.5 million in property damages (in 1921 dollars) sustained, and, according to the official toll, twenty-six blacks and thirteen whites were dead, although most unofficial estimates put the death toll much higher. The community was able to rebuild, eventually becoming a popular spot for jazz and blues clubs. However, eventually it succumbed to many of the same forces—middle-class flight and economic despair—that killed thriving black urban communities across the country. Older folks in Tulsa still like to use Greenwood as a model for what black people can accomplish when we stick together and help one another. It is still a teaching tool, ninety years after its height. The older folks are trying to pass on the idea to young folks that you have no excuse not to be everything you can be, because you come from a place and a people that were able to create something as beautiful as Black Wall Street. I heard that over and over growing up. Some of the markers are still there, used to create a Greenwood Historical District, but the city built a highway right through the area, so it can't be fully re-created.

Yao Ming is one of the most famous basketball players in the world and a source of immense national pride for the people of China. National pride has always been something that was important to Yao, even when he was a child in school. In this piece, Yao talks about how proud he was to carry China's flag at the Olympics— and how eager he is to teach his daughter about his homeland.

When I was in high school in China, history was always my favorite subject. My mother and father really wanted me to know everything I could about our past, our family, and our country. They would buy me a lot of storybooks about the history of China and the heroes in our country's past. The books had stories about famous generals and leaders—the good ones and the bad ones. They would point to the bad generals and tell me, "We don't want you to be like that."

It was a big dream come true for me when I got the chance to play on the Chinese national team. In China, the Olympics is such a big thing. Representing your country is considered very important. When I was little and watched the Olympics on television, those people for me were heroes when I saw them carrying the Chinese flag during the opening ceremonies. That is still a big thing in my memory. It was also a big thing because of my parents. My friends, uncles, aunts, and teachers always used to tell me that my parents were great basketball players in the 1970s. My mom played on the national team for nine years. I heard that ever since I was a little kid, and it always made me proud.

When I got to carry the flag and lead the Chinese team during the Olympics in Athens and also in Beijing, it was a dream come true. I think that was because of what happened when I was a kid going to school. Each Monday after the weekend, we would all get to school at seven in the morning and watch our classmates raise the flag. Each class would vote the week before to decide who in the class would do a good job. There were about twelve to sixteen classes in the school, and every class would have one child go out and raise the flag. It was an important job. But I never got voted to do it. So when I was picked to carry the Chinese flag for the Olympic team, it was important to me.

Even though my parents played basketball, to be honest I didn't really like to play until I was about seventeen or eighteen years old. Before that, because of my size, the coach would put me in groups with kids who were two and three years older than me. I had size, but they pushed me around easily. At that age, one year makes a big difference. I didn't feel like I had any success, so it was frustrating. But I was honored to follow in my parents' footsteps.

I'm excited about teaching my country's history to my daughter, Amy. I still remember things my father taught me when I was just three years old. He would tell me to always be nice to people and always say the magic words: "Thank you." I will try to copy that with Amy.

A few years ago there was a big earthquake in China in the Sichuan province. It killed sixty-eight thousand people. It really hurt me to see not only how many lives were lost but also to see how bad it was for the kids. They should be treated better than that. I donated a lot of money [$2 million] and started a foundation to rebuild quality schools, buy books and computers, and give people a chance to rebuild their homes. Last year when I went back there to see how the kids and schools were doing, it had a huge impact on me. Where I live, Shanghai, is on the coast; it's like New York or San Francisco. But this area is deep in the mountains; it's very difficult to get there. It's one of the poorest areas in China. After I left,

*twelve hours later I was back in Shanghai, but it made me wonder
how many years it would take those kids to travel out of that place.
Maybe it would take a hundred years for them to climb out.*

*It made me realize how we have to appreciate everything we
have. This is something my daughter needs to know. When she gets
a little older I will take her there. That's the kind of education you
cannot get from school.*

My grandfather was such a source of living history for me that
I used him almost like a human Google when I was growing up. I
would sit with him for hours in his room in Harlem and talk with
him about different eras and events in history. I would throw out a
person's name and just sit back and listen to him talk. Hearing history from the mouths of people who lived it is so much more compelling and powerful than reading it in a book. It's especially
fascinating when talking to older African-Americans, because their
view of history is often so divergent from the official histories that
are presented to schoolchildren. Their perspectives on the impact of
important legislation or the legacies of different presidents and leaders can be eye-opening, as I discovered with my grandfather. It was
especially fun to talk to him, because he had so much enthusiasm in
teaching me. I could tell he was excited that I wanted to know this
stuff, so that made me even more eager to ask him questions. On
and on it went. We were quite a pair.

When I think back on my childhood, I remember so many guys
around me who had no connection to their past, no knowledge of
the history that surrounded them even on the streets of Tulsa. They
were lost souls, with none of the drive or self-awareness that they
could have had if they simply knew their history. I've seen some of
them start to do the reading and make the connections when they
get to prison, sort of in the tradition of Malcolm X, who found his
wisdom and his voice after he became an inmate. They research,
they study, and it's like a shade is pulled up and the world is suddenly

bright and clear to them, like they can really see for the first time in their lives. But I find that somewhat tragic, that we let so many of our young people get to that desperate state without telling them who they are. You should not become an adult in this country and know nothing about your culture and history. That's absurd.

Sports agent **Arn Tellem**'s memories of his own childhood are so vivid that when you read the following essay, you can almost feel like you are taking the trip back into his past with him, walking along the Atlantic City boardwalk and feeling the same goose bumps that cover Tellem's arms as he reminisces. Clearly, his Jewish culture is and has been a powerful force in Tellem's life, a major factor in forming the person he is today.

My grandpop Ellis—the father of my mother—came to this country from Lithuania in the 1890s and settled in Philadelphia. Southwest Philly was the neighborhood of choice for new Jewish immigrants. Whenever I think of him, I'm reminded of the virtues by which he lived: caring and perseverance, fairness and integrity—virtues that defined his everyday life. Honesty was more important to him than how much money you made, where you lived, or what school you attended. Titles, degrees meant bubkes—your true measure was the impact you made on others.

He and I had breakfast every Sunday. Whether strolling to his southwest Philly synagogue or on the Atlantic City boardwalk, he always had a simple message for me, one he repeated end-lessly. "Arn," he would say, "you must work hard then play a little, then work hard and play a little." During lapses in our conversa-tion, he would surprise me with, "Arn, what do you do after you play?"

"You work hard," I would answer.

"Arn, what do you do after working hard?"

I said, "Play," and he would add, "You mean, play a little."

In spite of the long hours he kept, I spent lots of time with him, at Phillies games, at Army-Navy showdowns, fishing down at the shore. Baseball was his favorite sport, and Jackie Robinson and Hank Greenberg were his favorite players. To him, the black man of Brooklyn and the Jew of Detroit were both pioneers, and living proof that nothing was impossible. Baseball's history, he told me, encompassed a hundred years. The history of the Jews, he said, was even longer. Jewish survival depended on maintaining our heritage, traditions, and education.

Throughout his sixty-five years of marriage, Grandpop Ellis and my grandmother, Fanny, were active members in the wonderfully inclusive Beth Am synagogue. During services, I always sat beside him. We'd visit my grandmother in the choir booth and listen raptly to her lovely solos. Then we'd all walk down Warrington Avenue. I would look around, amazed that the entire neighborhood seemed Jewish. Everyone stopped to talk and argue and smell the aromas wafting from the Jewish kitchens. I felt as if I had relatives in every house.

Grandpop Ellis liked to remind me that the fate of being uprooted and exiled from one's homeland had been suffered by other peoples, not just the Jews. Yet the Jews were the ones who had not disappeared. What was the key to our survival? For my grandfather, it was family. And my grandparents were the pillars of our family. It was in their home that we celebrated the holidays, that I received my Jewish education. While my grandmother provided the warmth, the smells of holiday cooking, and the songs, I looked to my grandfather for context and meaning. He never failed me.

When I was thirteen, my father died of a heart attack. He was forty-one. Grandpop Ellis stayed with me, comforted me, and, through his own example, showed me how to live. After my bar mitzvah, I often questioned my faith, but I never questioned his teachings.

Not long ago I was in Atlantic City on business. I hadn't been there for almost forty years. Back then, Ventnor was the summer Riviera for the Jews of southwest Philly. My thoughts drifted back to that time, so much so that I could hardly keep my mind on my business meeting. I excused myself and caught a cab to the corner of Washington and Ventnor, the summer meeting place of my great-grandparents, grandparents, aunts, uncles, and cousins. When I got out of the taxi on a cold, dark winter day, it was as if I were back in 1960. The street was deserted; the only sounds were the howl of the wind and the breaking of the waves. I thought of Burt Lancaster's great line in the film Atlantic City: *"You should have seen the Atlantic Ocean in those days."*

I found the old house, which was the same as it always was. I felt chills. I had goose bumps, and goose bumps on the goose bumps. The side yard where on summer nights I had played catch with my father and grandfather was still a side yard. I paced the property, peered through the basement window, and swore I saw Grandmother gutting the flounder I had caught with Grandfather. In the back of the house were the steps that led up to the kitchen, the steps I used to scramble up to have breakfast with Great-grandfather. The front stoop was there, too. Great-grandmother would sit on it in the late afternoon, waiting for us to return all sandy and tanned from the beach. I crept up to the porch and squinted through the windows to see the musty living room where we used to gather to watch TV.

I shuffled down to the beach of my youth. Each step had a familiar echo; each evoked a memory. I thought of the time I forgot my sandals and had to walk barefoot on the molten pavement. I thought of my grandmother, my parents, my sister, my aunts, my uncles sitting on the soft sand, laughing and smiling and singing. I thought of my cousins, Warren, Bruce, Alvin, Sherman, Henry, Harvey, and Kenny, running on the beach, young, lean, confident, full of hope and ambition. I looked out at the crashing waves and saw my grandfather, with his calm, comforting smile. He was holding a young boy's hand, telling him in a soft, reassuring voice, just above a whisper: "Don't be afraid." He didn't let go of the boy's hand. "Soon," he told him, "soon you'll swim just like your cousins."

Grandmom Fanny used to say a family is like a colorful patchwork quilt—all bound together with love. She was right, of course. Some of those patches are now memories, but they continue to brighten the world long after they have faded. The lights of my grandparents are lights that will always shine in the darkest times and illuminate a path to follow—no matter how perilous it appears.

As I watch my little ones grow, I've got the lessons all lined up, the books dusted off, the stories poised on the tip of my tongue. I can't wait to tell them about their names, about their people, about the wonderful ancestors who came before them. I can't wait to bring them with me to Grenada, to show them the land where their great-great-grandmother walked, the structures that I helped rebuild after Hurricane Ivan. I can't wait to bring them out to Oklahoma and show them Black Wall Street and tell them that horrifying story of hatred and jealousy. I can't wait to take the trip across the Atlantic Ocean and show them the motherland—a place that they will already know intimately by the time we get there. How powerful it will be for my daughter Sierra to stand on the land from which she got her name, the place of her ancestors, to kneel down and dig her hand in the soil, her soil.

My grandmother and my grandfather are gone now, but they will live on in my family, because my children will know all about them. I've got so many stories, I'm not even sure where to start. Then again, maybe I'll just start at the beginning.

"Malcolm, Imani, Sierra, let's talk about your names. . . ."

To close out this chapter, we turn to one of the pioneers of hip-hop and the spoken word, **Abiodun Oyewole** from the Last Poets. The importance of the black father to family and culture is movingly conveyed in this piece, a poem that transports us, makes us travel back through the centuries. Fittingly, it is called "The Black Father."

Ripped from the womb of mother Africa
The drums tell the story
Of a man beaten down
But would not die
Of a man chained and shackled
Still standing tall
With the yoke of slavery on his back
He was a mule
He was a plow
He was sugarcane tobacco
Cotton and rice and indigo
The drums tell the story
They have been witness
To the rape of his mother
By creatures who never believed in God
They've heard the screams
And drank the tears
That have become the salt of this Earth
But this man would not die
Whipped and beaten and castrated
Just for fun
This man was left bleeding to death
In a puddle of his own waste
No name no face no life
Just a Black thing
To produce more Black things
To make white things better
The drums tell the story
Of how he tried like Harriet
To talk to the trees

Consult with the stars and the moon
To return once again to his greatness
But he was separated from his family
And forced into a battle
Against himself
And the African pride he wore on his heart
But his woman turned away
The children didn't know him
And his name became foreign
But he would not die
The drums tell the story
Each beat is a reminder of who he is
A master of sound
A lover of life
The torch and the blackness
The sun and the rain
Each child he sees is his child
And they come to him
With open arms
And smiling faces
Feeling the traces of his history in themselves
This man will always be a father
Standing tall like a lighthouse
For other men to see
And find their way back home

CHAPTER SIX

SKY IS THE LIMIT: HELPING CHILDREN OVERCOME FATHERLESSNESS

I couldn't believe what I was hearing. There I was, sitting in Spike Lee's fancy hotel suite with an impressive gathering of black intellectuals and celebrities—men like Spike and football legend Jim Brown, men I've been idolizing for most of my life. We had just finished a heated panel discussion on black athletes. Some of the panelists had gravitated to Spike's room, where we continued the discussion. Jim Brown was stating, in his usual forceful way, that any black child who grows up without a father in the home is doomed to failure. Spike and the others in the room were agreeing with him. If you've never been in the presence of Jim Brown, you should know that when he says something, everybody else either agrees with him or shuts the hell up. To call Jim Brown intimidating is an understatement.

But I couldn't sit there and let him go unchallenged. It would have been a betrayal of everything I had come to believe as a black man, as an NBA player, as a husband, and as a father. I found myself defending the entire younger generation to a group of black intellectuals. I have all the respect in the world for Jim Brown. He has always been one of the athletes I've looked to as a pioneer, someone who stood up for what he believed in no matter whom he was standing against. On this night, the person standing up to him was me. He wasn't pleased. But I just couldn't sit quietly and allow them to say what they were saying.

It's funny, because the older generation gets so frustrated with the younger generation when they don't think that we are listening. However, listening is a two-way street, and sometimes it's not that the younger generation is not listening, but simply that we have an opinion that differs from the older generation. There is no reason that opinion should be discounted or discarded because of our youth. My grandfather, who reminded me a lot of Jim Brown in that they had similar personalities, would always say while we were debating, "Aw, y'all young people think you have all the answers." Or he would say something like, "Y'all don't know nothin', 'cause you ain't been nowhere." It always made me laugh, but on a serious note, that unfortunately is the reason why it is so difficult for both generations to work together.

I remained unmoved from my position, arguing, as every other black intellectual in the room spoke against me, that fatherlessness is not a one-way ticket to a future of crime and misery. My position was that each child always has a choice. When people say that your destiny is a downward spiral straight to catastrophe if you didn't grow up with a father, I will always vehemently object. There are simply too many examples of great men who conquered the hurdles associated with not growing up with a father.

When I walked out of Spike Lee's suite, I thought to myself, *Is this the message that our most influential leaders are passing on to young people, that they are doomed if their father isn't in the home, that there's no room for hope? Really?* How would this work in the black community, where more than 65 percent of young people don't live with their fathers—indeed, how would it work in American society at large, where an estimated 30 percent of young people now live without their fathers?

I knew I had to do something to fight this harmful message, and also to try to push more young men into being involved and responsible fathers. I decided to put my thoughts into action and write a book that would serve as the answer to those men in Spike Lee's suite. It would be the book I desperately needed when I was growing up without my father in the house.

So that's how I got to this point, spurred on by Jim Brown to fight against the hopelessness that for too many of us describes the future of fatherless kids in our community. Of course we need fathers to step up, as I have implored them to do over and over in the chapters of this book, but I wouldn't be speaking truth if I left it at that, not after I have lived this life for the past thirty-three years. We need to be sending out dual messages in this country—messages that may seem almost contradictory, but both of which are equally important: While we are exhorting our fathers to be present for their kids, because if they aren't the results can be disastrous, we also must be encouraging our youngsters that an absent father doesn't necessarily spell disaster in their lives. If we are going to overcome this problem, we all must be able to hold both of these thoughts in our heads at the same time.

When I speak to young guys in the correctional facilities, I feel a duty to leave them with some hope, an action plan for how they are going to turn things around. The action part is important, because, for most of them, things can look pretty bleak from where they sit. Our society doesn't have a lot of tolerance or understanding for people who have been caught up in the criminal justice system. And that is a disgrace, because we are essentially saying we are willing as a society to throw away millions of lives that could be extremely productive and valuable to us. Lives that could be adding funds to our tax coffers, rather than draining our federal and state budgets at every turn.

We've heard the numbers before, but I think they bear repeating, because they are so dramatic and damning. In the United States, the average cost to keep a prisoner in a correctional facility is well over $40,000 per year. By comparison, this country spends between $10,000 and $12,000 per student every year on education. Not hard to see where our priorities are. And where all of our money is going. As they say, if you want to get to the bottom of a problem, follow the money. There are many critics of our criminal justice system who argue that the system leans so far toward incarceration because the prisons have become a jobs program for small towns all across America. This may be true, but when I view these men from up close, really dig down under the surface, I get angry, because we are squandering so much talent, letting so many possible resources go underutilized.

We incarcerate far more people in this country than any other country in the world. And the numbers for black men are staggering. While an estimated one in eleven African-Americans in this country is under correctional control (in prison or on probation), for black men in their twenties, approximately one in every eight is sitting in jail. That number just boggles my mind. What a waste. It represents an enormous loss of fathers—basically the draining of entire communities of fathers, being sucked away from their young children, and altering millions of lives in the process.

In the following essay, rapper turned actor turned movie mogul **Ice Cube** passionately describes, in his own inimitable voice, the horrible existence that men face in prison—and the futility of sitting around and feeling sorry for yourself because of your missing father. While reading this, you can practically feel the heat of his words coming off the page—and you can easily imagine the Ice Cube scowl.

With life, you can get duped into excuses if you take them. You can always blame circumstances; you can always blame what you don't have and not focus on what you do have; you can make a lot of excuses for yourself and give yourself an out in life. It's up to you as an individual to play with the cards you're dealt and win with them. I think the world is filled with obstacles. And the fact of the matter is, just because a person has two parents in the home doesn't mean that he is going to be successful. That's not a guarantee. Just because a person has all of the resources or a person is rich, that doesn't mean that he is going to be successful. And on the flip side, just because a person has one parent in his home and doesn't have access to all of the resources or is poor doesn't mean that he is going to be unsuccessful. Everybody has to take control of their life no matter what cards they have been dealt. People are always going to give you built-in excuses for why you can't be successful, and if you believe that nonsense, you will fall short.

We also have situations where people are looking for so much from the world, and what the world owes them, and when are they gonna get theirs. The world don't owe you nothing. Not a damn thing. And you're lucky to have one parent there to give you some guidance; a lot of people have no parents. You can always find someone doing worse than you are. So don't take any of these built-in excuses. Look at them as obstacles, and that you have to take these hurdles, and you have to win. You can't let the obstacles win, because you know what? If they win, then that means you lose. Life in itself is one big obstacle course.

A lot of people drink the Kool-Aid that's fed to them. But when you shoot a statistic out, for instance, that says something like 40 percent of young black people this, that, and the other, what about the other 60 percent that's not doing bad? If half the kids are dropping out, okay, that's horrible, but that means the other half are graduating. We have become fixated on the negativity. When you look at these so-called statistics, a lot of times I question how this information is obtained anyway. Like the political polls, I always question, Who are they polling? Who are they asking? I don't even know anyone who has been polled, and they are reporting statistics about my neighborhood. But anyway, people focus on the negative and ignore the positive. There are a lot of people in the black community doing the right thing, but they are always ignored in the statistical analysis by the so-called experts. There are more people doing good in the community than there are doing bad, so don't be fooled by their statistics. Now, do we need to figure out a way to weed out these people who are doing wrong? Of course, but we don't need to act like it's everybody, because that simply is a lie. Bottom line, no matter what they say, you have to be an individual. Young people follow each other too much. Even if it's something as simple as, "This dude got these kind of shoes, so I want shoes just like that." Naw, do what you like. Stand on your own two feet.

You have to understand that no matter how you look at it, we are a kidnapped people. Behind enemy lines. We are being kept and our entire lives have been sabotaged since we were brought here. And the thing is, the same person who enslaved you is not going to free you. You gotta free yourself. The first thing you have to do is free your mind from the grips of what they are pushing, preaching, and promoting. What they have been instilling in us. We have to wash ourselves and stop waiting for things to be fair. They are never going to be fair. We have to make them right, and if we don't make them right, nobody is going to make them right for us. They're not going to pass a law to make it right for us, no amendment; all they're going to do is give us lip service. Everything they give us today, a few years down the road, they're going to take it away. That's the reality. We have to understand that, and stop looking to them to solve our problems. We're waiting for a life check that ain't coming. All we got is a rope that is dragging us through the water.

Of course, you don't let them off the hook for putting us in this position in the first place with their evil intentions and plans, but at the same we have to use that knowledge to not continue their plans and destroy ourselves. We have to be dedicated to bettering ourselves

*as a whole, and when we become really dedicated to each other—
won't nothing in the world be able to stop us. We will be able to
overcome any obstacle, no matter what it is. We will no longer be at
their mercy. We will no longer be constantly fooled or tricked into
thinking whatever it is that they wish for us to think. We won't
be their puppets. We will be able to move freely. We just have to
understand that. I hear dudes in prison say things like, "It ain't
right how they're treating us in here." Of course it ain't right. They
ain't never gonna be right. We have to get this delusion out of our
minds that things are fair and square now and we can just pull ourselves up by our bootstraps. It ain't never been fair, and it ain't never
gonna be fair. We're relegated to the bottom, and ain't nobody gonna
help us up, so stop looking for that, period.*

*The haters are always going to be there. I think the most im-
portant way to combat their hate is not to give them so much power
over you. Look at it like this: When you were just sperm, you had
thousands of haters all around you. They wanted to be first; they
wanted to be a life. But you made it. You outswam all of them.
You're a life; they're not. They're waste. So what I'm saying is that
the haters have been there even before you were born and will always
be there, so you can't let them hold you back or have any effect on
you. Haters don't even fuel my fire, because I don't give them that
much power. They're just there. They're there like grass is there.
And they will always be there, but you can't give them any power
over you, and they'll just be invisible. Let the haters hate.*

*If you want to experience hell on earth, you want to go to
prison. It's like how you treat your dog. That's you now. You're the
dog. "Sit your ass in this cage, here's the food in a bowl on the floor,
you can go s#%t in this corner, and don't come out till I tell you to
come out. You're a dog now." So I don't know how anyone, coming
out of the 'hood, with all the freedom that you have, would want
to go to jail and make it even worse for themselves. If you want to
experience being forgotten about completely, then you go to prison.*

People may not accept your phone call, they won't visit if it's not convenient for them, and people don't take the time to write letters, so they will forget about you. Even family. So if you want to be forgotten about, thrown in a hole with a bunch of musty-ass men, if that's what you want for yourself, go 'head and stay on the path you're on. Everyone knows right from wrong; whether you grew up with a father or not, you know right from wrong, so this ain't no baby lecture or anything like that. Everyone knows when they're doing right; everyone knows when they're doing wrong. But the thing is, if you want hell on earth, then you want to go to prison. And when you go there, don't expect no sympathy, no mercy, none of that. People think, Aawwww, I'm down here; I'm in prison; my friends are gonna care about me and hold me down. Man, don't nobody give a f%#k about you. Maybe your mama, daddy, and your kids. Everyone else will talk a good game, but at the end of the day, they will move on with their lives. Treat you like you don't even exist anymore. May even delete your number from their phone and holla at your girl. Don't think that don't happen. So if you care about yourself, you wouldn't want to be in that position in the first place. And to take it a step further, if you don't care about yourself, you should be dead or in prison, because you're no use to anybody, not even to yourself, so what good are you? Who would actually want to be a person that is thrown away? That's what you are when you go to prison. You're thrown away in the trash can. And it's not like I don't feel for the brothers who are locked up and are innocent. I know there are innocent people in prison. But a lot of the people who are in there deserve to have their ass in there, because they've done some evil stuff unfortunately to someone who looks like them. And you can't expect mercy when you do that.

And that's when people let money become their God. People go to church and say they love God and pray and everything, but really they love that money, and will do any- and everything to get it. The fact of the matter is, money isn't everything. It's not. Ev-

erybody needs it, but you can't fall in love with it to the point that money becomes more important than life. It can't be more important than your family or your freedom or your life. And that's what you're doing if you go down that road; you're saying that obtaining riches is more important than your life. Playing Russian roulette with all the bullets in the chamber. It's not going to end well at all.

Bottom line, it's up to the individual and what you want out of life. There are a lot of people who come out of the 'hood, had no father, dirt-poor, sleep-for-dinner poor, and they don't end up in prison. It doesn't have to be that way, so don't let anyone, no matter who they are, tell you that it does. Because they're lying. You can control your own future.

The odds for these guys in prison to become productive members of society are overwhelmingly against them. In one experiment conducted by University of California–Berkeley public policy professor Steven Raphael, a black male without a criminal record applying for a job had a 14 percent chance of getting a callback for an interview, while a white male applying for the same job had a 34 percent chance of getting a callback. If both the black male and white male had criminal records, the callback percentage was 5 percent for the black male and 17 percent for the white male. With odds like 5 percent, it's easy to see why so many of these young cats feel the game is over for them. But the game is not over.

One of my favorite movies when I was growing up was *Higher Learning,* directed by John Singleton. (Ice Cube was also one of the stars.) In that film, Laurence Fishburne asks Omar Epps what he does when he comes up against another track star who is faster, stronger, more big-time than him. Fishburne's character then asks whether the answer was for him to quit. Omar Epps replied, "Hell, no." Then Fishburne repeats the question: "Then what do you do?" And Omar Epps simply replies, "Run faster." This is the message I try to bring with me when I speak to the guys in prison. People are going to be underestimating them, discriminating against them, ignoring them, disrespecting them, and rejecting them for the rest of their lives because of their criminal records. I tell them that many other men have faced odds as seemingly insurmountable as theirs and still managed to make it. For instance, President Barack Obama. When I mention his name, their heads all pop up. They are curious and skeptical. What kind of odds could the president have faced, with all his intellect and fancy Ivy League degrees? But when I start telling them about President Obama's story, how he saw his father for only one week during his entire life, how he tried drugs and was a bit aimless as a student at Occidental College in California, but turned it all around and graduated from Columbia University with a degree in political science. He went on to Harvard Law School, where he graduated magna cum laude and was the first black president of the *Harvard Law Review,* and later became the forty-fourth president of the United States. So if he could make it to that point, any of you can make it as well. They then begin to see my point. I predict that President Obama's story will be inspiring and transforming kids for many generations to come, as will the many other stories about people who were able to overcome fatherlessness— which was why I disagreed so vehemently with Jim Brown and the rest of the room. I am more apt to embrace the philosophy that it is possible to reach the young people before they make the choice to end up in prison. Jim Brown's position was that they had no choice. I am fully aware of his tireless efforts with Organization America. I've read that he works with gang members to give them opportunities and resources to be successful in life, and I admire that. I believe that work is so important and vital in this day and age, because he is changing the lives of young men whom society has long since given up on. But my question to him was, How can we reach them before they get to prison? How can we redirect their actions and choices before they go down the wrong path? His position was that we can't. That without resources or a father, they don't have a choice.

He actually sounded a little irritated at the notion that they did have a choice. I am in no way discounting the importance of resources. I am a firm believer that too many young men are in a vicious cycle of poverty, crime, and imprisonment that has systematically been put in place for their destruction. However, I also feel that you always have a choice. We have to be careful in destroying the arc of our young people's dreams. They don't have to be pigeonholed into anything. They are, in fact, the authors of their own destiny. That is the message I want to implant in their minds. To quote Michael Eric Dyson, "For black folk who have often been dismissed, stigmatized, or silenced without a hearing, we should be wary of repeating such rituals of repression with our children."

Film director **Michael Moore** is one of the most insightful and controversial filmmakers in the business. In films like *Roger and Me*, *Bowling for Columbine*, *Sicko*, and *Capitalism: A Love Story*, and in books like *Dude, Where's My Country?* and *Stupid White Men*, Moore has managed to put a finger on Middle American outrage and also create a great deal of his own. Moore has also spent a lot of time thinking about the plight of the poor in America, particularly those who come from so-called "broken homes." In the following essay, he explains why the system has been set up to make people believe that they have no chance at success unless they have a perfect American childhood. As Moore says, if you believe that, "You're getting played."

One of the "Big Lies" that we are told in our society is that there's something wrong with you if you come from a "broken home" or a home with a single mother. It's meant to put a stigma on you, when in fact many kids who came from so-called "broken homes" or single-parent homes wind up doing quite well or even better, for any number of reasons—it made them stronger, made them more independent; they learned to take care of themselves at an earlier age. So you can't really make this judgment.

I think when the statistics are thrown around and these labels are placed on homes and young people, there's a race- and class-based nature to them. For some people, it's a way to get around saying what they really want to say. We just lived through thirty years of the so-called "family values" era, perpetrated by Republican leaders, who, we've now learned, have no family values and are the worst offenders. From Newt Gingrich on down, we can list name after name of people who don't believe in the sanctity of marriage, who don't believe in any of this stuff, but who have actually worked to pass laws to make it difficult for people who don't fit into any of their so-called "Christian" values.

What we need to acknowledge first of all is that the so-called broken home or single-parent home is created in part by economic conditions. There's no getting around the fact that if you are able to have the basic essentials while growing up—a roof over your head, food on the table, the basics of a decent life—that is definitely a helpful thing for a child. But I have felt for some time that those in charge, the captains of industry, the political leaders (who are essentially the paid employees of the captains of industry), it is to their benefit that they have most of society scrambling like rats to get whatever piece of the cheese they can grab. It is to their advantage that most Americans now live from paycheck to paycheck, have no savings in the bank. The more they have you in want and in need—the more you are thrown into this place of just trying to survive from week to week—then you're basically being controlled by those who run the show. You're going to do what they say. You're not going to talk back at work; you're not going to question the morality or ethics of something at work or what your business is doing. You won't form a union; you won't do any of a number of things, because you need that paycheck. Because if you don't have that paycheck, you are doomed.

What I would say to young people right now is that your current conditions are not an accident. When you're sitting there in your dilapidated school, reading textbooks twenty or thirty years out-of-date, and you know you're not getting the education you deserve to get, you have to pause and say, "Is this just an accident, or is it to the benefit of those who run society to make sure we're not too smart? 'Cause if we get too smart, they probably know we will get together, we will organize ourselves, and there will be hell to pay for them. They only want us just smart enough so we can work the cash register at McDonald's. They need us to know how to read and do simple math." That's why, when you take those state-mandated tests every year, they're testing mostly your reading and math skills. They are not testing whether or not you understand that you have a right in this democracy to participate and control your own fate. They're not testing your ability to communicate with your neighbors, not testing your ability to be creative, to see what artistic skill you may have. You might be a great writer, artist, or poet. The school is doing nothing to find that out. The state doesn't care if you can write poetry. The state only cares whether they can keep selling a billion burgers a year and that you can flip them.

I encourage young people to be citizens in this democracy, because if everybody started trying to participate as citizens, if everybody had the idea that, "You know what, I'm a part owner of this government! I'm a one-three-hundred-millionth owner of this government, and I'm going to show up; I'm going to get off the bench and stop treating my democracy as a spectator sport"—if that ever happens, then those in charge know that would be a very dangerous thing. Those in charge don't really like democracy very much; they want the power concentrated in the hands of very few people. The four hundred richest Americans have more wealth than a hundred and fifty million Americans combined. How do they get away with that? You would think the hundred and fifty million would say, "What the hell? I'm scraping to get by, I got the landlord banging on my door, I have to water down the soup so it can last until tomorrow—and just four hundred billionaires own more than half the wealth in this country?!" What is preventing the hundred and fifty million from rising up and saying, "We live in a country that believes in equality and we don't consider this equal. We're going to do something about it!" The four hundred richest Americans are deathly afraid that if "we the people" ever come to the realization that "there are more of us than them," it will be over for the Wall Street elite.

Just imagine that you are one of the one hundred people who were on one of the planes on 9/11 that flew into the Twin Towers. One of my producers was on the plane that left from Boston, and I think about this a lot. I think about what I would have done. I guess I would have done what everyone on the first three planes did—sit tight and wait for someone else to work this out. There were three hijackers standing at the front of the cabin with box cutters who told everyone to stay in their seats. Why didn't the people on the first three planes try to overpower those guys? Because they were afraid, naturally. Because they thought someone else—the authorities on the ground—was going to take care of this problem and save them. What if the seventy to one hundred people on the plane had rushed the three hijackers? Who would have won that fight? They did rush them on that fourth plane—but only after they had learned what happened to the other three planes, in other words, only when they themselves were faced with certain death.

Now, replace those three terrorists with the three big banks on Wall Street who are making sure your neighborhood stays the way it is, that your school stays the way it is, who are funneling your family members off to prison so they can make huge profits. Once you realize they are trying to hold the box cutters on you, you will rise up and overpower them. That is their biggest fear.

Young people, you need to know that you will have to stand up and fight for yourself. No one is coming to rescue you. Those in charge are hoping you will sit back, check out, do nothing. They're praying you will not fight back, that you will not get out of your *seat. They are hoping you will, in fact, take it out on yourself, abuse yourself, take drugs, get involved in bad stuff. They have a whole corporate system waiting to funnel you into prison. Nothing makes them happier than getting more inmates! That's just dollar signs for them! They are playing you like suckers! Every time you get involved in something that breaks the law, do you really think they are upset? They love it! You are a profit-making machine for them. The system is set up so that you won't even get your day in court— they have a whole plea system in place to run you through a court-room faster than shit through a tube. You make their day when they can send one more of you off to prison, one less rebel to deal with, one more payday for the Man as you scrub the floors of his private, profit-making prison.*

You have to tell yourself, I got dealt this lousy card, but, dam-mit, I got a hundred and fifty million in my army! You need to start organizing everybody around you. You're a citizen in a democracy. Use that power. If you organize ten people in your neighborhood, or a hundred students in your school, their heads will start spinning so fast they won't know what to do. You already have the power in your hands, even if you don't have a dime in the bank. They know you hold the power, because of the numbers you have.

The only people who don't know that you hold all the power is you.

As I've said, I didn't grow up completely fatherless, but I do understand the confusion, displacement of anger, frustration, and destructive method of thinking that can be associated with a child not having his father around as much as he would like. I experi-enced a divorce at a young age, and although I did have a relation-ship with my father growing up, I can understand.

My personal story is an example of someone who overcame his single-parent childhood. For me, there was always the opportunity to join the gangs or run with the drug dealers, but from a young age

I somehow understood that there wasn't a future in these choices. They were all about the short-term gain. I remember guys pointing to my sneakers when I was working at a Mexican restaurant called Casa Bonita and telling me they had a way for me to trade in my raggedy shoes, a way to make some quick money. But even though I would come home smelling like tacos and enchiladas, taking two paychecks to make what the dope boys were making in a day, I was able to turn my back on that stuff.

Yes, I made it to the top of my profession, having a long career in the NBA, but I am still chastened by the knowledge that there were always guys better than me, guys who should have made the league but didn't. I know I wasn't the best player coming out of Tulsa. I can name twenty guys off the top of my head who should have made it before me. The same thing with the guys in New York. When I played AAU ball, I'd see a steady stream of these guys. They were amazing, but for one reason or another they just couldn't get it together, couldn't make it through high school, couldn't stay on the team, couldn't put themselves in a position where a college would be willing to take a chance on them. I'm not even talking about an NBA career—if they just got a full ride at a university, that would have lifted them out of their circumstances and their environment and put them on the path to a good job and a better life.

Sometimes when I go speak in the correctional facilities, I take some of my teammates with me. It's funny, because shortly after I got to the Atlanta Hawks and asked the front office staff to help me set up a prison visit, there was a lot of hesitation on their part. This was something new for them; they don't have many guys asking to go to a prison. They asked if I was sure this was something I wanted to do—maybe I might be interested in going to a school instead? I explained that this was something I had been doing for more than a decade. They finally relented and I was able to bring teammates Josh Smith, Jamal Crawford, and Marvin Williams to the Metro

Regional Youth Detention Center, and speak to a group of about a hundred young men.

I'm very clear when I go into these facilities that the guys cannot be shackled when I talk to them. That just will not work, me trying to make a deep connection with some cats sitting there in chains. I want them to be comfortable; I need for them to be relaxed, to know that they can open up to me. In some places, the guards can be a problem. If that's the case, I will have the guards removed, because they don't need to be present if they are going to be a source of tension or intimidation. In all the years, I've never had an issue with my safety. When problems arise, it usually has something to do with the guards.

One of my goals when I am speaking to them is to recount the stories of my life and other lives that I know they will be able to relate to. If I bring other players with me, they do the same thing. I tell them how I grew up, the similarities between my life and theirs. I do some spoken word, read some of my poetry. I have a poem called "Wasted Talent" that I usually do, in which I talk about a particular guy from Tulsa who didn't make it. He got caught up in drugs, crime, and guns, got strung out, and never made it to the NBA. They all can relate to that story; they know exactly what I'm talking about. I even tell them about some of the discussions I've had with black intellectuals who don't think any of them have a chance because they didn't have fathers in the house. I ask them to raise their hands if they grew up with their fathers in the house. In the last group I did, of the hundred or so guys in the room, only twenty raised their hands. That's about the same percentage I usually see. I try to appeal to their competitive nature, to tell them that they have to beat the odds, to show everybody they're wrong. I tell them there are people out here like myself who are fighting for their side; they aren't necessarily in this alone. I go through more examples of people who were able to turn it around, people like Jay-Z, who grew up in the projects and talks in his songs about how much his life changed for the worse when his father left the family. But Jay used his gift with words and he didn't let his circumstances stop him. He could have ended up just another great rapper in prison for the rest of his life, or even dead, if he had continued in the dope game. But eventually the lightbulb came on for him. I'm trying to get a lightbulb to come on in the heads of these guys sitting in front of me. I figure if I give them enough examples, throw enough encouragement their way, for some of them something might click.

I had a lightbulb moment when I was in middle school and Wayman Tisdale visited our school. Wayman was a great basketball player and a great human being. He starred at the University of Oklahoma, had a great NBA career, and then, incredibly, went on to have perhaps an even more impressive music career. He was a pioneering jazz bassist who recorded eight albums and made it to number one on the *Billboard* jazz charts. When he came to my middle school and spoke in the early 1990s, we were hanging on his every word. This was during his NBA days, before he retired to concentrate on music. I think I remember every single word he said that day. He told us how he was a student at the same middle school (Carver Middle School); he walked the same halls we walked; he would stand at the same intersection of Pine and Peoria we hung out at; he played ball in the same Y we played in. It was incredibly powerful for us, because we had never met anyone as famous as him, someone who basically had lived the same life we were living and who had become hugely successful. What it did for me was make the idea of success so much more tangible. It really made all of us believe that we could actually make it; there was a path laid out for us. After I got to the NBA, I met Wayman again and told him how much his words impacted me. He was pleased to hear that. The memory of that day was one of the things that pushed me to want to speak to young people myself. I knew that I could actually make an impact, because that one visit from Wayman had such a profound impact on me. It is really meaningful for young people to hear from someone who went through the same things they are going through, who walked in the same shoes they are walking in. If the young people feel that you understand them, can relate to them, can feel what they're feeling, they will listen to you.

Baron Davis, a longtime NBA star, beat impossibly long odds to make it to the league. Both of his parents were drug addicts and, at some point, his family was homeless, squatting in abandoned buildings. If anybody knows about the challenges of overcoming fatherlessness and poverty—and the immense joy when you finally do succeed—it's Baron. He is truly a living embodiment of this chapter's title, "Sky Is the Limit." He says he had been to nine or ten funerals by the time he was thirteen. That's unbelievable. Most of us can't even imagine going through such a childhood. In this piece, he talks about the mind-blowing obstacles he overcame and how they have motivated him throughout his life.

I grew up on welfare. My mom and dad were never married, and they turned to a life of drugs and, with my dad, a life of drugs and crime. By the age of four, when I could recognize what was going on, he was never around. We went from my mom having a good job and being a single parent to all of a sudden being evicted and basically living on the street if it wasn't for my grandparents taking me and my baby sister in. I can recall living in burned-down houses and motels. My dad was the dude who was never around. Like with anyone on drugs, there were lies and infrequent visits. I just never knew who he was. As a kid I had no connection to the dude that made me.

I grew up in South Central Los Angeles, in a Bloods neighborhood, but we were surrounded by Crips. A lot of people in my family grew up in gangs. I was a first-generation gang member, from the time I was able to walk and talk. I was in it, lived it, was part of it. But at the same time, as a kid I was innocent. All I wanted to do was play. When I was a child, basketball was my escape, my therapy for not having a stable lifestyle or parents or anybody to talk to or communicate with or turn to. I was a kid living in my own world, having to deal with a lot of adults. Basketball was the only thing that helped me stay a kid.

I was always the youngest one on the block, in the neighborhood. Everybody I hung with was a lot older. I got to study their life, the choices and decisions they made with every year as they got older. There were many guys from my neighborhood alone who got college scholarships, who had opportunities to further themselves using basketball and football as a tool. But they fell victim to the neighborhood grind, the neighborhood ritual of not doing anything. As a child looking forward, I could see my future every year with the decisions my friends were making. When I was ten, two of my best friends went to jail for life. When I was eleven or twelve, one of my good friends I went to elementary school with was murdered around the corner from my house. There was always all kinds of crazy stuff happening. Each and every year, I could look around and say, "I know not to do that over there; I know not to do this over here."

As I grew up, my instincts were mainly based on survival. I loved basketball; I thought it was my future, but I was just trying to survive year to year. You're constantly faced with negativity all around you. There's no optimism. It's hard to be optimistic when you're focusing on staying alive. You have to somehow find a place that's safe, to go to a place where you can visualize the future and be optimistic. The basketball court was the time I had to do that. I would stay on the court for hours and hours a day. If you're embraced by the 'hood, you're embraced by the negativity around you. You see it every day. Staying on the court kind of numbed me to all of that. But when I wasn't on the court, I faced the same negativity everybody else faced. Once I was off the court, all I wanted to do was go home and sleep so I could get up and play basketball again.

I had to find different ways to numb myself to all the negativity of the neighborhood and just survive it.

But the negativity definitely pushed me to be more focused. That happens when you're going to funeral after funeral. By the time I was thirteen, I had been to, like, nine or ten funerals. When you see the people you play cards with, the people you grow up with, and now they're not here, it shocks you as a child. That was something I didn't want to do. I enjoyed life; I wanted to live. That was really my motivation, to make it out of the negativity that surrounded me and do something positive for myself. Once I allowed that to happen, once I started thinking that way, more and more people started coming into my life who would lend a helping hand. They would give me an opportunity to get out the neighborhood, to go see a college, maybe go to a football game or to a professional basketball game. To travel outside of South Central and see different things. My world started opening up.

Anytime I talk to young males who are growing up in the situation I grew up in, I always challenge them to do the hardest thing. Gangbanging, selling drugs, all that's easy, the easy way out. If you want to be hard, tough, really be gangsta, have a gangsta mentality, then try something that's hard, which in their case is to work on doing right. When you're focused on doing right, you learn more about yourself; you grow as a person and become stronger mentally as an individual than you ever can taking the easy route, which is gangs and drugs. Doing what's right each and every day is probably the hardest thing to do. It's even hard to do as professional athletes, getting up and knowing we are doing the right thing each and every day.

During my prison talks, a topic that I always know will get their attention is when I bring up the haters. I tell them that for the rest of their lives they will be encountering people who will be hoping they will fail. I had them growing up myself. There was one memorable incident I recount to them, when I was on my way to a big basketball game in high school and I got stopped by the Tulsa Police Department. The cops said they thought they had seen me in a mug shot, so they held me and made me late for the game. It was against one of our biggest rivals, Central High School. I had to just sit there on the curb while they searched my car with three police cars behind them. I remember all of their lights flashing and cars passing by and people looking at me, and how embarrassed I was. I was so upset, I felt like I was going to explode. But I had to calm myself enough to get out of the situation, even though I knew the police were wrong for what they were doing to me. I knew I had to exercise enough self-control to make it to my game. When I finally got to the game, I was so mad I took it out on the court. I had one of the best games of my career. Indeed, when you figure out how to get past this stuff, the sky is the limit.

Of course it bothers you, but I tell them that if they are going to emerge from their circumstances, they have to figure out a way to come to terms with these things, many of them unfair, that undoubtedly will happen to them. Incidents like these seem to follow black men around. When I did speech and debate in high school, the first speech I ever wrote was about stereotypes. I talked about how it felt whenever I walked into a store in my baggy jeans and Timberlands and had the police follow me. I opened up the speech describing the incident I had with the police on my way to my game. Even as an NBA player, I still have to deal with the stereotypes. That wasn't the last time I was stopped for no reason by the police. I don't know how many times people are amazed when they hear I am into poetry and politics and have a passion for writing. People have this little box where they want to stash NBA players— they turn on the TV and see the tattoos and the scowls; they open up the newspaper (or open their browser) and see stories about DUIs and baby mamas, so they believe they know all they need to know about every guy in the NBA. When they meet me and I don't fit their expectations, they're surprised. You can either play to the stereotype or prove it wrong. But I will go into more detail about the destructiveness of stereotypes in the next chapter.

At Syracuse, I knew that I needed a plan B, just in case the whole NBA thing didn't work out. After all, I could twist a knee stepping off the sidewalk and it would all be over before it started. So I majored in business management, even though it required me to take some business classes that were hard as hell. I hated algebra in high school, but I couldn't avoid the math classes at Syracuse. One incident in particular immediately comes to mind. I had exhausted my brain for about two weeks straight for a calculus class. I studied harder than I had ever studied in my life. After I completed my exam I was confident that all of my hard work had paid off. However, the next day of class my professor greeted my hard work with accusations of cheating. He told me that three-fourths of the class had flunked this exam, with many receiving below 30 percent, so how could I possibly have managed to get the grade that I got (a respectable B-minus) without cheating? I was stunned. But I was able to keep my cool. I can say that not all of my professors were cut from this same cloth, but I had my share of encounters. I remember one professor asking me on the first day what I was doing in his classroom, and shouldn't I be in remedial English or Rocks for Jocks or something? I was left with the options of reacting to his insult or proving him wrong. I am thankful I chose the latter, but of course I shouldn't have had to.

Why did I have to prove myself worthy of being in their classrooms? But these are the same obstacles that confront all too many men who grow up without fathers or come from rough circumstances. If you can manage to not let them hold you back, you can soar. These incidents were certainly not indicative of the vast majority of professors at Syracuse University, but the sting of disrespect resonated with me and still stays with me today, as a reminder of the hurdles I had to overcome. When they happened, I couldn't threaten these guys or respond with a stream of carefully chosen curse words. I couldn't run to the dean and say that so-and-so professor hurt my feelings. If I was going to succeed and thrive, none of these reactions were going to work for me. No, what I had to do was use the words as a spur to work hard and prove that his stereotypes were off base. I received a respectable C in the calculus class (hardest-earned C I ever got). In my mind, my C might as well have been an A.

When I talk to young people, I tell them that while they can't control the school system or the criminal justice system or people's reactions and expectations, they can control their choices. If they get caught up in the system, they will find booby traps at every turn. It's not a game they're going to win. They're not going to get the dream-team lawyers—they'll get the court-appointed attorney who was handed the case twenty minutes before the trial. Their lawyer's not going to care whether the police officer's search was illegal—he's going to accept a plea bargain and move on to the next case. There is a big stack of chips aligned against them. Chips put there by the haters. But if they can run through those chips, there's no limit to how far they can rise.

Rising NBA superstar **Kevin Durant** had a rocky relationship with his father over the years, but he was fortunate to have other men, including his brother and a godfather, who both stepped in to fill the void. He was able to get past the difficulties with his father and still manage to thrive. In the following essay, he talks about how he used basketball as a tool, almost like therapy, to help him overcome obstacles.

My earliest memories are of my parents not being together. It was just me, my brother, and my mother. I would see my father maybe once a month, if I was lucky. That was the visitation schedule that was put in place. That was the nature of our relationship from age four to about eleven. Then when I was eleven and in middle school, my parents began to get back together. It was a little strange at first, because I had lived apart from him for so long, but my mother seemed happy, so I was happy for her. I began to develop a closer relationship with my dad during that time. I was beginning to enjoy some of the things that came along with having your dad actually live with you. It's different from just seeing him once a month. You don't really know each other. For example, I don't think he could have told me my favorite TV show, what classes I was struggling with, if I had a problem with someone in school, if I woke up with a nightmare in the middle of the night or got in trouble because I didn't want to eat my vegetables, or just regular stuff that kids go through growing up. So when he moved back in, it was like we were getting the chance to really know each other. Things were good for a while, but then they had a big fight and broke up again. They were separated again for about five years, until I was sixteen. So for the most part, I really didn't grow up being close to him.

But after I turned sixteen and really started playing a lot of basketball, we began to get a little closer. He was trying to be there for me and my brother, to teach us things, not just about basketball but life in general. Maybe he was trying to make up for lost time; maybe he felt bad about not being in our lives for such a long time. But whatever the reason, he was there and we appreciated it.

Lucky for me, I had an older brother whom I kind of viewed as a father figure. He taught me a lot and I owe him a lot. He was a good example for me and took care of me. I can't say that I didn't have any anger about the situation, but I think I got my frustration out playing basketball. I loved it. I could really play all day if you let me. Maybe if I didn't have basketball or some type of outlet, I would have been affected a lot more. I've seen it happen to people I grew up with. They don't have an outlet like basketball, so other things begin to become their outlet—and most of the time those things aren't very positive.

I also had a godfather, Torris Brown, who did all of the things for me a father would do for his son when I was growing up. He would talk to me, take me to movies, get on me when I was messing up, play catch—you know, regular stuff that people living with their fathers who get that every day take for granted.

I would definitely disagree with all of those people who predict that kids will fail if they don't have two parents in the home. There are too many examples of people who have made it and are very successful who didn't have any relationship with their fathers. Most of the guys I know came from single-parent homes. They could have gone in different directions, but it was something that they chose not to do. You have to grow up quick when you don't have a father around. Even as a young kid you have to be able to choose between right and wrong, and kids know the difference. Even little kids. I don't think not having a father is automatically going to send you in the wrong direction. I don't believe in that. And there are other people who can serve as a father figure—it doesn't always have to be someone negative. Maybe a coach or a teacher. Kids have to put themselves around people who will help them, not hurt them. All my friends knew I had a goal and were supportive of that. I knew they had goals and I was supportive of them. Why would you be around someone who only wants to bring you down? But I wasn't about to blame my father's not being around for any bad choice I made. I knew right from wrong. Sometimes you don't have to have both parents around to be able to succeed. I am a living testament to that.

There aren't enough older, wiser heads talking to our young people, and I think it's because too many older folks are afraid of the younger generation. Some of these guys cultivate that fear, wear their scariness on their sleeves, because it's the only way they've ever known how to be. There wasn't a lot of benefit to presenting cheery smiles to the world where they come from. But once you pierce that sullen outer layer, you often find bright, sensitive guys underneath—

guys we shouldn't be afraid of, guys who could be swayed, moved, pushed into better lives if more of us just let them know we care. Sometimes these guys will ask me why I am so interested in meeting with them, why I'm not afraid of them like everybody else. I tell them that I've been talking to guys like them seemingly my whole life, and I've grown up around a grandmother who worked in a facility like theirs, around a mother who made a career out of trying to reach guys like them. It's become an essential part of who I am; it's just in my blood.

One of the thoughts I try to leave them with is the need for them to start breaking the generational curse. Many of them already have kids and are seeing the early signs of the curse being passed on to the next generation—the curse of kids drowning in fatherless families, kids adrift in a world where they don't feel supported, where they don't feel like anybody has their back. As I said before, that last phrase is what this all comes down to: Does anybody have their back? Because that's what fatherhood is: making sure your children know that wherever they go, however far they travel, whatever tight jams they might find themselves in, there is always a strong dude out there who has their back. Always. Once their children know that and believe it, they will be well on their way to breaking the curse.

I want to end this chapter with a poem I wrote called "Fatherless Children" that was inspired by my debate with Jim Brown. I actually wrote it that very night.

They'll tell you that you can't make it
That you began life's test with an F pasted to the top of your exam in
*   bright red ink*
They'll show you links through studies and statistics
Lifetime sentences
Force-feed you with facts of fiction
Aimed at predicting the outcome to your destiny

As if they can see into your future
And God created you to fail

They'll tell you that you're on a downward spiral to hell
Unfit for survival in a societal jungle

Unable to live in a world without morals
They'll spoil your fruit if you allow them to

They'll magnify the distant thunder to rain down on your mentalities
Flood your hopes and dreams
And wash away your possibilities

They'll snatch away your cloud nine without realizing that it's your
*   mind's sky*
And your potential is limitless

I wish I could close your ears like eyelids
Shutting out the light of their lies and allow you to enjoy the darkness
*   of your possibilities*
See, some light can be detrimental
Without UVA protection you can burn the outer layer of your reality

It's hard for me not to get disgusted
When I hear young minds encrusted with lines of dusted dreams
Rusted pipes of corroded outlooks
Crusted contraptions fastened to impressionable realities
Dragged around like luggage to burden one's capabilities

Deceiving your mentality like the son of the morning
Poisoning your spirit with a serpent's tongue
Slithering in and out of your kingdom
A bite that stung more than it burned

Residual effects that churn the foundation of your emotions
Creating potions of failure

Don't let them fool you
Don't allow their miseducation to school you
Through distorted lessons of defeatist sessions
More lethal than injections
They'll lay your mind to rest
The best-kept secret is
No matter what the situation
You are more than a conqueror
And this is only a test

You can be whatever your heart desires
Moving forward toward the unwritten chapters of your lives
You can make liars with their pants on fire eat their words
Curve past the obstacles in your path and crash directly into success
Head-on collisions to happiness
Learning from the mistakes of fathers who were far from the best
   examples
You can trample their crowds of negativity
See they want your passion to go up in smoke like a chimney
But your will to succeed can still burn relevant
Cooler than peppermint your anger can cease
Avoiding the bellies of the beast you can reach for the stars
As far as your eyes can see
You don't need to be anybody's statistic
So don't miss your chance

You can dance to your own tunes
Cats get it twisted like pretzels, thinking they have to accept those
   passed-down generational patterns
The scattered cowards that showered their family tree

You don't have to be that automatically
So don't tell me you had no role models in your life
And you had no choice
You always have voice in the matter
You can be anything under the sun
Even the worst father can stand as an example of
  what not to become

CHAPTER SEVEN

DON'T BELIEVE THE HYPE: FIGHTING THE STEREOTYPES THAT CAN OVERWHELM YOUR CHILDREN

As a man, as a black man, as a father, as an NBA player, as a fan of rap music, I have faced the sting of stereotyping all of my life. When people see me coming, big, black, bearded, and dreadlocked, maybe clothed in baggy jeans or sweats, probably in a hurry, their minds start making assumptions and assigning me to boxes—some of them wrong and many of them hurtful. Sometimes I get put in a box whose existence I wasn't even aware of.

One day in Los Angeles, when I was walking down the street with a few friends, I passed a group of young boys. They thought they recognized me and I could overhear the dialogue that was going on among them. "He plays basketball—I know him," one of them said. But then his boy responded, "Nah, how can he be a basketball player? He doesn't even have any ice on." (For the uninformed, "ice" means jewelry.) That's what that young cat said. I was so taken aback, I had to stop and investigate.

I asked them, "Is that what y'all think?"

They said, "Well, that's what we see."

I was so upset. "Aww, that's horrible, absolutely horrible," I said.

But that is the destructive, mind-warping, brainwashing power of stereotypes. We all have to deal with them—soccer moms, blond women, Asian students, Spanish-speaking Latinos, headscarf-wearing Arabs . . . the list goes on. It is the way our minds work, a handy categorization system that makes life a bit easier to process as we make our way through our days. I understand that. But some stereotypes are more harmful than others—and some stereotypes are the handiwork of a media and entertainment culture that seems to have no concern for the damage it leaves in its wake. As a father with a son and two daughters, I have been spending a lot of time lately thinking about the images that fly at my children on a daily—hell, an hourly—basis.

When my son, Malcolm, was three years old and I was playing outside with him, Bob Marley's song "Buffalo Soldier" came on the stereo and drifted out into the yard. Before I knew what was happening, Malcolm's cute little voice started singing along with Bob. I stood there and watched in amazement as my little boy sang *all* of the lyrics. Somehow he knew the entire song. I had no idea. I know I listen to reggae a lot around the house, but I had no idea that Malcolm knew all of the words to "Buffalo Soldier." It was an eye-opening incident for me, because it served as a timely lesson: Kids listen to lyrics. A gong had sounded. I knew from that moment forward, I would have to become ever vigilant about the kind of music that I listened to around my son. It was as if Malcolm had issued a warning, like those traffic signs you see flashing on the highway, telling you there's congestion ahead: WARNING, DAD! NO MORE RAP FOR YOU!

As I've said in previous chapters, I've always been a huge fan of music. Hip-hop, reggae, jazz, R & B, I listen to it all. But since I came of age in the 1990s, rap has always been my particular passion. As far back as I can remember, I paid close attention to lyrical content. I was always powerfully drawn to the lyricists in rap, those artists who could paint a picture and tell a story with their words—

artists like KRS-One, Rakim, Digable Planets, A Tribe Called Quest. So I was a bit stunned, as I began to work my way through the lyrics of some of my favorite artists, that virtually none of it was appropriate for my kids. My perspective on hip-hop culture has changed as I went from a consumer to a father—and I have to say, what I see around me is a virtual tidal wave of negativity that flows at our children. Negativity that becomes a breeding ground for all types of harmful stereotypes. I feel the need to shelter my children from the same culture I wallowed in when I was younger, and it's not a good feeling. I can't turn on the radio when my kids are in the car, because the music is inappropriate. I can't turn on BET, because the videos are so scandalously inappropriate. I even have to be careful with VH1 Soul, which used to be my channel before my kids came into the picture. This all gets daunting in my house, because I just love to have music all around me. When I'm moving around in the morning, I'm playing music. When I want to pick up the mood in the house, I play music. A vigilant parent can never let down his guard—even while we are watching the show *Run's House*, a favorite in our household because of its wholesomeness and uplifting messages provided by Reverend Run and his adorable kids. During a break, a commercial came on for a lingerie football league. Who knew there was even such a thing as a lingerie football league, which features women playing serious football in— what else?—lingerie. It's not hard to imagine what they were thinking when they came up with the idea for this: football, near-naked ladies—a guy's dream, right? But not so much for the fathers of young children. It certainly caught Malcolm's eye. He knew right away that there was something a bit bizarre about what he was seeing on the screen. "Daddy, why are those ladies playing football in their underwear?" The commercial lasted for only a few seconds, but already the damage was done. *Damn!* I paused for a moment. I wanted to say to him, "You know, Malcolm, that's a damn good question!" I wanted to say: "Because our society is unforgivably sexist and ridiculous. But your job is to make it a better place, Malcolm." But I didn't say either of these. I can't even remember what halfhearted answer dribbled out of my mouth.

One day Malcolm came home from school and asked me to teach him how to "dougie," which is the name of a popular dance. My first thought was, *Where the hell did he learn about the dougie?* And my second thought was, *I don't know how to teach this boy to do this crazy dance.* But being the dutiful dad that I am, I went on YouTube to see if I could figure it out. I saw a video with these young cats doing the dougie—and then the unedited version of the song starts up, sounding like an innocent little nursery rhyme, except it's filled with curses. With Malcolm standing right there next to me! I couldn't hit the stop button fast enough. And I suppose that's how little kids are supposed to learn how to dougie. It was just another lesson to me about how nearly impossible it is as a parent to totally protect your little ones from these potentially harmful images. As a father, I know that at some point I'm going to have to let him hear the stuff so that I can then break it all down, but he's still far too young for all that.

If you have little ones, you know how they're now taught to memorize everything using songs. The times tables, the U.S. presidents, the months of the year, the days of the week in Spanish—they all come with a song. It's a very effective technique; Malcolm absorbs these songs like a sponge. But I quickly learned that one consequence of this technique is that they are particularly attuned to song lyrics. When they hear a song now, they immediately focus on the lyrical content. This is not a good thing for a dad who loves his hip-hop. I keep repeating the fact that I love hip-hop, because I don't want to come off here sounding like C. Delores Tucker or Anita Bryant, a prude looking for some kind of ban. But I have to admit that I see the music in a much different light now. As I said, even the so-called positive rappers use language that's inappropriate for young ears. I turned on the satellite radio to the old-school hip-hop station, thinking my favorite rappers from the eighties and nineties would work just fine. Right away, I get a shock when a song from Dr. Dre's *The Chronic* comes on. Wow, I guess *The Chronic* is old-school now. It is a brilliant piece of work, but I don't think a rap album can get more profane than *The Chronic*. And let's not even talk about the videos. BET's *106 & Park* is supposed to be geared toward young people, like teens and tweens. But the videos shown on this show are raunchy enough to make a grown man blush. They compile a list of the top ten videos, voted on by the kids. But of the top ten, eight or nine of them will be inappropriate for them to be watching. I wish there were some kind of rating system on videos like we have on movies, warning a parent whether a video is appropriate for their children to watch.

My point in talking about the music and hip-hop culture is to bemoan the awful stereotypes they are now creating about black males, black females, the black community. And these are stereotypes that affect us all, creeping into other aspects of our society that have nothing to do with music. As a father, when I see this stuff now, I feel like I want to gather up all the babies in my arms and sit them down to do a mass teach-in. To explain to them exactly what they're seeing and what the consequences are of their steady diet of these images. In a sense, this is what my mother did to me. One day, a friend of mine handed me a tape (yeah, we were rocking the cassette tapes back then!) called *Straight Outta Compton*, which was NWA's debut album. He said, "Hey, man, check this out. These cats are saying some crazy stuff." I took it home and my mother happened to see it. She confiscated the tape and listened to it herself. But instead of taking it away and telling me I was forbidden to listen to it, she again grabbed the teachable moment. She sat me down and talked to me about NWA. She said they were rightly frustrated by a system that had severely limited their opportunities, but she said they were wrongly taking out their frustrations on their own people, which was the worst reaction they could have. She listened to one of my Public Enemy tapes and said she liked what they were saying, because they were focusing on self-awareness and consciousness and history. She also liked the jazz blend of Digable Planets. But when she saw me watching Salt-N-Pepa's "Push It" video, she explained to me why the video was inappropriate and how it objectified women. She said I was supposed to have more respect for women than that. To show how far we've fallen, that Salt-N-Pepa video now looks tame, almost quaint and innocent, compared to the images in the run-of-the-mill rap video today.

The leader of the seminal group Public Enemy, **Chuck D,** has always been known for his outspokenness and his perceptive insights on American culture—one of the primary reasons Public Enemy instantly became a national phenomenon. In the following piece, he talks about what happened when the record industry figured out that negative images outsold positive ones.

When Public Enemy came out, we were more reflective rather than this coined term "positive," but I'll take "positive" because it's something we can stand to see more of, considering the imbalance of negativity out there. The negativity going across the airwaves, with TV, consumer products, all realms of social life, especially in America, is an imbalanced portrayal of imagery for commercial reasons. This came about once the industry found out bad can outsell good, especially when it comes to a people and culture that was less understood. These commercial interests can think this way because they don't understand the history of black people; they don't understand our makeup; they don't understand how we feel. If you don't do enough research in that area you can just make a blanket statement, saying, "Gangsta seems like it is where the appetite or familiarity of black folks is, so we can sell two million. But if they say things about their neighborhood or positive things, we might sell one million or less." This is the 1990s story. The problem with that is artists were quickly written off, because it requires them to be reflec-

tive based on what commerce says instead of the reality of the matter. And the reality of the matter was that the images were skewed, imbalanced.

There's more positivity coming out of communities of color than negativity, but negativity is what's making the front page, because it sells newspapers, it sold TV shows, sold news programs in competition with each other, it sold cable TV, satellite. Even sports got to the point where it was starting to reflect aspects of that negativity. I remember as a fan it got to the point where the NBA was mimicking what was happening in the street. Cats were wearing big dookie earrings on court. Then David Stern said, "No, we're not going to have this. You can reflect your culture, but not in this game." But it didn't happen like that when it came down to arts and culture and television. People said, "We're just going to make sure it works— makes money. If it doesn't work, it's out of here." At the end of the story, black negativity, black death, has always been profitable in America. It's always a reason to put something on.

When we came out in the 1980s, we just covered it as we saw it. You got the government over here, the thugs over there, and Mom, all here on the same album. But that balance of positivity and negativity was thrown off when they began to see black imagery was even more profitable when it was on the bad tip. There was a time that whenever there was a fight in the NBA, it would make the highlights. Then they realized, "Hey, with these black people fighting on the court, if we keep showing highlights, these white people aren't going to keep coming to the games. They're the ones paying for these tickets. We have to figure out a better way. This ain't hockey. We need to clean this thing up."

But that never happened in the area of music. Well, I should just say rap, 'cause in R & B you didn't have the Temptations rolling on the Four Tops. We just lost this young cat from a group called the Cali Swag District; he was shot in Inglewood the other day. I just saw a TV documentary on twenty rappers who died from gun violence in the last twenty years. From Scott La Rock on up to now. When you don't have control of your reality, the fantasy world can take over. If the fantasy world is delivered to you by way of commerce, you're out there trying to buy your status, because you don't know yourself. Persons who don't know themselves can go out there and assemble themselves by putting together things on the outside with their wallet, their credit card. Over the last twenty years, the image of a people has been put out as a brand. We've been branded all over again. When we have our culture and our blackness being made into a brand, look out. I tell artists all the time, "If you're going to be true, be true to the whole game." They say that won't sell. But if they really want to get real, I say we're in the digital age and none of this is going to sell anyway. So be yourself. This has been a wake-up call for artists. They say, "I can't lose for nothing, because there's not a business model out there selling like we were selling five or six years ago. I truly have to figure out how to find myself, and it's not going to come from some sales count."

As a parent, you have to navigate these images. Number one, it's not so much the artists. The artists can do whatever they want. But the companies in charge of the images and the artists have to be held in check. The community has to hold a BET in check, which is owned by Viacom. The community has to hold accountable the radio station, which is probably part of a conglomerate from someplace other than that community. But the black community is viewed as being powerless, so anything goes.

I've got a twenty-two-year-old daughter and an eighteen-year-old daughter. They'll tell you, when they got in my car when they were younger, they listened to Martha Reeves and the Vandellas and the Supremes. There was no way we were finding anything recent that we could all share and relate to. They knew what hip-hop was because of their friends. When I was growing up, Stevie Wonder, James Brown, Curtis Mayfield, they were like Barnes &

Noble. My mom could play them; I could hear them and there were things I could relate to. Now you have a radio station trying to get listeners based on some survey, talking about, "We got a teenage audience of twelve to seventeen." But the average age of the artists they're playing is somewhere around twenty-five to thirty-two. So you got a twenty-five- to thirty-two-year-old younging himself down with topics he thinks teenagers are going to reach for. The imagery is what young people are reaching for, but there's a gatekeeper they have to pay. A gatekeeper like the BET show 106 & Park. I tell people all the time that 106 & Park ain't an after-school show for kids. It's an adult show for the twenty-five-year-old postcollege crowd, but they won't sell it that way. They want the most impulsive audience. The most impulsive audience is middle schoolers, sixth to ninth graders. They want to be grown, they want to be older, they got expendable income, and they are impulsive. They think, We gotta get that audience.

We just had a baby and we're going to expose her to a lot more than the limitations. The effects of exposing our children to a limited world—that will be an issue coming up in the next five to ten years. You have to extend the gamut. So many great musicians, athletes, singers are doing the right thing; you have to work harder as a parent and reach down into the Internet and different parts of the music and expose them to that. If you just say, "Okay, child, you're black; here's your culture thrown to you from 106 & Park," your child will be very limited. What you should say to this child is, "You are a world person, a child of color; a black American is something you should stay rooted in and move on to higher ground from that point on, rather than saying this is all you're going to be, all you should be, and your life is rooted here in this box as this person the United States deems you as, based on your birth certificate."

These corporations know they have you. They have your imagery; they have your history; they have your culture figured out;

they will sell you yourself. When you don't have yourself and are looking for yourself in other places, that's no different from slavery. When somebody knows more about you than you do yourself.

I grew up in Long Island, outside of New York. My parents are from Harlem. I grew up in a black town, and I grew up having a foundation of my family history, black history, but at the same time they were like, "The world is yours." My mother especially encouraged me to be a world citizen first, instead of saying just American. It's not saying anything derogatory against America. I grew up when Vietnam was the thing, the assassination of presidents, Dr. King, Malcolm X, RFK, the Panthers. I had to have an open mind to get past those atrocities. It wasn't a bitterness. If you're going to tell the story, tell it all. Don't truncate and say we got a whole bunch of bad stuff happening in black neighborhoods.

I can't wait to do for my kids what my mom did for me: to dissect hip-hop for them, to show them that there's an entire genre of rappers who are writing songs with depth, that challenge the system, uplift the community, and make us think. Rappers like Common and Mos Def, Talib Kweli and the Roots. I want to show them that there's so much more to hip-hop than what they hear on the radio and see on television, which only seems to be the most offensive, sexual, and inappropriate images for people their age. Again, this is not an attack on hip-hop, but as a parent, you become more aware that this is not for young ears to hear. Adults can listen to it all day, as I do. As parents, I believe we all have a responsibility to teach and interpret, to sit our kids down and explain to them why some of the music is harmful, why some of it degrades women and perpetuates painful stereotypes. I know I'm going to have to do this with my son, because he's already asking the tough questions about things he hears and sees. I like the flow of questions—it reminds me of myself when I was a boy. The questions are a must, because there's no way I can keep the negativity away from my kids forever.

I know my daughters are going to see those women gyrating in the videos. There will come a day when I will not have the ultimate power over their time and the remote control. I wish I could put them in a bubble for safekeeping until the day of their marriage— I'm sure every father of daughters has the same thought at some point—but it's more important for me to teach than for me to shelter. I will have to tell them that no video image, no rap lyric, no aggressive boy or gossipy girl can define them if they refuse to be defined by others. Parents can't sit idly by and let their children passively consume the culture with no interference or interpretation from the parent. That's akin to child abuse—or, at the very least, gross negligence. You can't turn on the television or radio and walk away, unless you don't mind your kids being raised by rap lyrics and *106 & Park*. And you also can't snatch the CD away or just turn off the television without explaining what they have heard or seen and telling them why it's inappropriate. If my mother had simply taken the music away from me, I would have been even more intrigued and eager to get my grubby little hands on it.

There was a scene in *The Cosby Show* that I'll never forget, because it demonstrated a parent perfectly running interference. Rudy, the youngest daughter, played by Keshia Knight Pulliam, was listening to music with the headphones on and singing along to the lyrics, which said something about "do it to me all night long." Her disturbed father asked her if she knew what the lyrics were talking about. Rudy said the song was about "holding hands and kissing." But Bill Cosby corrected her. He said it meant "do my homework with me all night long." Now, I know we can't lie to them, because they are eventually going to find out what "do it to me all night long" means. But when they do find out, we have to be there for guidance and teaching.

Fathers and mothers certainly need to do a lot more talking to our daughters. We need to be telling them why it's crucial for them to respect themselves, to protest when someone tries to objectify them or exploit them. I know I must sound like an old man now, the crotchety dude on the corner complaining about "these young folks," but I can't help it. When I see the stuff they are trying to throw at my daughters, the images and stereotypes that threaten to overwhelm them, as a father it, in the words of author Nathan McCall, "makes me want to holler."

Sometimes stereotypes are so powerful that they can have their strongest effects on the kids who are members of the stereotyped group. In other words, if a young black boy gets a steady diet of the wrong rap music and videos, he might start believing that these are instruction manuals on how a young black man is supposed to conduct himself. This trap can be especially dangerous for the sons of the well-to-do, who might not get a lot of close-up interaction with characters in "the 'hood" and may feel desperate to prove themselves. This phenomenon has been well chronicled in many essays and books. Instead of pointing my kids in a direction where they might feel the need to acquire some sort of fake authenticity, what I plan to work on is keeping them humble. This is the card that I believe will trump the quest for hardness or street cred. I've already started with them, bringing them to homeless shelters during the holidays to help feed those less fortunate than themselves, having them distribute toys to needy children. It's important for my children, especially my son, to realize how blessed they are, for us to help them fight off the inclination to be spoiled. I want them to see it as a duty to help others, and I want them to grow up around all types of kids, not just the well-off. It's okay to be proud of what you have, but you can't give in to complacency or a sense of entitlement. Humility will enable them to always have an inner drive, to want to keep working on behalf of themselves and others. I think this outlook is important for young people nowadays, because somehow a lot of them seem to be born with a sense of entitlement—even the ones who don't have much. It seems to be an unavoidable part of the deal with childhood, like it automatically comes in the kiddie package, whether they live in Beverly Hills or the projects. I have seen a few rites of passage programs in action, and they seem to go far in battling this sense of entitlement, because they show young boys the importance of history, the responsibilities and expectations that come with manhood. My hope is that my children will one day look around them and see the prevalence of negative images, the inappropriateness of the youth culture that seems to pervade our society—and they will start to ask difficult questions and demand change. I want them to be able to see for themselves, without my continual prompting, that Daddy's favorite rappers hardly ever get any airplay on the radio, that video channels have little interest in more uplifting material. I'm not trying to knock anybody's hustle or stifle anyone's creativity, but can't somebody give us something positive, if just to act as a counterbalance? Who knows, it might turn out to be a genius marketing strategy—rap for the conscious-minded, videos for people who want more than titillation.

My concern over the music and the images is closely related to the plight of athletes, particularly in my sport, because it is with the rappers that we pro basketball players seem to have the most in common. I daresay the popular image of NBA players is not positive. That's how I could walk up on a group of young black boys and have them wonder why I'm not draped in any "ice." If we're not driving drunk, then we're abusing our girlfriends. If we're not getting busted with drugs, then we're carrying a weapon. If we're not fathering kids scattered across the country—a baby in every NBA city—then we're wasting our millions and declaring bankruptcy. The media can't get enough of these stories—each one gets blasted across the airwaves as if it's life-or-death news. Gossip is now the engine that drives the twenty-four-hour media cycle—a recent *New York Times* report said gossip was a $3-billion-a-year industry—and heaven help you if you happen to be a celebrity who gets churned up and spit out by the gossip machine, like so much TMZ or MediaTakeout.com roadkill. Even the *Huffington Post*, the once progressive Web site where you could see various opinions on politics, has included a gossip section of tabloid news and pictures to the right of their main page. Your life may be in ruins, your name a national joke, your career in tatters—but oh, well, the machine is already on to the next story. And no retraction necessary if all the stories turn out to be wrong.

Back in 1998, when I was still at Syracuse, *Sports Illustrated* ran a scathing report on professional athletes having multiple children with multiple baby mamas. The cover of the issue featured a cute African-American toddler gazing at the camera, with the headline blaring, "Where's Daddy?" The blurb on the cover stated, "Pro athletes have fathered startling numbers of out-of-wedlock children. One NBA star has seven by six women. Paternity cases have disrupted teams. What's happening and what does it mean for the kids left behind?" To give the story's premise some authenticity and scale, the *SI* writers quoted former NBA star Len Elmore, a Harvard Law School graduate, ESPN analyst, and college professor. "For numbers I would guess that one out-of-wedlock child for every player is a good ballpark figure," Elmore said, as if he had done some type of statistical analysis. "For every player with none, there's a guy with two or three." This all came amid the crisis of fatherlessness in the black community that has resulted in an estimated 69 percent of black children living without their fathers. The fallout from the report was immense and devastating. That story became the nation's working template for the black male athlete and fatherhood. From that day forward, it would act as a superstereotype, haunting us for decades to come. Just as Bill Clinton after Monica Lewinsky became the national spokesman for the randy chief executive, black male athletes became the model for the tragically irresponsible dad. Every story about black athletes and fatherhood—to some extent, every story about black men and fatherhood—was set against the backdrop of the *SI* cover story. So when Derek Fisher decided to be with his daughter during her operation for eye cancer instead of playing in the NBA semifinals, he was hailed for his heroism. Derek certainly should be commended for his decision, but as he would say himself, it was a no-brainer of a decision for any committed and loving father.

Billy Hunter, executive director of the NBA Players Association, said the *Sports Illustrated* story painted a portrait of NBA players that didn't resemble the huge majority of players he has come to know in the league.

In 1998, Sports Illustrated *published what became a controversial article titled, "Where's Daddy?" It depicted an unsavory story line of NBA players whose fame, wealth, and unstructured lives were resulting in the promotion of endemic absentee fatherhood, a phenomenon that is commonplace in African-American communities. Using a few, specific examples of publicized child-support cases, the article painted an image of athletes who operate as rolling stones: performing on the court, partying everywhere else, impregnating women, and abandoning their children.*

Indeed, there are some athletes who lack maturity and an understanding of personal responsibility. And there are those women who prospect celebrities for financial gain by actively seeking to bear their children. But all in all, the article was a very harsh projection of what is not a standard among the athletes I have come to know through the NBA Players Association. While it may be difficult to maintain two-parent homes, given the demands of being a professional baller, most guys I know are affectionate and devoted parents to their children.

I'd venture to say that even those players who fall short of heroism do manage to exceed the expectations and standards of the underserved communities where they were raised. What they lack is an understanding of what matters in life. They are not driven by malice, but instead a one-dimensional focus on the lure of notoriety. I don't want to deny that there are specific issues related to father absenteeism troubling African-American communities. However, I hope to pose that athletes are a greater part of the solution than ongoing fuel to the fire.

There ought to be more coverage of the good stories that are simple, yet true anecdotes of men who have a devoted love of fatherhood. To name just a few, players like Charles Smith, Karl Malone, John Stockton, Dikembe Mutombo, Patrick Ewing, Michael Curry, Alonzo Mourning, Etan Thomas, Derek Fisher, Keyon Dooling, Theo Ratliff, Chris Paul, and Ray Allen exude a respect for the demands of fatherhood. I recall that Buck Williams, relentless and focused on the court, almost always had his sons, Julien and Malek, with him at games. As fierce as his rebounds, his affection and attention to his kids were exemplary. There is no doubt that, along with his wife, Mimi, his passion for parenting was an inspiration to other players. There are many instances of responsibility, but such stories don't make headlines.

Since that *SI* story, we've endured more than a decade of reports in the same vein. When the media gets wind of another baby-making machine in the sports world, they go after him like sharks smelling blood—while the hundreds of great dads in the sports leagues go unreported and unexamined. The Internet was abuzz in 2010 with the news that New York Jets cornerback Antonio Cromartie had fathered nine children with eight women in six different states. According to reports, the Jets had to give him a $500,000 advance to help him make child-support payments. There was even a widely circulating video that showed Cromartie taking more than thirty seconds—they actually counted out the time—to name all his kids. There was an undercurrent of glee in these reports, as observers shook their heads once again at those ridiculous black male athletes and their abundant spawn.

Turn on the radio and hear even reputable news organizations like National Public Radio doing a report on why so many professional athletes squander all their money, with the correspondent theorizing that players must not be paying attention during rookie camp when we are given seminars on money and investing. I thought rookie camp was great; I got a ton of useful information from the experience. And while there were a few guys who weren't paying attention, most of us were. Most of the players in the league are not bankrupt. In fact, I actually got a reputation from my teammates as a spendthrift because of my refusal to spend money. I was acutely aware of all the stories of players going bankrupt and I was not going to be one of them. So I went in the opposite direction—I didn't want to spend money on anything. My rookie year, I bought my mother a house in the suburbs and I bought one of Baron Davis's old cars, his Navigator. That was it. I tried to hold on to everything, to save everything, to invest everything, using the strategies I learned at Syracuse as a business major. In the beginning, my investments were so conservative, I would have made a Buddhist monk look like Donald Trump.

Television commentator and sportswriter **David Aldridge** has been around the NBA for decades and has seen up close the workings of the media. In the following essay, Aldridge claims that the sports media has no interest in portraying athletes in a bad light—rather, he says the negative reports are part of a general societal trend to go after the most sensational, explosive stories around. He says more athletes should use social media to tell their own positive stories.

People tend to be much more interested in people's failures rather than their successes. There's no question that there are more negative things written about everybody in our society these days—not just athletes, but entertainers, politicians, even the man on the street. That's why reality TV is such a big hit: People like to see other people in situations where they're not comfortable and where they're not doing what they should be doing. My journalism professor told me a long time ago, "We don't do stories on planes that land on time; we don't do stories on people who make it across the street without anything happening to them." Unfortunately, people generally tend to be more interested in things people do wrong rather than things they do right. Journalism falls into that trap like everything else. But there are guys who do a lot of good things, and I think they do get covered. I don't believe that good things never get covered. But I agree that more negative things get covered than good things.

This is why it's great we have social media outlets like Twitter and Facebook. I think it give athletes themselves the opportunity to present unfiltered their view of the world and how they want to be perceived by the world. When I started in journalism, newspapers were dominant. Television had influence, but it wasn't the way it is now. Now the Internet is the great democratizer when it comes to journalism. Everybody can be a journalist. You can be a journalist; I can set up my Web site and be a journalist. What has to happen is athletes—and I think you're seeing it already—have to take more control of their image, more control of their message to people. They might be able to bypass the media altogether. It is true that an athlete's relationship with his child or children is an aspect of his life that is not part of the narrative you see in the media.

I don't think most sports reporters have animosity toward athletes. I'm sure some do, but to me it's a job. It's not, "Man, I wish I could drive that car; I wish I had that suit, had that girl, had that bankroll." It just doesn't register. I'm sure there are some reporters who do not like covering athletes for various reasons—some of those may be jealousy; some may be racial. I can tell you, in my experience in doing this for the last twenty-five years, for the vast majority of reporters of all races and all genders and all age groups, it's a job. It's a job I feel like I have some training in and some ability to do. I don't look at the athletes I cover as "them." I just don't.

But I do have a frustration with the media and the people I work with. We as African-American reporters talk about this among *ourselves all the time. When the Sprewell incident happened with P. J. Carlesimo, I was asked to do an interview with ABC News. I remember being asked, "What does this say about the professional athlete?" I said, "I don't think it says anything about the professional athlete." They said, "You know what I mean; it seems like they are out of control these days." I said, "You are not talking about a group of athletes. You are talking about one athlete who had an incident with his coach. I don't think you can take that one athlete and make a value judgment about the other four hundred and fifty people who play in the NBA who haven't had any incidents with their coaches." And we went back and forth on this, and I finally asked the producer, "Look, what is it you want me to say? Obviously you have an idea of what you want me to say and I'm not saying it. If you can just tell me what it is, I can either agree to say it or not say it and then we can move on." Believe me, that's a frustration I have. And I'm sure athletes feel it twentyfold. When one person does something bad, it's a judgment on everybody who plays that sport.*

It's kind of a running joke with some of my friends in the media. When we see an athlete mess up, we joke with each other, "Why do all these baseball players hate their managers?" If a baseball player gets arrested for DUI, we say, "These baseball players are all thugs, aren't they?" We understand it. We joke about it. We try to fight it when we can. It is out there. I tend to be an optimist. I think that speaks more to laziness on the part of people who do that rather than malice. I may be naive on this. The one thing I think you can correctly accuse reporters of on occasion is being lazy. That's true, whether we're talking about athletes or politicians. Some reporters are lazy. They do not do the work required to speak or write with some sense of accuracy about the things they cover.

During the last NBA lockout in '99, there was a story in the New York Times *about Kenny Anderson, about how he had eight cars, that he spent all this money on cars and things, asking how would he survive a lockout, because he was lamenting that he had to pay all these bills. It was a caricature of athletes, but it resonated with a lot of people. They say, "See, look at all these NBA players. They have all this money and they spend it on cars. They don't take care of the money they have; why should we be sympathetic toward them?" Those types of stories do have resonance with people who aren't paying attention. If that's the only time they look at a subject, it will resonate with them. That is absolutely a problem in my business I hope we can do better at. It plays to an easy and facile way of looking at the world. The world is complicated.*

Let me make clear that my intent in this chapter is not to point the finger at everybody else and cry about how bad we athletes have it. Of course the community of black men who are athletes, musicians, and rappers have a responsibility to act like grown men and not play into the stereotypes. But it can sometimes feel like you're swimming against a tidal wave. And I am especially concerned because of the impact it has on the way the public perceives us, especially the young people who idolize us and seek to emulate our every move. Kids have to know they are being shown only one image, one side of the coin. When I have posed this question to media types, I often get back the response, "This is what the consumer wants." But I'm not so sure about that. I say that's all you're giving them. Do they have any other option? In the movie *Malcolm X*, the Elijah Muhammad character pours iodine into a glass of water and says, "If this is all you give the people, they have no choice but to drink it." Then he pours clear water into a glass and says, "If you give them a choice then they can choose which one they want to drink." All we are giving our kids is the dirty glass. That becomes their reality, their truth. So whenever they see an athlete or rapper, they have been trained to think a certain way. My wife says she has been told at least a dozen times from different people when they meet her that she is nothing like the women on the *Basketball Wives* reality show. She doesn't throw drinks in people's faces; she doesn't curse anybody out in public; she doesn't walk out of the house draped in jewelry. That show has become the public's shorthand for a basketball wife, so wives like Nichole have to contend with the fallout. It's even happened when I am with her. I wanted to respond by saying, "You do realize that's a reality show—it's not supposed to be representative of every basketball wife, right?"

Dave Zirin is a sportswriter who has never shied away from analyzing the intersections of sports, politics, and culture. Zirin is not a guy who pulls punches. And he feels quite strongly about the negative stereotypes that plague professional athletes. In this essay, he says that the negative coverage of athletes is the result of a calculation by the sports media that negative stories will attract more attention.

> There's a kind of Superman fantasy, a macho fantasy, that goes with being an athlete in the American male mind. Part of that fantasy is having lots of kids by lots of women. At the same time, most sane people realize that while it might be a cool fantasy, it's a pretty awful, harrowing reality. What it allows the reader to do is both be titillated—"Wow, wouldn't that be amazing [to have all those women]?"—but at the same time to look down on athletes, tut-tut with their fingers wagging, and think, Aw, what a terrible role model they are. I have been inside newsrooms and this is a calculation that is made. It's the opposite of laziness. It's a calculation about what they think sells, what they think will titillate readers. But there is some laziness that comes in. I think stories that are more positive could do well, but that takes work; it takes journalism; it takes building trust, having editors willing to take chances on those stories. Those things are in very short supply. There's so much mistrust between the modern athlete and the media—and for good reason.
>
> How does it change? It takes breaking down those walls, having the athletes trust that you won't exploit their situation, won't make

them look bad, won't put their career at risk, but actually display them as a three-dimensional human being. It's a lot easier to deal with one dimension, and, honestly, in a society with so much racism in it, it's a lot easier to deal with racist archetypes than it is to deal with three-dimensional human beings. It's easier to deal with the color of skin than the content of character. It plays on a ton of racist archetypes to talk about black athletes with lots of kids who are bad fathers. That's easy and it touches buttons and it gets it out to an audience quickly and it supplies content in a twenty-four-hour news cycle, which is the god of all things media—"How do we fill up twenty-four hours?" It's a lot harder but much more rewarding both for the individual and for society to say we're going to actually peel the onion a little bit. We're going to get beyond color and stereotypes and actually tell some real stories.

Considering that my relationship with my kids is the most important thing in my life, when I think about how it would feel to be portrayed all the time the way athletes are portrayed, it would create some serious rage. Not only is an athlete who happens to be a good father being ignored as a role model and as an example, but the media portrayal also ignores the fact that the athlete who is a good father has to be away from his kids a great deal to provide for the family. That's the sacrifice I'm in awe of. Knowing how Etan feels about his children and how other athletes feel about their children, I'm really in awe of the sacrifice they make, that Etan's wife, Nichole, makes, to make the family unit work. The fact that that's given such short shrift I would see as a slap in the face. I see it as another reason why there are just reservoirs of mistrust between the mainstream sports media and athletes.

In 2005 the NBA instituted a dress code to help rehabilitate the players' public image. Players are required to wear "business casual" when engaged in team or league business. Players in attendance at games who aren't in uniform must wear a sport coat and dress shoes.

When leaving the arena, players must wear business casual or "neat" warm-up suits issued by their team. And this is the list of items players can never wear on team or league business: sleeveless shirts, shorts, T-shirts, jerseys, sports apparel (unless appropriate for the event), headgear, chains, pendants, medallions over the players' clothes, sunglasses while indoors, and headphones (unless on the team bus or plane and in the locker room). Whew. I was against the dress code when it was announced, but I have found the public's reaction to it to be interesting. I've heard people say things like we are "less threatening." I have to tell you, hearing something like that bothers the hell out of me. First of all, we're the same guys we were before. Was everybody scared of us before we put the suits on? Are we also threatening in our uniforms, or just in our everyday clothes? Are we threatening in sweats? Of course, I can acknowledge that guys do look nicer in their suits, but the psychology behind the move and the messages inherent in the public's reaction are disturbing to me. After the November 2004 brawl at the Palace in Auburn Hills during the Pistons–Pacers game, the league felt like it needed to take action, to ban the chains and medallions and disassociate itself as much as possible from hip-hop. Otherwise people who had never met a professional basketball player, had never had a conversation with one, would feel like they were within their rights to walk around calling us thugs. What's ironic is that I constantly have people come up to me, just like they go up to my wife, and say things like, "We see you on the court and we thought you were totally different." I feel compelled to ask them, "You do realize that basketball is my profession, right—and that there's no reason for me to act the same way off the court when I'm not playing basketball?" Watch a basketball game and hear how many times the commentators will assure us that somebody like Kendrick Perkins, who plays with a perpetual angry scowl, is really a nice guy off the court. It is a bit odd to me, as if I should expect James Gandolfini to walk around with a gun in real life, whacking people like he did on *The*

Sopranos, or to think that Kim Cattrall is just as promiscuous and sex-crazed in real life as the Samantha character she plays on *Sex and the City*. People have such a hard time separating us from our on-court demeanors, but I contend that it wouldn't be difficult at all to quickly transform the public image of basketball players. Not long after the completion of every game, when we leave the locker room, we are inundated by our wives and kids running up to us and giving us an abundance of hugs and kisses. After all the love, we take our kids by the hand and all walk toward the car, together as a family. It happens every day in every NBA city, yet I have never seen it shown on television. Instead what you get are the players stalking into the arena with their headphones on, deep scowls on their faces as they are trying to get hyped for the game. That's all you see. It sometimes almost feels like people don't even think we're human. If it weren't for the NBA Cares program and the commercials the league produces to advertise it, the public would virtually never see us smile. It gives people such a false impression of who we are and allows the public to swear by the truth of their stereotypes.

Too many people want to tell me that I'm an exception in the league because I read books, talk about politics, seem aware of the world around me. But I thoroughly reject that notion. I am not an exception. I'm not the only person in the league who reads and thinks. I'm not the only athlete interested in politics. When I tell people that we have political discussions in the locker room all the time, they're like, "Really? About politics?" I'm stunned that this is so surprising to people. For the sake of all of our children, we—the public, the media—need to stop trafficking in these easy stereotypes and dig just a little bit below the surface. In the case of professional athletes, the public might be surprised to find some real human beings down there.

In popular culture, it is common now to see not just athletes, but fathers and men in general depicted as inept, idiotic, and downright mentally impaired. Turn on the television set or go to the movies and see how long it takes before one of these images of the incompetent man is thrown at you. Political commentator and syndicated columnist **Roland Martin** says he is tired of the stereotype, tired of people looking at him and assuming that he is clueless about everything outside of sports and beer. In this powerful essay, Martin attacks popular culture's stereotype of the inept father—a stereotype that he says was belied in his very own household while he was growing up with his father.

Remember during the election in 2008, then-senator Barack Obama won one of the primaries and he brought his family out, and when Michelle Obama walked on, he said to the entire audience, "Doesn't Michelle look nice? Isn't my wife looking good?" Here is a man running for president; he took the time onstage, cameras running live around the world, saying how good his wife looks. When you see the president affectionate with his wife, when you see him spending time with his kids, what does that say to America about how a daddy should behave?

Other politicians need to understand that folks are watching them, too. So when John Edwards gets indicted for taking money to pay off his mistress, breaking campaign laws allegedly, when it becomes public that while Arnold Schwarzenegger was touting his marriage and his children, at the same time he had slept with the housekeeper and had a love child, when you see the same thing happening with Bill Clinton having an affair with the intern, what does it say about trust, virtues, and accountability? What message is that sending to young people about fatherhood and what it means to be a man? I'll never forget this. I was reading Jack Welch's book. Everybody talks about how Jack Welch is America's best CEO. And in his book, he talks about how important trust and character were to the officers and the employees whom he surrounded himself with. Then in the very same book, he talked about cheating on his first wife, and the woman he cheated with became his second wife.

Then he cheated on his second wife and the woman he cheated with became his third wife. And I found it interesting that when he talked about leadership and his leadership ability, he talked only about corporate leadership and corporate responsibility, but would not touch personal leadership and responsibility. Rudy Giuliani wrote an entire book on leadership, but Rudy Giuliani did not touch on his failings personally. So what does this say in America about the expected character and virtues of our leaders? I think politically, it says a lot about a person's character that they will sit here and demand such loyalty and such power politically, but then make excuses personally. That to me completely sends the wrong signal to Americans both young and old.

I think this overall negative depiction of fatherhood that is being projected to not only young people but to society as a whole goes so much further than athletes and music. There are a few commercials that immediately come to mind. It's a commercial, I believe it's OnStar, and the baby is in the back crying. A white father, white baby, so it's not always about color, but the baby is in the backseat crying; the daddy is absolutely frustrated with the baby crying and presses OnStar to reach Mommy, and as soon as the baby hears the mommy's voice, he immediately stops crying. So what does that say about a daddy's relationship with a child? There's another commercial where the kids (again all white) are all gathered in the kitchen and are whining and complaining and being loud, like kids do. There is one point where the kids spill some cereal on the table. And the exasperated daddy says, "Where is your mother?" So what this commercial is saying is that Daddy has no control. He has no clue how to deal with his out-of-control children. So when you're watching these commercials where Daddy is inept, where Daddy can't fix anything, where Daddy does not even know how to make the family some food, what they are driving into the minds of everyone is that daddies are sorry, are weak, and haven't the slightest clue about actually taking care of children. These commercials feature whites, feature blacks; they don't discriminate, but the overall message they are sending is that daddies today are a bunch of incompetent, good-for-nothing imbeciles.

The image projected in most movies, as well as television, is that old buffoon Daddy can't do anything right. He can't be an actual benefit to the everyday occurrences of the family. I remember the movie Just Wright, *and this is not a knock on* Queen Latifah *or* Common; *I think they both did great in the movie and are great people. But I remember in the movie,* Queen Latifah *is living in her own household and Daddy is helping her fix things around the house. And she's complaining that the door handle is not fixed, the windows aren't done right, the kitchen sink isn't done right, so she yells, "Daddy, can you call someone to get this done right, please!" If you remember* The Cosby Show, *there was this running joke that Cliff Huxtable could do nothing right. He couldn't fix anything in the house. And this was probably the most positive all-around image of a father we had. But he couldn't even take care of his own body as far as eating the right foods, and he was a doctor. Claire was always telling him how to eat healthy and he always wanted something unhealthy.*

Now, are there men like that? Of course there are. But I will tell you right now, there are also a lot of wives out there who could be characterized in a negative light. But the culture has accepted as the norm that Daddy is the one who is the good-for-nothing in the home, that Daddy doesn't help Mommy do anything around the house in order to make it truly function smoothly and properly, and it is Daddy whom Mommy has to in essence take on the responsibility of helping, just as she would help the rest of her children in every facet of their lives.

One of the reasons I am so cognizant about this is because of how strong a father I have. I know the man he was and is. One day, a woman comes to my mom on her job and says to her, "Why is it that every time I watch TV, Roland is always talking about his daddy and he is never talking about you? Just 'Daddy this' and 'Daddy that'?" And my mom didn't pay it any mind at first, but when she mentioned it to me, I told her that the first thing she needs to tell her coworker is to stay out of our business. The second thing I told her is that I love her dearly, and I more than appreciate everything that she has done for me in my life. She has been a wonderful mother, and I reminded her that I have written about that and spoken publicly about that. But I then explained to my mom that growing up, I have watched men say, "Thank you, Mama," "Hi, Mom," "I owe it all to Mom," and Daddy is missing in action. God put it on my heart a long time ago to always tout and speak positively about the fact that my daddy was and always has been in my life. That he stayed married to my mom. That he raised his kids and was the best daddy I could have asked for. And how important and special it is for a son to always affirm his father. I remember Tim Russert would always talk about "Big Russ," his daddy, and I would always talk about mine, and it was nothing against his mom, but it was something about that daddy-and-son relationship. That is why I feel the need to not always speak highly about my father but about all fathers. That's one reason I am glad that Etan is doing this project, because not all fathers fall into the "sorry" category the way they are depicted.

Finally, we close this chapter with a poem by **13 of Nazareth,** called "The Blak-Salaam-Man-D.E.R.," cleverly utilizing the metaphor of the salamander to make its point about perpetuating stereotypes versus deciding to make your own path. Thirteen explores the lightbulb that goes off once one realizes the limitations that have been placed on one's future, and the transformation that takes place when one sees his potential.

The Blak-Salaam-Man-D.E.R.
Crawled from under the rock of propaganda

And felt the reflection of the truth in the light of the moon
But he ignored because it was hotter to be cool
And gather in the mainstream with the nocturnal fools
But one night his ears were caught by the wise owl the dropped
*   jewels*

Perched on a branch with a single question
Whooooo?
Are you beneath the surface?
Followed by what is your life's purpose?
Where are you headed?
When are you going to accept that life in a creek is worthless
And, finally, how does it feel to be touched by something real?
The salamander was wordless
And he continued on in the soil of ignorance, although he heard this
But the wise words sparked something new
Something taken for granted by many and understood by few

So the black salamander approached the wise owl one night
*   in secret*
On his journey to the creek and
Said what is this thing?
This thing moving inside my head?
The owl grinned and said
That is a thought
For you see a thought sparked correctly
Might make you respect me
But if you don't respect yourself then your perception is incorrect

So the salamander still hung in his nocturnal slum
But it wasn't as fun because he now viewed it from
A new perspective
Spent more time pondering, becoming more perceptive

Realizing that the mainstream is actually a swamp in one's
     environment
Is reflective of personality

So the salamander spent more time with the wise owl
And occasionally took a casual stroll down to the swamp
But instead of being wild like he once was he was calm and reserved
Instead of partaking in the festivities he chose to observe
The actions and the words of his peers
The water moccasins living there
He said it's been a while since I've seen you here
The salamander said listen mister moccasin
I no longer mock your sin
So get thee behind me and return to your hell and swim
With the murderers and whores where there's rumors of wars
Of those who refuse to put the lamb's blood on the post of their doors

The snake became angry, yet riddled with fear
For the salamander's aura stood too bright to stand near

So the black salamander disappeared between the bushes and leaves
Feeling free of conformity
He remained under his rock and he was thought of abnormally
The next morning he
Crawled from beneath the rock of doctrine and
Inhaled his first breath of daylight oxygen
The son of righteousness shining on him in complete truth
His slimy skin would begin to secrete a juice
His body stretched
He grew arms and legs
His tiny little head popped open and sprouted dreads
A full-grown black man naked from the swamp he fled
Until he came upon a garden

Beautiful a place of splendor
A broken vessel fell to his knees meaning his mender
The Black Salamander
Or should I say the Blak-Salaam-Man-D.E.R.
The black peaceful man destroying evil with righteousness

You see, the owl was the prophet
The swamp symbolizes the street
The snake symbolizes the many devils ever ready to sink in their teeth
The rock is the veil of ignorance that we all hide beneath
And the Black Salamander
Is me

CHAPTER EIGHT

REDEMPTION SONG: OVERCOMING ANGER—YOU HAVE TO LET IT GO

Ever since I got the idea to write this book, I have been thinking about this chapter, brooding over it, picking at it. Anger. From the day my father first walked out our front door when I was six years old, anger has been a constant in my life. For so long it bubbled just below the surface, affecting and changing me even when I wasn't aware that it was there. In many ways, finding strategies to channel and redirect my anger has been one of the most important developments of my life, allowing me to get out of my own way on the path to success, ensuring that I wouldn't be stunted by hostility and destroyed by the implosions that I have seen destroy so many men around me.

When you grow up without a father in the home, the void and emptiness can elicit a range of emotions throughout your childhood years, from self-pity to loneliness, from insecurity to depression. But with each of these, the road always seems to make its way back to anger.

"Why me?"

"Where is he?"

"How dare he leave me!"

As I observed the young brothers around me growing up, and as I go into correctional facilities now as an adult, I can honestly conclude that anger is one of the most pivotal issues facing young black men in America today. Often the anger can seem to be omnipotent, unguided, a general hostility that they aim at everything and everyone in their paths. But in my travels, I have come to understand something: When you peel off the layers and burrow down below the surface, the source of the anger reveals itself: fatherlessness. It is like a hidden underground spring that supplies a fresh flow of fury to all the tributaries around it.

And no matter how much money and fame you manage to accumulate, how many degrees you acquire, you never totally escape it. You may learn to control it, even thrive on it, but you can't dodge it. I remember watching a documentary about the NFL running back Ricky Williams, the 1998 Heisman Trophy winner. Ricky was talking about how much he hated his dad for not being there when he was younger. He said when he was little he wanted to grow up to be a police officer so that he could shoot his father and get away with it. The way he looked when he said it was scary. The anger was seeping through the television screen. When I saw it, I sat back and said, "Wow. That is hatred."

I saw another memorable scene on television during the reality show starring NFL wide receiver Terrell Owens called *The T.O. Show.* In this particular episode, T.O. goes back to his hometown in Alabama and we learn that Owens grew up in a house directly across the street from his father—yet he didn't know who his father was until he was nine years old! Surrounded by his sisters, cousins, and aunts, Owens sits in his father's house and waits for his dad to show up while the cameras roll. When it becomes clear that his father isn't showing up, the pain on T.O.'s face is obvious—it is agonizing to watch. T.O. finally has a face-to-face talk with his father a bit later, and his father tries to apologize for the anguish he has caused T.O. and says he didn't want T.O. to think he was a bad person. He even tells T.O. that he loves him—bringing tears to T.O.'s eyes. After T.O.'s many years of anger and disappointment, now at thirty-six, sitting across from his father, who is now an old man, T.O. still looks like a little boy desperately seeking his father's approval. He still has that need to have a connection to his father, after everything that has gone on. It was riveting television—and almost unbearable.

I struggled mightily as a kid to keep my anger under wraps, but it was tricky business, because I never knew when it would pop up, unleashed by some unexpected trigger. I would push it to the side and try not to think about it, but then something would happen, I'd hear a song or see a TV show, and it all would come rushing back. I can still vividly recall my reaction to a memorable episode of *The Fresh Prince of Bel-Air*, which was one of my favorite shows when I was younger. I was in middle school when it came on, and it had a profound impact on me, because I identified so strongly with what the Will Smith character—also named Will—was going through. His father, played on the show by Ben Vereen, has breezed into town and is trying to reestablish a connection with Will, who hasn't seen him since he was four and his father went out to buy cigarettes and never came back. Uncle Phil and Aunt Viv are leery, but his dad, whose name is Lou, says he's ready to be a father again to his son. Will is giddy. He has a great time with his dad, going to parties and laughing and joking—much to Uncle Phil's chagrin. Will even goes off on Uncle Phil, telling him that he's not Will's father and that he can't stop Will from taking a road trip with his dad, who is a trucker. Uncle Phil tells Will that his father makes a lot of promises but doesn't deliver, and he resents Lou for trying to come in after all these years and woo Will. In the end, his father says that Will can't go with him—and he was even trying to leave without saying good-bye. Will didn't even call him "Dad" anymore in that scene; he called him "Lou." All these little details really mattered to me as I was watching. When his father is gone, Will is talking to Uncle Phil, trying to play it off, acting like everything is fine. He says he learned how to play ball by himself and got through this problem and that problem by himself. The tears start building up and he yells, "To hell with him!" He breaks down. Uncle Phil wraps him in a big hug. Seeing that, I was like, *Wow.* I could feel everything that he said; every word felt like it was directed straight at me. I think that episode was especially meaningful for a lot of boys like me, because we don't talk about that stuff, keeping it all bottled up inside—until we explode. I did that all the time when I was little, acting like nothing bothered me. "I'm fine; I don't need my dad." You just kind of shrug it off. The young guys I work with in prison do the same thing.

After that episode, I was angry for the rest of the night. It just stayed with me. I was thinking, *Things are not supposed to be this way.* Shortly after that, I heard a song by the rapper Tupac called "Papa'z Song." I can still recite all the lyrics, nearly twenty years later, because I listened to it so many times that it was seared into my memory. Tupac raps about how he had to play catch by himself because his father wasn't around, and that he prays to have a father sent to him before he reaches puberty. The song continues: "It's a wonder they don't understand kids today / so when I pray, I pray I'll never grow to be that way." He says that he's heard God doesn't like ugly—and then says, "Take a look at my family." When he says, "I pray I'll never grow to be that way," I really took that to heart. I told myself, even at the age of fourteen, that I never wanted my kids to feel the anger toward me that I felt toward my father. I went line by line, breaking down those lyrics as skillfully as a college English professor dissecting Shakespeare. I just kept telling myself that my situation was all wrong—my mother wasn't supposed to have to work this hard; I was supposed to be able to talk to my dad whenever I was having problems in school or going through regular boy stuff; I was supposed to have a relationship with him that was more than his being some cat I saw twice a month. What I had didn't feel like a father-son relationship; it felt like a dude I was cool with whom I saw a couple times a month. And I'd think about all this stuff and get angrier and angrier; then I'd listen to the song all over again and get even angrier.

Triggers are so unpredictable; that's why they're so dangerous. In one of the prisons I spoke at, one young cat told me that he snapped one day and unleashed his anger on some unsuspecting guy, an authority figure, because the guy had on the same cologne that his father wore all the time. He got a whiff and he lost it. I have certainly been there. It's a don't-know-what-I'm-going-to-do anger, an I-feel-like-I'm-about-to-explode anger. Mine got triggered once when my brother cut himself shaving. As I discuss in more detail in the next chapter, my mother was the person who taught me how to shave. She gave me the option of using a razor or using clippers. When I saw that razor, I said, "Nah, I'll stick with the clippers." But my little brother, when his turn came, for some reason decided to go with the razor. And why did he do that? He cut his whole face up. When I say he cut his whole face up, I mean it— Julian did some serious damage. When that happened, I got really mad. I thought, *This is something a father is supposed to teach us!* My brother wasn't supposed to have to figure it out himself, helped by my mother, who obviously has never done it before—the blind leading the blind.

Rapper **Styles P** was mad at the world as he sat in a jail cell, trying to figure out how he had gotten there and what he was going to do about it. Like so many of us, he had been living with anger his whole life. In this next piece, he talks about how he managed to get out and use the energy of that anger to forge a successful career.

My father passed away when I was younger, so I was raised by my mother in a single-parent household. I know what it's like to be poor, to reach into your pocket and find nothing but lint. I ran wild as a youth and landed in jail. I distinctly remember sitting in my jail cell and making the conscious decision that I wanted something better for my life. I didn't know what that something was, but I knew that jail wasn't it. I had anger in my heart for a lot of reasons—I was mad that I grew up poor, mad that my father wasn't in my life, mad that I was in jail.

But what I realized when I was behind bars was that there are plenty of people who had it way worse than I did. I wasn't the only one who faced difficulties. There were places in the world where people had literally nothing, where they were a whole different type of poor—no home, no food, no shoes, tin-roof houses. So I had to make a decision. I decided to turn everything around and strive for the best, because otherwise I was really cheating myself. It took prison for me to have that wake-up call. I had to find a way to exert that energy and transform it into something positive.

See, jail is like the second coming of slavery. You are an animal. You have no rights, no privileges; you are less than human. People treat their animals better than people are treated in jail. Imagine someone telling you as a grown man when to wake up, when to eat, when to sleep, when you can see your loved ones, being strip-searched, having to lift your nuts, open your mouth, lift your underarms, squat, spread your cheeks so they can make sure you're not transferring any contraband. And imagine someone being able to do that to you anytime they want. They don't have to have a reason or probable cause. They can do it just because they feel like strip-searching you. That is no system for any human being to live in. So I had to figure something out quick.

So many people have the mind frame that we can't make it, but we can. We just have to put our minds to it. There are too many examples of people who were in worse situations growing up and they made it. Now, there may be a long, hard road, but it's definitely attainable. It all starts with youth having high self-esteem and knowing that they can do anything they put their minds to. But that has to come from them; it can't come from anyone else, because everyone else is probably going to be trying to pull them down or discourage them. So they have to know that they were put here for a reason, they are important, and they have a purpose. If you are breathing, you have a chance. I didn't want any part of prison. I put my focus into music and that's what worked for me.

I am focused on hopefully one day writing screenplays and films. I also wanted to become an author, and I've accomplished that with my first novel, Invincible. *I have a lot of goals that I wanted to accomplish and still want to accomplish, and I couldn't get them done from the inside. So that's what worked for me. But it doesn't have to be just rapping or playing ball. Whatever it is that you want to accomplish, you just have to set your sights on that goal and not let anyone keep you from attaining it. You can't let not having a father or being poor keep you from being successful, because you would only be cheating yourself. And take it from someone who has been there and is speaking from experience, not from watching movies or TV or anything like that: Prison is not the place you want to be. It took actually going to prison for me to realize that, and hopefully through my experiences, young people reading this will not only believe in themselves, but will take my word that they don't have to go the route I did. They won't have to be locked up to realize the sky's the limit for them.*

At some point, my mom caught wind of what was going on with me and my anger. She saw me listening to the Tupac song all the time; then she saw some of the stuff I was writing, things that helped me get the anger out by putting it on paper. She was really worried about me. She pulled me to the side to talk. "You can't be angry like this. You have to be thankful, because there are lots of people in situations much worse than yours." But I couldn't see that at the time; I didn't want to hear that at all. In seventh grade, I had a memorable teacher, Tyrone Wilkinson, who began to read some of the poems and other stuff I was writing. He thought the words were meaningful and important. He gave me a quote that had a profound impact on me over the years. I still use it to this day when I do workshops with young people. He said, "Any man can serve as an example—even if it's an example of what not to become." With those words ringing in my ears, I pledged that I would do better than my dad when I had kids of my own.

In those years, writing became such an important tool for me to work out my anger. It was my psychotherapy. When I wrote my first poem, the anger was raw, palpable. I would go back to that poem from time to time over the years, adding to it. I wrote on it in middle school; I wrote on it in high school; I wrote on it well into adulthood. It was a really long poem that took me through the different stages of my feelings about my dad. My mom stumbled upon it by accident in those early years. I never intended for her to see it. When she read it, she cried. She said, "You have to let go of this." But I told her that the writing helped me deal with it. I wasn't going to sit down on some therapist's couch and unburden myself. It would have been a waste of time to even try to get me to do that, because I wouldn't have talked. But I could write.

When I look back on those years now, it's almost startling to me how purposeful and self-aware I was about this stuff. I got invited to a father-son event and I decided to invite my mom, who didn't realize what was going on. When we got to the event, where all the other guys were either with their fathers or some other male in their life, my mother asked me why I didn't tell her that we were going to a father-son event. I said, "Because you're my father." That really hit her hard. On Father's Day, I would give my mom flowers or some other present. I wanted her to know how much I valued the extra mile she was forced to go for her boys because my father wasn't around.

Writer **Kevin Powell**, who became famous when he appeared on the debut season of MTV's *The Real World*, was forced by his university to go to therapy because he had so much anger. But Powell said the therapy wound up changing his life, and he became a staunch advocate of its powerful effects, writing about it in essays and his own books. He describes the revelation in the following essay.

When I was growing up, and I see the same thing now as a grown man working with a lot of young boys and men, there were not many outlets created for young men to express themselves. So a lot of things get bottled up. Growing up tremendously poor with a single mother, my father not being married to her, and not really seeing him after I was eight years old, all had a profound effect on me. When you're going into school and you're made as a boy to sit still and cross your hands, and that's not really your cultural experience, you're going to have a lot of eruptions. That was certainly the case for me, and it was the case for a lot of boys I encountered. All we had was sports. I was artistic; I drew before I wrote, and I loved visual arts, but that wasn't really supported.

Anger, to me, stems from not having spaces to speak freely about what's on your mind, about what's hurting you as a male. If you couple that with a lack of a father figure or consistent mentor in your life whom you can bounce things off of, you're going to have what we call in our community a bad temper. The issue is how to get to the roots of where the anger comes from. That's the problem. Now that I'm in my early forties, I do workshops and sessions with black males all over the country, and overseas as well. Everywhere I go it's the same thing: Brothers don't ever have spaces created for them to get to the root of what has made them angry all these years. When you start unpacking that stuff, there are a whole range of reasons—they could be a child of divorce; maybe they had no father there; maybe a parent died young; there may have been economic issues in their home; there may have been something that happened in their lives around violence, some sort of child abuse or molesta-

tion. I've even had brothers come to me privately and say they were angry because they don't know how to read.

When I think back to my own life, anger had a lot to do with my going from school to school, getting in trouble with police as a teen. It had a lot to do with the politics I took on in college. I think in retrospect it was righteous to become a student leader activist, but one of the things I say to a lot of young males now is that we have to understand the difference between proactive anger and reactionary anger. Unfortunately a lot of us engage in reactionary anger. In my lifetime, it's led to my getting suspended from school, getting fired from jobs. It led to my burning bridges instead of being a bridge builder. The anger has to be dealt with. That's why I'm a big advocate not just for therapy and counseling, which is something I've done for over twenty years and I still do and believe in firmly, but also for creating circles of spaces where men can come together and talk. That's really, really important. Not just counseling or going to a therapist, but having men, regardless of their backgrounds, with whom they can have discussions about stuff beyond sports and sex.

Therapy is tremendously important. When I was in college at Rutgers, I got in trouble in my fourth year. Out of anger, I ended up pulling a knife on a female student. I wasn't going to use it—I would swear on my grandmother's grave I wasn't going to do that. In the world I came from, if you felt threatened as a male, you reacted with force; you reacted with anger. So I got kicked out of college. I got suspended from school for a year, and the stipulation for me to go back to Rutgers was that I had to sit out a year and had to go to counseling. I was like, "What?" I was twenty-one years old, and I was thinking, I'm not going to counseling. It was the late eighties, and there was still a stigma around therapy, particularly in communities of color: "If you're going to therapy, you must be crazy." I didn't tell anyone I had to go. Ironically, the person they sent me to, Dr. Owen Isaac, was a black man in New Brunswick, New Jersey. He was an older brother, like the Denzel Washington *character in the movie* Antwone Fisher. *That was the exact dynamic we had. It was mind-blowing. It was the first time in my life, at age twenty-two, that I ever had open, honest conversation with any black man or any older male about anything that was hurting me. When I look at it now, that's unacceptable. Even if a boy is not going to counseling, you've got to create spaces where these young boys, preteens and teenagers, are talking about what's going on in their lives, because otherwise they will become self-destructive and self-sabotaging in the way I was. The session probably lasted half a year. It wasn't long, but a couple of things struck me: One, he told me I was a prince. No one had ever said that to me before. He took away my apprehensions, because he sought to lift me up, while I went there thinking, He's going to tell me something is wrong with me. That was very important. And the other part is that I had never heard a man speak that calmly. Growing up, the few men I was around were the gym teacher, the sports coach. I played baseball for ten years; I ran track all four years in high school. They were always yelling at us. For the first time, a male was talking to me in a calm fashion. When I think back on it now, he was actually giving me an alternative way of looking at masculinity and manhood: "You don't always have to be this aggressive, loud cat; you can actually talk in a calm way and still get your point across." Those things stuck with me.*

Within a year or so I was over in New York, pursuing a writing career. But I never stopped going to counseling. It's now four counselors later; half of them have been women, half men. There's no way I could have written all the stuff I've written—poems, essays, books—if it hadn't been for therapy over those years, because I had to go back and unpack all those wounds. Bell hooks once said to me, "A lot of times Americans don't realize that if we don't deal with the stuff from our childhood, the anger, the trauma, we become adults and pile adulthood stuff on top of childhood stuff—and we wonder why our relationships are screwed up."

Counseling really had an effect on me. Now I'm a different kind of person. People say to me, "Kev, you're so calm." I say, "You have no idea what I had to go through to get to this point."

We've got to create some spaces for men. Men are looking for solutions. I've had so many men send me e-mails—white brothers, Latino brothers, Asian brothers—and the common thread is, "I need help; I don't know what to do as a man." Women have women's studies at colleges, the feminist movement, Oprah, but there are very few books out there for men that present some practical solutions. When I went on MTV, I went on there saying I would be myself. This was just a couple years after Rutgers. I was going on as a conscious black male and I was proud of that. I wasn't going to be shuffling and jiving. I had studied the works of Donald Bogle, Oscar Micheaux, Melvin Van Peebles, Malcolm, and Martin. But you can't control what people do, how people portray you, because you're not the producer—which is why I like working for myself these days.

I talked in an earlier chapter about the controversy that erupted last year surrounding the ESPN documentary on the University of Michigan's "Fab Five" basketball team of 1991. In the film, Jalen Rose opens up on his feelings about the Duke team at the time, saying he hated Grant Hill because he was so jealous of him, with his loving family and successful, distinguished, wealthy parents. He said he thought Duke was a team of "Uncle Toms" because they recruited only middle-class black kids, not poor kids like him. Jalen caught a lot of flak for his comments, but when I saw the documentary, I could totally identify with what he was saying. I would have the same jealous reaction back then when I saw kids with their fathers. Their fathers would be picking them up from practice, teaching them different things. They would be telling their fathers about their day. I couldn't do any of that, not when I saw him just once or twice a month. We did not have that kind of relationship.

When I got to high school, my friends became a very important part of my life. This is also where I got lucky. I had a group of friends who were all good influences on one another. This was not a given. We easily could have been a group of cats getting together to do something negative. I've certainly seen that happen. The people around you can either help the situation or hurt it. We all know peers are one of the biggest influences on young people. There were five of us—Kendall, DeJuan, Robbin, Zee, and me—and we bonded in high school. We are all still really close today; they were all in my wedding. We've always been able to tell one another the truth. If one of us does something stupid, we can say, "Dog, you're messin' up. You know that was stupid, right?" We used to take these road trips in high school, maybe down to Dallas, or to somewhere like Six Flags. In college, we would drive down to The Essence Festival in New Orleans and just kick it. During the trips, we'd usually have one session where it turned serious. I remember this one trip where we were laughing and joking, having fun, and then Tupac's "Papa'z Song" came on my little mix tape. Everybody got quiet. There was no more laughing. Then we all started talking. We started bouncing our different anger off one another. We were all in different situations with our fathers—situations that weren't what we wanted them to be—and we all let our anger out. Dealing with these kinds of feelings can be tough, because normally we didn't really have an outlet for them. For us, this was a release. It came pouring out. It was intense. After we were finished, we were like, "Whew, we need to pull over." We still have these sessions now, when we have our guys' weekends. Those are my guys; they always will be. We appreciate one another's differences and we help one another. We tell one another the truth. If you can't tell your friend, "Dog, you're trippin'," and have them respect it, then they're not really your friends. Friends can't just go along with any bad decision you make. That's a hype man. I see guys who have hype men around them, or yes-men. Whatever they say, the guy says, "Yeah, you right, man."

Those aren't your real friends. I'm blessed to have a great group of real friends.

When I go into the prisons, the sessions usually follow the same pattern—at first the guys come into the room acting all tough and hard, like they don't want to be there. You can just see it written all over their faces: "What is this bulls★★t I'm about to listen to?" Then we get into the session, start tapping into their feelings, and next thing you know these tough guys are crying. It blows me away. I realize most of them are just little kids who want their daddies. With well over 65 percent of us growing up in this situation, we have a whole generation who are messed up, with all this anger brewing inside. I can recall one of the guys telling me his story, how he wound up in the correctional facility, and it was so simple, so commonplace, that it was painful. Another case of a trigger popping up at the wrong time. His dad had just forgotten his birthday. He didn't get a card, a call, nothing. He was so angry that day. One of the teachers picked that particular day to single him out in front of everybody. He snapped. He picked the teacher up, pinned him against the wall, dropped him to the ground. Next thing he knows, he's locked up. A clear displacement of anger. He wasn't mad about the situation he was acting on; he was mad about something completely different. That's why it's so important to figure out a way to get beyond the anger. And it's why I have such a passion to work with these guys. That so easily could have been me. I was right there, in a similar situation, angry and brooding. If I had gotten the wrong trigger on the wrong day, I could have been sitting in that facility right where he was sitting.

When I'm talking to the young guys in prison, I try to use personal examples they can easily relate to. I have made my share of mistakes, even as an adult. I have been in situations where I didn't simply walk away or turn the other cheek, but rather came back with fists of fury, like many of these guys did. I was actually suspended from the team when I was with the Wizards for punching a teammate in the face. It was in retaliation for his throwing a cheap shot at me during practice. Did he deserve it? Maybe. But was it the right thing to do? Definitely not. What if I had knocked him out, he hit his head on the floor, slipped into a coma, and I was brought up on charges of attempted murder? It can happen that easily, and I have talked to cats sitting in prison cells for doing something similar.

I can't even imagine what kind of anger must lurk in the hearts of cats who had someone close to them brutally taken away from them by forces beyond their control. Such is the case with veteran actor **Lamman Rucker**. Before Rucker starred in movies such as Tyler Perry's *Why Did I Get Married?*, his brother was murdered in 1992. In the following piece, he talks about the anger he harbored for many years over the killing of his brother, and how he currently helps other young men deal with the anger in their lives.

If anyone has a reason to be angry, it's me. My little brother was murdered in 1992. It took everything in my power to not go to the street and hunt the guy down who was rumored to have murdered my little brother. But I had to think about it. I had to think, What could come of this? If I jump out there in the same streets that murdered my little brother, I will lose either way. If I do get him, my family will end up losing me one way or another. We already lost my brother; I would either wind up in jail for murder, or I would be murdered myself. That would be a selfish move on my part. So, as a result, as difficult as it was for me to live with the fact that I have never avenged the murder of my little brother, whom I loved with all of my heart, it is a decision I am thankful I made. However, I would be lying if I said that it doesn't still bother me to this day. But I have to clear my head and remind myself that I turned that day from being one of the worst days of my life into the first day of a new chapter of my own self-discipline and self-determination. There would have been no Tyler Perry movies for me, no acting on televi-

sion or onstage, no college, no nothing. I wouldn't be here to do any of those things if I were six feet deep or behind bars. My entire life would have been completely different had I not made the decision to walk away from a situation that still haunts me to this day. And that's why I do the work that I currently do. That's why I work to encourage other young boys to not fall into the same traps.

I can remember so many times growing up when I had to use self-control. Whether it's somebody stepping to me trying to start a fight, or one of your boys getting into it with somebody, and before you know it all hell is about to break loose. Without having that mechanism of self-control, or trying to talk things out no matter how somebody is threatening you, you can ruin your entire life. I know it's hard to not let your ego get in the way, especially if they are challenging you in front of a lot of people. What happens is that people get caught up in the moment, they get caught up in the emotions of the situation, and honestly, they simply don't want to look like chumps in front of their peers or their friends. And they fall into this trap of having to prove themselves to other people, when the only people who matter are you and your family. They don't think about the ramifications of what they are doing beyond that moment. The short-term gratification of, "Yeah, I punched him in the face," or, "I got him back for what he did to me," or, "I shot him at point-blank range for murdering my little brother" is not worth it at all. Those are realistic and natural inclinations to have, but after that moment has passed, there is nothing but regret. Even if you got even, no good can come of it. It's funny that people think that walking away from someone trying to provoke you, or from being in a tough situation, is punk behavior. But I consider the punks the ones who are sitting in jail because they couldn't walk away. It's easy to retaliate, but what's harder is having the courage to walk away. Allowing that person to have that type of power over you is being a punk. You may have lost the little insignificant battle, but you will win the war if you're still here. You have the self-discipline and the *self-love and self-worth to say, "This isn't worth it, and I will control my behavior and control my aggression so that I can take my life to another level." And even if that's considered a short-term loss, that's a loss that will benefit you as a long-term gain. The ones who took the short-term gain, those are the ones who have the long-term loss. Every cat I know locked up will tell you there are so many regrets that they have. So many situations that they wish they could have done over. They will tell you in a heartbeat that it was tough, but they will also tell you that the short-term gain they got for reacting, not having self-control, allowing their emotions to dictate their actions, was the worst mistake they have made in their lives. Everyone always has all this insight and clarity after the fact, but what good does that do you if you are sitting in jail? You have to just take a step back and think before you react, and believe me, as I speak from experience: That is not easy to do, but it's crucial.*

I started a theater company in L.A. called the Black Gents of Hollywood. We use the arts and the theater as a backdrop to teach young men what it means to be a man, teaching principles that will be effective and helpful for their entire lives. We encourage this creative mechanism as a way to express themselves, the same way that Etan does with poetry and the kids he works with. The first play that we have done, called WEBEIME, *is about a young man who is angry and is coming from a very disadvantaged situation that includes a cycle of abuse. There are eight men who are all expressing the anger and pain and frustration and emasculation and everything that comes along with this boy growing up in this situation. He's looking back on his life while he is going to be executed for a crime he has committed, and he's thinking that he wouldn't be in the situation he is in if he had gotten a handle on his anger. And the overall theme is, Am I a victim or am I responsible for my own choices and my own actions? The conversation is that while there are things that I don't have control over, such as the role my father takes in my life, the economic circumstances I am born into, etc., what I*

do have control over is the choices that I make in my life. I have
control over how I respond and the direction I choose to take my life.

When I speak to cats at the correctional facilities, an ideal case for me is the story of Allen Iverson. When he was in high school, Iverson got caught up in a situation that he didn't even start. He was involved in a racial confrontation at a bowling alley in Hampton, Virginia, where he grew up. The face-off between the group of black teens and the white teens grew into an all-out brawl. When it was over, only Iverson and three of his friends, all black, were arrested. The seventeen-year-old Iverson, star of the high school football and basketball teams, was convicted as an adult of a felony charge called "maiming by mob," a rarely used Virginia statute ironically intended to fight lynching. Iverson and his supporters claimed that he wasn't even there anymore when the trouble began, because he had left the bowling alley. When I talk to these guys, I tell them that if it weren't for Coach John Thompson at Georgetown, who was willing to give Iverson a chance, nobody would know who he was—he would be just another cat locked up who could play ball. We don't even know how many other guys there are like Iverson whom we will never hear of. The key point I try to make is that they will sometimes get in situations where they will even be correct, their outrage will be justified, but they still have to think first before they react. That's really hard for young males— we, myself included, just react.

Sometimes I will hear from some of these guys later on, particularly the ones from the Free Minds writing program that I worked with in one of the Washington, D.C., prisons. They write me letters or I see them in person and they tell me, "You were right. It was tough to hear, but you woke me up. You told me about the system, about how unfair the law can be, and now I want to be a lawyer. I want to help other people." When I get stories like that, it makes me feel the same way my mother feels when she runs into her old students. It's a wonderful feeling to know you're having an impact. What's upsetting to me is how quickly society will push these ex-cons aside. We should want them to be able to turn their lives around, get a job, go back to school, right? We should want to help them so they don't go back to doing what got them into trouble in the first place. But we make it so hard for them to do that. A lot of them get discouraged, get angry—and fall right back into the pattern, the trap.

Former NBA star **Derrick Coleman** was raised by his grandmother and his uncle. He never met his father, and it's something that has bothered him his entire life, that has made him carry around an ever-present anger about his situation and made him wonder why his father didn't even consider Derrick worthy of having a relationship with. In the following piece, Coleman talks about the quest he is currently on to locate his biological father, if just to ask him a simple question: "Why?"

I'm originally from Mobile, Alabama. I was raised by my grandmother. When I was thirteen, my uncle Robert came and got me and had me move with him to Detroit. It's ironic that Etan is writing a book on this, and I have to really commend him for doing this, because it has a special meaning to me personally. Right now, I am in the process of trying to locate my father. All my life, growing up to this date, I have never met my father, and I am trying to find him this minute. I don't want anything from him; I just want to get the opportunity to see him and bring closure to something that has been bothering me my entire life.

There is a saying that I have permanently etched in my memory: "The chains remain." It's a reminder to me that I don't want to grow up to be like my father. Those generational chains from him will not be placed on my children. I don't know the reasons he didn't stick around or why he never wanted to have a relationship with me and be a part of my life. I can't tell you that it didn't hurt me and anger me. When I was young, I would ask my mother questions. She would either change the subject or give me the short, short version, so I eventually left it alone. But the curiosity never fully went away. I remember thinking to myself, Well, what about me? Regardless of what y'all were going through, I was still your son, and you didn't care enough about me to want to see what was going on with me? How I was doing, what I looked like, if I looked like you, if I was okay, if I needed anything, nothing? You didn't care about any of that? It made my blood boil. But it also made me vow to never be that way with my kids when I had them, regardless of what happened with the relationship with the woman. Because I understand relationships don't work out, but it's not the children's fault. They had nothing to do with y'all's mess. So I vowed to always be involved with my kids.

It bothers me to this day, which is why I'm here, a grown man—some might say an old man—still having the need to actually meet my father. No, I don't want anything from him, but I have to admit I want to ask him, "Why?" Why he never called. Why he never checked on me. Why he never wanted me. I want to ask him all of those things, but I know I don't want to grow up to be anything like him.

It's crazy that today you see all these sporting events, basketball, football, track and field, and you see all these single moms out there supporting their babies. No fathers. You see mothers out there carrying football pads and water bottles. That's supposed to be the fathers doing that. So I vowed to never be that deadbeat, poor-excuse-for-a-man type of a father when I had my kids.

I always had a strong family structure. I had a strong grandmother, and I always had a lot of uncles, aunts, cousins who were there to give me the guidance that I needed. My uncle was no joke. I actually feared my uncle. Not that I was scared of him like that, but I was scared of—if I did something wrong—what he would do to me. I think kids need to have that type of fear. I think it's a good thing.

My neighborhood in Detroit, 12th Street, was considered a gang at the time. Anyone from Detroit around my era knows exactly how tough 12th Street was. But sports always played a huge role in keeping me away from all of that. It gave me a goal to work toward. A lot of kids who aren't working toward any goal, who don't see any light of opportunity at the end of the tunnel, of course are going to look at the present and not the future. Why would they? How could they? They look ahead and see nothing but darkness, so where's the incentive? I had basketball, and that really occupied my time.

Society is always going to tell kids from single-parent homes that they can't make it. But it's a mind-set. I'm not someone who ever bought into the statistics or the negativity. Now, I'm not in any way saying I didn't make mistakes. I definitely did. Anyone who knew me growing up and all through my college and professional career will tell you that I was no angel. But my point is that I believed in myself no matter what anyone thought, said, or tried to do to convince me otherwise. I always had the mind state that, given the right opportunity, I could excel in anything I wanted to excel in, and nothing on planet Earth had the ability to stop me but me. It put me in survival mode at a young age, because I knew that everything was against me. I had the mentality of me against the world. So, yeah, I had everything stacked against me, but there comes a point in everyone's life where they have to make a decision. To either let themselves be defeated or to not allow themselves to be defeated.

I think one of the main things we need to do with our young kids is to partner them up with mentors. Men who can talk to them and tell them, "Hey, I'm from the same environment that you are in, I had the same anger in me that you have, I had the same social problems that you have, but that didn't stop me from being the *person that I wanted to be." Men who can actually show them that they were able to overcome their obstacles and be successful. It's not about sitting there and complaining. Nobody wants to hear about your trials and tribulations anyway. What are you gonna do about it? Sometimes you gotta simply look in the mirror, not blame anyone else for your problems, even though it may be someone else's hands that directly or indirectly were responsible for your being in the situation you are in. But how can you learn from that and turn a negative into a positive? How can you turn someone else's evil intentions into something that only makes you stronger? Isn't that what Tupac said? "That which does not kill me will only make me stronger." I don't think he was the first one who said that, but it's true.*

Our people have been put through so much, but we're still here. So young people have to figure out, How are you gonna get yourself out of that situation in a way that is good for the long term? Not a way that may work for a year or two, then have you ending up dead or in jail, but a way that will set you and your family up for the future. Yeah, you have a right to be hostile, like Public Enemy said back in the day. Hell, I had a right to be hostile. I never even met my dad. But you know what? I didn't let it stop me. I think young people need to have more men actually tell them that personally, and make that personal connection with them.

I feel so comfortable talking in the prisons, partly because I've been doing it for so long. I started when I was in college. I don't ever remember being nervous or scared—maybe that's because my mother used to have me speak to her high school students when I was still in high school myself. To be honest, her school was so bad, speaking at the prison didn't feel that different. When she first asked me to do it, I asked her, "Mom, what am I going to say to these cats?" She said, "Just talk." So that was what I did. As I got older, my talks gained more depth and sophistication. Eventually, as I started adding the writing workshops, I was able to encourage them to use writing as a vehicle to vent, just like I did. What I try to do is get them to start thinking about their lives from the perspective of their own children, for those who already have them, or of their future children. Sitting there in a cell, far away from their growing child, they are well down the road to repeating the same cycle of fatherlessness. I tell them to close their eyes and go back to their childhood. I ask them to remember the moment when they were the angriest at their fathers—maybe he wasn't there for something important to them, or he had done something mean to them. Each of them gets to that moment without much difficulty. "Now," I say, "imagine your son feeling that exact same way—about you." That immediately wakes them up. It's like a light comes on. These guys are often like children who grow up in a house where they are the victims of abuse—chances are they will be abusive themselves. With fatherlessness, so many of us are now trapped in the same cycle of anger and dislocation—until we decide we are going to break out of it.

It wasn't until just before I got married that I finally finished the poem that I started in middle school. I knew I had to get past the anger, or do something with it, before I got married. I couldn't bring that brooding anger into my marriage; I wanted to start fresh, with a new beginning. I wanted to use the experiences with my dad as something to learn from, rather than something to be burdened by. I also had to recognize that although I didn't have the ideal situation with my father growing up, things could have been a lot worse. There were cats who would have given anything to have a portion of what I had. A crumb of the meal I refused to eat. It's like the saying, "The man with no shoes never knew how good he had it until he saw the man with no feet." Sometimes in life, it takes seeing situations worse than yours for you to appreciate what you have.

I had been struggling over the years with forgiveness. Forgiving was hard, real hard. I knew it was something I was supposed to do, something God wanted me to do, but I wasn't sure if I would ever get there. I knew what the Bible said, but, despite knowing that, I still could not bring myself to actually forgive. How deep is that? I knew the scriptures, I knew Matthew 6:14–15 (KJV):

> *For if ye forgive men their trespasses, your heavenly Father will also forgive you:*
> *But if ye forgive not men their trespasses, neither will your Father forgive your trespasses.*

I was fully aware of many scriptures along those lines, but I still couldn't bring myself to actually forgive, even being fully aware of the consequence for not forgiving.

I finally confronted my father about it right before the wedding. I told him, "I am saying, 'I forgive you,' because that is what God commanded me to do, and I don't want to go into a marriage with this anger." When I confronted him, my father didn't really know how to react. I remember him telling me that he never knew I felt this way. He told me that he was under the impression that everything was good and that all of the weekend trips and times we got together every month meant something to me. What he didn't understand was that although I was thankful for those memories, nothing could replace his actually being there. No amount of toys, gifts, trips could replace that. Which is why I could still relate to the anger of a young cat who has never met his father. Not that my situation was on that level, but I could definitely relate, because I too felt the anger.

I actually kept writing on the poem after the wedding. I didn't finish it until my first child was born. That felt like a good time to finally move on, to close that chapter. When I was finished, I showed the finished project to my mother. This was almost fifteen years after she had read the poem in its beginning stages. She cried again, but she was happy that I was able to come full circle, to get past the anger, even to forgive. Lord knows it's hard, but it can be done. It must be done.

I'd like to close this chapter with my friend and three-time winner on *Showtime at the Apollo*, poet **Messiah Ramkissoon**, with a poem he calls "Anger Man-Age-Ment." It's about how we have to let it go if we are going to thrive—what Messiah calls "self-release."

Written for that Man whose Age Meant
a 6 foot grave or jail cell placement
One-word sentence; "Life" is the statement
On a one-way entrance; ice on the pavement
Streets and sidewalk outlined in chalk
Neither are safe when outside at dark!
To vacate pain,
some get high for pleasure
Influx of rain,
weight gain and high blood pressure
Viewing life as a torn love letter
Sweaters worn by cold hearts
in the warmest weather
Fingers sworn to go hard
A bond forever
The body and soul weren't born together
One is old, one from the modern era
The process of aligning both is perfect peace
To find growth one must self-release
To help decrease the taste of revenge
And shirts with deceased faces of friends
In danger is a man without a grip on his anger
Bound to sink like a ship without an anchor
Without a temper we will live longer
Anything else is to kill and self-conquer

When stress weighs and thoughts conjure
A man maintains principles like Kwanzaa
Hostility is toxicity
To those in proximity
Including self
It ruins health
No fulfillment in killing
No glory in gangster
The root to a villain's story is anger
Truth and wisdom is a warrior's answer
It's easy to get upset and be a bitter person
Two choices: Be a pet or be the bigger person
Puppet or puppeteer, the soul must cleanse
So body and spirit can become best friends
Manage your anger. Free your neck from the noose
Of suicide, murder, and domestic abuse
X the excuse of the cards we were dealt
Like ice, even the hardest hearts melt
On average some find in marriage a stranger
Time to let go the baggage. Manage your anger!

CHAPTER NINE

DEAR MAMA: HELPING SINGLE MOTHERS SHOULDER THE BURDEN

Some of you might wonder what a chapter on single mothers is doing sitting in the middle of a book about fatherhood. My answer is simple—because so many single mothers out there, including my own, are forced to take on the role of the father in the household. So this chapter is my tribute to them—and my thoughts on the implications behind our country being filled with so many mothers who are also acting as fathers. If 65 percent of black households are run by single mothers, it is now the norm for the majority of kids in the black community—and becoming the norm for the country as a whole, where the number of single-mom households is somewhere around 30 percent. It would be negligent to talk about fatherhood and not talk about them.

The struggling, overstressed single mother is now an iconic figure in our country, particularly in the African-American community. She's the subject of Hollywood movies—remember Cuba Gooding Jr. telling Tom Cruise not to "shoplift the pootie" by mistreating single mom Renée Zellweger in *Jerry Maguire*?—and the target of too many conservative political attacks to mention here. So much of "what's wrong with America" has been placed in her lap—as if she asked to be abandoned by the child's father, as if she grew up dreaming of the day when she would raise a family by herself. In a sense, it was my upbringing in a single-parent household that brought me to this juncture, writing a book about fatherhood.

Of course, it goes without saying that the job of the single mom is difficult—much more difficult than the job of mom in two-parent households. I don't think I would get much argument here—even from the wives who enjoy complaining to anyone who will listen about how little their husbands contribute to the maintenance of the household. I saw it every day, up close, in the household of Deborah Thomas. There are images from my childhood of my tired, over-worked mom that I will carry with me forever. I remember her coming home from school, wrung out, and she'd still have to grade papers, cook dinner, and then deal with me and my brother, Julian. But somehow she would summon the strength to work with us, or play with us, figuring out a way to raise us the way we needed to be raised. She was amazing. But it couldn't have been easy. As I look back on it now, a lot of it was unfair to her—and probably changed her life in substantive ways from what it would have been if she and my father stayed together.

For one thing, raising two boys by herself required my mother to be extra strict with us. Corralling two active, curious, vigorous boys is no joke. I'm getting just a taste of it now with my son, Malcolm. I can't even imagine Malcolm times two. But Mom was a master at keeping us in line. She didn't let us get away with anything. She was a schoolteacher, so we had to be on point with all of our schoolwork. If we started slipping, she would sit us down to talk. She just didn't take any mess—and that's the way she had to be. But I think that because of her need to remain vigilant and strict, she didn't allow herself to be as playful and fun with us as she probably would have been if my father were in the house. We would get flashes of it sometimes; she's a funny, joyful woman who likes to have a good time. But I know in the back of her mind she was always considering the consequences if she let up on us too much. There was too much at stake to let an excess of fun seep into the household. You can't give little boys too much slack—you let up for too long and they'll quickly take advantage. But as the father of three, I now see how much pure, unadulterated fun you can have with your kids if you just let yourself go sometimes and be silly and childish. I talked about this at length in the joy chapter. I think my mom might have missed out on some of that. Because she was so worried about keeping us in line, she probably denied herself some of that joy. It's funny, because I see it now when she is playing with my kids. She is Grandma now, or, as they call her, Mimi. My brother and I have both on occasion caught ourselves staring and thinking, *That's not the same lady we grew up with.* She really wasn't that playful. We joke about how being a grandmother has made her soft, because Malcolm and Imani can get away with things with her that we surely wouldn't have gotten away with. But her role is completely different now. It's relaxed and free. She is able to simply enjoy her grandkids without worrying about being the bad guy. She lets me and Nichole do that. She is the one who will spoil them. It's nice to see her at ease and no longer in a constant state of worry. Understand that in no way am I laying any blame at her feet. Rather, I'm acknowledging one of the steep prices single moms have to pay.

For most single moms, there's one issue that they never seem able to completely escape: money. A single black woman with children earns a median annual income of $25,958, while more than 40 percent of black families headed by a single mom are poor. Embedded inside these statistics are a lot of struggle and pain. My mom was a schoolteacher, so we weren't exactly poor, but a teacher's salary isn't a lot, particularly in Tulsa, Oklahoma. We always had enough, and we always had one another, but I certainly remember my mom struggling to make ends meet. She would spread all the bills out on the table in front of her and stare down at them with this stressed-out look on her face. She was getting child support from my dad, but it's not the same as having two incomes. This is an everyday reality for single moms in this country.

Atlanta Hawks star **Joe Johnson** calls his mom "superwoman" after watching her keep their household afloat throughout the rough years of his childhood. His father reappeared in his life after Joe was grown, but Joe felt that, in many respects, it was just too late—a subject he details in the following essay.

The first word that comes to mind when talking about my mother is "superwoman." My father wasn't around at all, and my mother had to do everything by herself. She worked two jobs to make ends meet, and many times, ends were far from met. I remember coming home and the lights being off, or the gas would be off, and they had to remain off for a week or so because she simply couldn't pay the bills to have them turned back on. But my mother somehow still had the strength and courage to do everything she could for me. For example, for AAU I needed gear, shoes, etc., and somehow she made it all happen for me. I tried not to ask for too much, because I knew how difficult it was for her to do for me. I knew that she would definitely try to figure out a way, but I didn't want her to struggle. I didn't want her to worry about my having new shoes for a tournament when we could barely keep the lights on, but somehow she did it.

As far as my father, he simply wasn't around. I can remember hearing my mother on the phone asking him for help in raising his son, and for whatever reason, he didn't give it. Later my mom would tell me that most of the times she reached out to him for help, he didn't even respond. As if he didn't get her message. He was in the same state, but I never even met him besides one time when I was younger that I barely even remember. Five years ago I actually met him, and all in all he's a good dude, but he just didn't handle his responsibilities. I try not to stay mad, because I'm grown now, but it's not really something I can forget. I can't completely let go of the past. I still think about it sometimes, because it's not the way it was supposed to be, and honestly, I don't feel he is entitled to enjoy any of this that me and my mom have now, because he wasn't there with us when we were going through the trenches. When I really needed him the most, he wasn't there. Would he still be trying to come around now that I'm grown if I were not who I am today? Of course not. So I try not to be bitter, and we talk probably once a month, if that, but he was never a part of my life, and now it's too late for him to try to make up for lost time. But my mom, she was there. I owe everything to her. Without her strength I don't know where I would be right now.

My mom played the role of both mom and dad for me, and she did an incredible job. I'm a living testament to a mother being able to play both roles. I know you hear all of the experts say how messed up a kid coming from that type of a situation is supposed to be, but actually I think it helped me. I saw how hard my mother was working, and it made me work that much harder. I saw my mother bustin' her butt to do everything she could for me. My love in return was to do my best so that she would never have to work again. That's not to say that it was easy, and there were definitely outside factors that were pulling on me to do wrong, but I knew how hard my mother worked and how much it would break her heart if I did wrong.

Growing up in Little Rock, Arkansas, a place that was really heavy with gangs, was tough. The documentary Gang War: Bangin' in Little Rock was filmed close to where I grew up. A lot of the gangs moved from L.A. down to Arkansas, and that element was around me, but I decided to use basketball as my way out. So that's where I put my focus. My mom had me on a curfew all through high school, and it was a little earlier than it probably could have been, but she knew what was around me and didn't want me to be sucked into that element. A lot of the kids in my neighborhood were going in that direction, and she wanted more for me. So I tried *to always do the right thing. I didn't want her to worry any more than she already did. I didn't want to put any type of burden on her mind, because she had a lot that she was already dealing with. She was and is my inspiration. She is my idol. To do what she did when I was younger, working two, sometimes three jobs, barely getting sleep before she had to get up and go to the next job, was absolutely amazing. My mom can have anything in life she wants from me. I love her that much. It makes me appreciate what I have now, because I remember when things were different. I remember buying my mom a house when I made it to the NBA. I remember her crying. I took her out to the suburbs for about two or three days straight and told her to pick out whatever house she wanted. There's no way that I can describe what that felt like. For me to be able to do that for her . . . Like I said, she can have whatever in life she wants from me, because I owe everything to her.*

Another everyday reality for single moms is the difficulty of trying to have some type of grown-up personal life—in other words, a love life—with meddling, prying, disapproving kids all up in your business. I was so protective of my mom at all times that any guy who was coming into our house was going to have a difficult time. Nobody was good enough for Deborah Thomas. There was one guy she was talking to for a while, but I wasn't feeling him at all. I had nothing against him personally, not really, but I saw myself as the head of the household. I was the bodyguard. I guess it's the same way it will be for me when my daughters get older—no man will be good enough for them either. I tried to take a step back at some point, because I knew I was being selfish, trying to keep guys away from my mother. But it was hard for me to get past it. Any kid who grew up in a single-parent home will know exactly what I'm talking about. You know that your reactions to potential suitors aren't fair and aren't even reasonable. But they're inescapable. My mom never did remarry. Maybe an apology is in order here. Sorry,

Mom. Sounds a bit weak, huh? She worked so hard anyway that I don't know when she would have had time for a man. At one point she was even working two jobs. After teaching during the day, she taught at night at a local college, the Spartan School of Aeronautics. Sometimes we'd have to go to the college with her and sit there quietly doing our work while she taught at the front of the class.

For my brother and me, our efforts to keep stress and strife away from our mother meant that we probably shouldered more burdens than we should have. As I got older, I started trying to handle all my problems on my own, because I didn't want to add any stress to her life, and I didn't want her to worry about me. My brother was the same way. She always wanted us to be involved in a lot of activities—piano lessons, karate lessons, drama, sports. She signed us up for everything. But it all cost money. As soon as I could work, I went out and got a job. It was at the Mexican restaurant Casa Bonita, a very well-known spot in Tulsa that I mentioned in chapter six. I was fifteen and walking around with a little cash in my pocket. But more than clothes or sneakers or electronics, what I really wanted to buy was . . . groceries. Yes, that's correct. It felt good to contribute to the household and buy things that would make it easier on my mother. Sometimes I'd bring home Mexican food from the restaurant. I was young, but I felt like the man of the house. My mother would constantly ask me if I needed anything, and my response would always be, "Nah, Mom, I'm cool." If there was a noise in the house in the middle of the night, I was the one who investigated. I'd tell my Mom and Julian, "Y'all wait here," and off I'd go.

That's supposed to be the father's job, not the teenager's.

A lot of people may wonder what goes through the mind of absentee dads over the years, as their children sprout into adulthood without a connection to their dad. Well, in his ministry, **Pastor John Jenkins** of First Baptist Church in Glenarden, Maryland—a church I've been a part of for many years—sees a steady stream of these absentee dads. But he sees them on the other side, when they are trying to reestablish relationships with their children many years later. As he explains in this piece, it is an exceedingly painful process for them.

The majority of families in our community are headed by a single parent, usually a single mother. It's not a scenario we desire, but these women are overcomers. Handed a debt, they learned how to deal with it, and we have to applaud them. A lot of the women I pastor find themselves in this situation. They could complain; they could cry. But they don't. They become homeowners; they send their children to college; they train them. I think God gave Etan's mother the grace to do it. The wisdom to know what to say, how to say it, so it would make an impact. His mother was able to do that. I'm proud of Etan. He had a lot of obstacles in his life, things that should have taken him out. But God gave his mother extraordinary grace. I applaud his mom; she's a wonderful woman.

While we celebrate women who overcome in that situation, and say, "Amen, you are raising your kids in difficult situations," we are not saying men are not needed. By God's design men are needed. I am pushing for men to step up to the plate. Even if you're not married to the mother of your kids, which is a growing situation in our community and culture, you still have a responsibility to your child, who needs the father to be engaged and participatory in his child's life. Whether you have a relationship with the baby's mother or not, you still need to have dignity and concern, spend time with your kids, love on them. A child needs that. On Men's Day at our church every Father's Day, we celebrate men who are doing what they are supposed to do—being fathers to their kids, being husbands, making the right choices, treating women in an appropriate way.

The absence of his father instilled in Etan a passion that never dies down, fueled by the experiences he's had in life. He hasn't allowed it to make him bitter. Guys have to learn that even if their life is not turning out the way they wanted, life is always about learning lessons. Everything we're trying to do, God is trying to teach us something. Whatever you have going on is an opportunity for you to learn. You have to make a conscious choice. Here's what I'm learning: My father is not here; I see the agony it's causing me, it's causing my mother; I'm not going to do that.

When I look back over my life, my father's a good guy, but he's not perfect. Nobody's perfect. We learn from what they do well and what they don't do well. We try to replicate what they are doing that's positive.

What's happening with a lot of these men—and I see this a lot in our church, which is heavy on family involvement with kids— I've seen countless times that they come back, and many carry a silent guilt. They don't want to talk about it; they want to keep it invisible. When you have an encounter with God, the spirit of the Lord speaks to you, challenges you in your behavior and actions. These guys come back and want to know, "What do I do?" They are calling me because they don't know how to respond. Many are recognizing a significant need they have to be engaged in their kid's life. They have an emptiness inside of them. It's the yearning inside of a man who wants to please God, a yearning to make all things right. You see these guys opening up their hearts to their children. There are countless stories like that in church. They feel guilty; they get restored, sowing into that kid's life, giving them advice. It's a touching thing to see. They get freedom, fulfillment. This thing they thought they could suppress, they recognize they have to do something about it. They get a level of fulfillment, and it's wonderful.

Growing up, I took on the burden of being a protector and father figure of sorts to my younger brother—even though I was only three years older than him. My mother said when I was little I was constantly asking for a brother, and when I finally got him, she always told me, "This is your little brother and you have to look out for him." I definitely took that to heart. In fact, I kind of went overboard with it. When we were in high school, I was a senior and he was a freshman, and I looked after him almost as if he were my son. It was way more extreme than it would have been if we had had a father in the house. There's a difference between a big-brother protector and a father protector. If he was having a problem with somebody, I would want to know, "Who was messing with you? Show me where they are!" Even if he were having a conflict with a teacher, I'd want to have a talk with the teacher. My mother would say, "Relax. I'll talk to the teacher." I think sometimes I didn't allow him to go off and try things on his own, because I always kept such a close eye on him. After I graduated, he was able to do more things on his own. But he never seemed to think of my protectiveness as a negative thing. I still have the same role in his life now, fifteen years later, and we're still tight. He knows I'll always have his back.

There are definitely repercussions later down the road for a kid who maybe grows up too fast and who keeps everything bottled up inside because he doesn't want his mom to worry about him. You are mature beyond your years, but you also learn that silence is your best coping strategy to deal with problems. This tends not to be the most beneficial mind-set to take into a marriage. I speak from experience. Ask my wife, Nichole. If something was bothering me, I didn't talk. I'm getting a little better now (in my opinion), but I'm still a work in progress. Of course, this is consistent with the male stereotype of the strong, silent type—who suffers alone in silence and isolation, letting things eat away at him little by little.

On the positive side, this need to keep things away from my mother is what led me to writing. I learned how to express myself with words on a page. The words became the vehicle I used to work out my problems. Poetry is a wonderful means for conveying emotion.

As I moved through adolescence, my mother had to be the one

who sat me down for "the talk." Yeah, I'm talking about sex. And it was an exceedingly painful, embarrassing experience. For boys in those preteen and early teen years, your mother is absolutely the *last* person you want to talk with about sex. But it was a natural role for my mother, who was always eager to put on her teacher hat. I can remember it all so vividly: She pulled out these books with pictures of people with the scariest-looking sexually transmitted diseases you could imagine. I was horrified. "Mom, I don't want to see this!" I protested. But she wouldn't hear it. "No, you need to know this!" she said. She'd start teaching me about a disease and trying to get me to look at the picture. But I'd have my head turned away, trying to get her to stop. She taught me about all the STDs you could get from unprotected sex; then she talked about condoms. She broke everything down. It was definitely necessary, but that's the talk you're supposed to have with your father.

My mom even taught me how to shave. Hey, somebody had to do it, right? I needed to figure out a way to tame the stuff that was growing from my chin. First we used the clippers. Then she pulled out the razor and showed me what that was like, how to use this incredibly sharp blade to slice and scrape the hairs from my skin. It did not look like fun. Any false move from my trembling adolescent hands and it could get real ugly. I wasn't having it. "Nah, I don't think I want to do that," I said. "I want to stick with the clippers." As I said in an earlier chapter, a few years later my brother was a bit more adventurous and decided to go with the razor—and he paid dearly for his adventure!

Al Horford, the Atlanta Hawks star, is still amazed by the incredible positivity his mother demonstrated throughout his childhood. We sometimes traffic in the stereotype of the mean, ornery black mom, stepping to any person who dares oppose her, but it does a disservice to the mothers out there like Mrs. Horford, who always managed to bring sweetness and light into the picture. In the following piece, Al tells how, like many other children of single moms, he was always committed to staying out of trouble so that he wouldn't bring any undue stress to her life.

My parents got divorced when I was five years old. My father stayed in the United States and my mother and I moved to the Dominican Republic in an effort to start out fresh. We went through tough times financially, but my mother was always my biggest supporter. The divorce made me mature at an early age. I realized what I had to do in life to be successful and to stay positive for my mother. It made me grow up as a person much faster, because I felt responsibility. My mother was always working, so at an early age I had to learn how to be home by myself. I learned how to take care of the house, cook, clean, and just function by myself. And when she came home, I saw how tired she was from work, and maybe she had had a bad day or a long day, so I tried to make everything as easy on her as possible.

One thing that always amazed me was how positive she remained in spite of the struggles we were going through. She wasn't a dismal, woe-is-me type of person at all, and I believe her positivity rubbed off on me. It taught me how to never get down or feel sorry for myself, but to always look at the positive side of things and enjoy life.

When I was growing up, Saturdays would be our cleaning day around the house. She would always have music playing, usually salsa, bachata, or merengue. One of her favorites was Juan Luis Guerra. His music was very positive, very upbeat, and just put you in a good mood. She would have the music playing and she would be cleaning, and the entire mood of the house would just be filled with positive energy. That's the way I wanted to keep my mom: happy, listening to music, and smiling. I didn't want to be the cause of bringing her out of that place, so I tried to stay on the straight and narrow almost for that reason alone.

However, like all kids, I definitely wasn't a perfect little angel who never got into any trouble. But when I did, my mother treated me like an adult. She would sit down, talk to me, and explain why what I did was wrong. And I wouldn't do it again. She didn't even have to raise her voice, or get mad enough that she had to spank me. I was always focused on not bringing any more worry or stress to her life, so I was determined to do what I was supposed to do. She would talk to me a lot and encourage me to do what was right. She would explain how there will be people who will try to bring me down and attempt to persuade me to do things that will keep me from reaching my goals, and that I should stay away from those people if I wanted to be successful. And I listened. I learned to not let anyone limit me as a person, that I was in control of my life. I had dreams, and I had the power and the ability to pursue them. But it was up to me.

I didn't have a father in my house, but I wasn't about to allow that to stop me from pursuing my dreams. Growing up, my dream was to play basketball. In the Dominican Republic, that really wasn't looked at as a realistic goal. Baseball maybe, but not so much basketball. But my mother supported me and encouraged me and told me that if that was what I wanted to do, I had to put all of my attention and focus into doing that. I believed in myself and set my goals. Because I had someone like my mother in my corner encouraging me, I never doubted whether I could achieve those goals. So my plan was to go to college in the States, work hard at my game, and if I was able to make it to the NBA, great, but if I didn't, I had an education to fall back on. I was focused. I didn't have time to be playing around or making some of the mistakes that I saw some of the other guys I played with make, because I knew that I would be letting my mother down if I messed up. The fact that my mother believed in me so much really kept me from even thinking about doing anything that would keep me from being successful.

I can definitely identify with every word in Al's piece. In my case, my mom was even my first basketball coach. She got me my first basketball hoop and showed me how to shoot. Then, as I got better, she made sure that I was playing against the right level of competition. For a while I attended a Catholic school in Tulsa called Monte Cassino. I didn't like that place at all—Catholicism was so different from what I had been taught at home about religion. But I did like playing basketball with the kids there, because I was dominant. I thought I was Kareem Abdul-Jabbar or something. Mom knew that wouldn't work for much longer. She brought me to the AAU team and introduced me to Reverend Potter, who became one of the most important male figures in my life. This was no accident or coincidence—it was part of her grand plan. When we went back to New York to visit, she also told my grandfather to take me out to the park in Harlem and see what my game looked like against stiffer competition. It didn't take long before I told myself, *Oh, looks like I need to do some practicing.* They were playing a totally different kind of ball. It was not Monte Cassino.

As I've said, my mother is truly a teacher at heart. It's what she's been doing for nearly forty years, and she's very good at it. This was one of the greatest gifts she gave me, teaching me to look at the world as a student—one who is always on a quest to keep learning. Man, the things we got into, my mother and I, as the world started opening up to me and I began to recognize unfairness, hypocrisy, and injustice at every turn. Just as a small crack in a windshield can eventually spread into a hundred cracks across the window, *The Autobiography of Malcolm X* was the small crack that started to blow my world wide-open. When I pulled that book down from my mother's bookshelf and started reading, it was like my eyes opened for the first time. Everything changed; I started questioning everything around me. Right in the middle of the book, before I was even finished reading it, I announced, "Okay, that's it; I want to be a Muslim!"

She said, "Hold on. You haven't even finished reading the book yet. Finish the book and then let's talk about it."

"No. I know I want to be a Muslim," I said. "So take me to the mosque. There's nothing to talk about."

She looked at me and laughed, because she had gone through the same process when she was younger. In her early years my mom was rolling with the Black Panthers and Stokely Carmichael, going to the meetings and functions. She used to tell me about the Panthers' after-school programs and the free lunches, when they would feed the neighborhood kids. She participated in all of that—including the questioning of authority. So instead of just telling me "No!" about becoming a Muslim, she went out and bought me a Koran and some other books on Islam. She took me to a mosque. I had a million questions, heavy stuff about Christianity and the Nation of Islam and Elijah Muhammad. She sat me down and answered them, one by one; then she took me to the pastor of the church we attended and she let him answer some. We read the Koran together. We read *The Black Muslims in America* by C. Eric Lincoln. She wanted me to have all the information and then to allow me to make my own decisions. (Though that did not apply to everything I wanted to do—when I thought it might be cool to have an earring, her response was clear and unambiguous: "No!" That was the end of that.) After I had gotten more information and done a lot of reading, then we talked. I liked a lot of the things Muslims did, like helping the community, encouraging men to walk upright and women to respect themselves and value themselves as queens, focusing on education, knowledge of your history and culture, responsibility, discipline, etc. But then there were other aspects that my mother didn't agree with. So we talked about it. Although she agreed that women should dress respectfully, she believed that they took it too far. She also believed that the white man was not the devil. She told me that white people had to choose to be devils, and while some did choose that route, many chose not to. She also stressed that, unfortunately, there were some black people who chose to be devils, too. That particular message was vital to my growth. She showed me the growth of Malcolm X, when he came to the realization that being a devil was a choice. So she encouraged me to take the positive aspects of the Nation and apply them to my life, but that it was important to always do the study and research for a full understanding.

After that process, I wanted to read everything. I was insatiable. My mother started bringing me all kinds of books—Frederick Douglass, Huey P. Newton, Nat Turner, Booker T. Washington, W. E. B. Du Bois, Marcus Garvey, Bob Marley, Maurice Bishop from Grenada. I started reading about inventors like George Washington Carver, Garrett A. Morgan, and Granville T. Woods. This was also when I was introduced to poetry, such as the work of the Last Poets. She was playing something by them and I was intrigued. "Who is this?" I asked her. So she started telling me all about them. She also played Gil Scott-Heron, so we talked about what he was saying in "The Revolution Will Not Be Televised." These were all things I wasn't being taught in school. My mother was providing me with the education outside of school that is crucial for black kids to acquire. Actually, it's important for all kids to learn, so that they become inquisitive, question the things around them. As a result of these sessions with her, I started questioning some of the lessons I was being taught in school. For instance, in Oklahoma every year on April 22 we celebrate the Oklahoma Land Run of 1889, when more than two million acres of unassigned land in the heart of Indian territory were opened to settlement, resulting in more than fifty thousand people all racing to claim land at precisely the same time. But when I began to think about it, I wondered, "Why are we celebrating this? They slaughtered all the Indians to open up this land, so this is a celebration of the time they slaughtered them? Is that what we're doing here?" My mother said, "Yeah, kind of." Then I started asking about how Christopher Columbus could discover a land when people were already here. My mother just laughed. She always laughed at me, because she said I reminded her so much of herself when she was younger. She said I needed to start doing extra studying, beyond what I needed to study for school. "You have to know how to play the game," she told me. "Understand that this is their history. They are celebrating it this way, teaching it this way, because it's the way they want to see it. We know Christopher Columbus didn't really discover America, because there were already people here. But you learn it for the test. If you want, you can put a notation by the side, next to the answer they want, and you can also give an alternative answer." So I started doing that. Some of the teachers didn't react too well. But there was one teacher who did. His name was Mr. Williams, and he was my favorite teacher I ever had. It was my freshman year at Booker T. Washington High School; he was extremely strict, a real disciplinarian. When I would question these things, he would smile at me. He said, "Okay, I will push you extra hard." He made me do more than the other kids in the class. He was strict as anything, hard as anything, but I loved him. He was a great teacher. I didn't mind people being strict when I was growing up; I just didn't want people to be unfair. I remember once in an economics class in high school, I told the teacher I didn't agree with him because, I said, we had to factor ethics into the equation when we were talking about Nike using sweatshops. So we had this big debate. The teacher didn't like that I challenged him. My mother always told me that it was okay to disagree, but I had to do it respectfully. I had some teachers who liked it, but other teachers who absolutely hated it.

Around this time I began to get some notoriety for basketball, but I wasn't looked upon as the typical jock, because I also was doing speech and debate. While we were winning state championships in basketball, we were also winning state championships in speech and debate. People had a hard time placing me in a box. And that, too, was from my mom. At a young age, she was always instilling in me and my brother the need to do something we were passionate about and not worry about what other people said. It was funny—all my boys would roll with me to the speech and debate tournaments. They'd be sitting there in the audience in their letter jackets or hoodies, cheering me on. Speech and debate is never going to be the cool thing to do in high school, but I loved it. I loved competing against other people, writing my own speeches, doing dramatic interpretations. I thought it was cool, even though it wasn't really looked at as cool in my school. But I was comfortable with it. Because of the principles my mother taught me, I never had a problem with peer pressure. Rather than fitting in and running with the crowd, I wanted to set myself apart and be different, make my own path. That was what she preached to me and Julian all the time: "Don't follow the crowd." She'd say, "You like Malcolm X so much—Malcolm didn't follow the crowd. He set himself apart."

With all these wonderful lessons from my mom, I would get so offended when I'd hear people say that you're crippled and doomed to failure if you're being raised by a single parent. I remember when I heard that the first time, watching some show on television around my middle school years. I was shocked, because I didn't feel crippled. When I look at it, I see so many positives. Yes, there were things we didn't have; there wasn't as much money in the house as there would have been with two parents, and there were things my father was supposed to teach me that I had to learn from my mother. But there were many things I got from her that have served me very well. She taught me to respect women, to cherish women, from an early age. Because of the responsibilities I had in the household, it made me grow up quick so that I could handle things myself. I was more aware of what was going on around me. I didn't get a summer job and just blow all the money; I had more appreciation for money than that. Even now, I have more of an appreciation for everything I have because I saw how hard my mom worked when I was younger.

Civil rights activist **Reverend Al Sharpton** is also convinced that being from a single-parent home often is a motivator that pushes many kids to succeed. It certainly worked that way for him; he never wanted to disappoint or upset his mom. But Reverend Al was also motivated by something else—the desire to prove to his dad that he could become successful and accomplished without his dad's influence. In the following piece, Sharpton talks about the difficult times he had in his younger years after his father left—and how they eventually reconciled, many years later.

I think it is totally inaccurate to say that young men in single-parent homes can't make it. I could give you fifty examples that say otherwise, starting with the president of the United States. I'm personally offended when I hear that. I was brought up in a stable middle-class family till I was nine years old. My father left us, and my mother had to raise me and my sister in the 'hood in Brooklyn. It was especially traumatic to go from a comfortable middle-class lifestyle with a two-car garage in Queens to welfare and public housing, because I wasn't familiar with that. I lost my father and a lifestyle at the same time. I felt a sense of rejection. It's one thing if he and my mother couldn't make it, but why did he have to reject me at the same time? I was named after him; I looked like him; a kid can develop all kinds of complexes and insecurities. Men aren't honest about that. We try to get past our own insecurities, have our own way of dealing with it all, and my mother isn't aware of all that's going on with me. She's reacting one way, dealing with it herself. With no man there, what I did was reach out to other men. I reached out to my pastor, Reverend Jones. I reached out to people in the civil rights movement. When I was a teenager I met James Brown, and he really became a father figure. In addition to his being a big star, one of the reasons I latched onto him was because one of the only memories I had of enjoyment was my father bringing me to the Apollo Theater to see James Brown. And my father also wore his hair conked. James Brown said, "I want you to wear your hair like mine." So in looking like James Brown, I was also looking like my father.

I wanted to be successful for my mother. I felt she was the one who didn't leave me, who did love me, and I wanted to vindicate her sacrifice. I would get up at five and walk her to the subway in Brooklyn. We lived in a high-crime area. She felt more comfortable if she wasn't walking by herself. One thing she would do is put her cleaning rags in her pocketbook so the other kids wouldn't know she was doing domestic work. She did this so the kids wouldn't laugh at me and my sister and make fun of us because our mother was a domestic.

I would challenge the sociologists about this. I think sometimes people who are single-parent kids may be motivated more than kids who grow up with a sense of entitlement. Sometimes it can be the thing that drives us, that motivates us. If we use it as a stepping-stone, it could work as a motivator rather than an obstacle.

As I got older, I wanted to become something to make my father wish he had never left me. About twelve years ago we started talking again. We really reconciled four years ago. A highlight for me was three years ago, when my father called me on his cell phone. He runs a car service in Orlando, Florida. He said, "Do you have a minute?" I said, "Yes, what's going on?" He said, "One of my workers doesn't believe you're my son. Can you get on the phone and prove it to him?" So I did it. He was in his seventies at the time. That was full circle. After all the awards and honorary degrees I've gotten, nothing meant more to me in my life than the fact that I made him say to someone that I was his son. Inside I had felt that rejection until then, and I was in my fifties. But at the same time I didn't want anyone to feel sorry for me. It's like an athlete who has a handicap. It can make you surrender or it can make you work out harder.

Even though I have other father figures, he's still my father. To *be completely whole, I had to one day deal with the fact that he is my father. I'm not James Brown's son; I'm not Reverend Jones's son. I'm Al Sharpton's son. But I proved I could make it with that one parent and become something he would never be. I didn't let everyone else become the appraisers of my value; I appraised my own value.*

When I made it to the NBA, the first thing I did was tell my mother she didn't have to work anymore, that I would take care of her. I brought her out to the suburbs and told her she could have any house she wanted. Every time we saw a house, she'd say it was too big; she didn't need that much space. We were eventually able to find one that she could live with. Then I told her she didn't have to work anymore. After all that she had done for me, it felt so good to be able to tell her, "You don't have to work again. You don't have to do anything; just sit back and chill." Of course, she didn't listen to me. It's now more than ten years later and she's still working. She has a passion for it and doesn't want to stop. A few years ago we were driving to the grocery store and she was telling me that it might be time for her to retire. There was crazy stuff happening in her school; some kid in a classroom a few doors down from hers brought a gun to school, and they had also had something like a race riot. She said, "I might have had enough of this." So we get out and walk into the store—and this girl comes up to her and says, "Miss Thomas, I had you, like, ten years ago and you changed my entire life! The way you stayed on me—if you hadn't done it, my life would have been different." The girl was crying, and she gave my mother a big hug. My mother came back over and looked at me. She said, "I guess I'll have to stay a little longer."

It might be a valid question to ask whether a mom has to be "superwoman," like Joe Johnson's mother, or a natural teacher like my mother, to be able to raise children successfully by herself. I don't think so. Of course, there are a lot of great moms out there, busting their behinds to care for their children. But when you call them superwomen, I think in some way it diminishes the incredible struggle and hardship they endure. "Superwoman" implies that there was an ease to it, that it was all a breeze. And that is the opposite of the truth. A lot of times my mother didn't do things for herself that she might have wanted to do, because she chose to do for us first. That's why I would pay for things myself as soon as I was able. But the situation wasn't supposed to be like that; she wasn't supposed to have to struggle and scrimp and save. Because a father is supposed to be there with her. She's not supposed to be the protector and the nurturer and the provider, all at the same time. Those roles are supposed to be split between two people. Of course, it can be done, but a woman shouldn't have to do it alone. With the way things are going in our community and in society at large, too many women are finding themselves in this situation, through no choice of their own. Once they are there, they make the best of it. That's what my mother did—she made the best of it. She taught us what we needed to know. And it was just two of us. I can't even imagine how women with four or five kids can do it. The way I see it is this: Men should try to make their kids' lives as wonderful as possible— but when the men mess up, or the relationship doesn't work out, the kids and the mom need to know that all is not lost.

After watching my mother all those years, I would say that the number one weapon that a single mother needs in her arsenal is strictness—with both boys and girls, but especially with boys. I'm a firm believer that kids will do whatever they are allowed to get away with. You've heard that saying that nature abhors a vacuum? Well, kids are the same way. If there's a leadership void at the top, a lack of a strict, respected adult telling them what to do, kids will fill that space with all manner of craziness that will turn out very badly for them. In my house, we could watch only two television shows a day.

I liked *Diff'rent Strokes* and, when I was a little older, *The Cosby Show*. That was it. I had a curfew all the way up until the time I left for college. I could never come and go as I pleased. A lot of kids didn't have that. At a certain time I had to be home. No ifs, buts, or explanations—you know, "The movie ran late," or, "I was almost here on time." No, none of that was acceptable. And my boys all knew. If we were out and it was getting close to the time for me to go home, they'd remind me—"Hey, man, it's getting close to your time." So I'd have to leave the party, no matter what was going on, how much it was jumping. Looking back on it now, I think it's great that she did that. You can't leave kids to discipline themselves. And my mom didn't have the luxury to say, "You wait until your dad gets home." My wife does that now sometimes to my son. I'll walk in the house and he'll be sitting there, looking all pitiful. I'll say, "Okay, what did you do?"

My mom didn't believe in sparing the rod. I know kids now are getting time-outs, but I didn't get those. I didn't have a sparing-the-rod household. As I shared in chapter three, when my mom spanked me, she would sit down and talk to me afterward. She would make me hug her and then explain to me what I did to earn the spanking. That's the word she used—"earned." She made me reiterate to her exactly what I had done, so that she made sure I had a full understanding: "That's what you chose to do; this is what you get afterward. Your actions have consequences."

As I got older, my mom did a great job at keeping me humble. That was a big thing with her: to always remain humble. She would point out different guys who were great ballplayers but didn't make it, never even went to college. They were still playing at the Y in Tulsa or the parks in Harlem. I needed to know that it could all come crashing to an end if I weren't appropriately humble. She said people were going to start liking me just because I played ball. I needed to be aware, conscious of what was going on around me.

"You have to be smart," she'd say.

That was her mantra, the words that will stay with me always: "You have to be smart." That was Deborah Thomas, single mom. Always teaching.

I want to close this chapter with a poem from my brother, **Julian Thomas**. It's his tribute to our mom, called "It's a New Dawn; It's a New Day."

It must've been one of those nights.
It must've been one of those jazzy kinds of nights,
When the sidewalk sweats with the anxious heartbeat
*   of a sultry neighborhood.*
A no crystal stair kind of neighborhood
Where the brownstones are resigned to their joy in secret,
Submitting to their lot like the innocent without pardon.
Proud brown Harlem.
Yeah, it had to be one of those nights.

One of those electric funky nights
When the Barrio forgets about the weekday's commute,
And the street lamps flicker a syncopated tune.
When the six train moves with the exhale of the
*   working class,*
The sway of lavender relax,
Like a Coltrane giant step into a steamy bathtub soaked in
*   Epsom foot powder,*
Enough to handle the work of the spirit, and the work
*   of the field.*
One of those lazy sunset nights,
Where the fading sun sparkles the East River an amber glow
And the birds are flying high,
And the breeze is drifting by

And you know how I feel.
That is how I picture you.
Aquarian queen in a concrete jungle,
Strolling the wisdom of the ages in B-flat.
Shielding me with favor earned decades before I was a
    twinkle in your eye,
Or a thought beneath your hat.

The teacher who walks in the shadow of the garden gives
    not of her knowledge,
But rather of her passion for learning,
Her thirst for peace.
She gives inspiration to manic young minds like good
    tidings from the East,
Soothing a troubled past with freshly carved hope for
    a sturdier future,
Sculpting foundation like granite rock from quicksand.
Plan your work,
Work your plan.

Aquarian queen in a valley of thickets and thorns,
I would give you the world on a golden platter
Yet still it would not be enough.

It was you who taught me how to lead by example,
And to treat every soul with respect and concern.
Whether I grew up to be the prince or the healer,
The pastor or the politician.

It was you who taught me how to give without want in return.
To use my gifts not for the sake of acclaim,
But for the chance to be a lighthouse in the dark of the storm.

FATHERHOOD

It was you who taught me how to live by the spirit,
Trusting discernment to leave the salty chaff
And take only the nourishing grain.

It was you who taught me to love without keeping score,
To be the protector, and a pillar of strength.

We've never spoken of these things, yet you've shown me
all the same.
It's in the way that you speak with dignified grace,
The way that you walk into a crowded room with noble stature
And discreet nobility.

It's in the way that you lead a classroom with patient tolerance,
And honest enthusiasm that is always exalting, and never
condescending.

It's in the lift of your chin, the resolve in your eyes,
The insight in your voice, and the straightness of a spine
That would never cower to unworthy authority.

The philosopher can explain to you the science of thought,
But he cannot give you his wisdom, nor the strength to do
what is right.

A master architect may design the most fabulous house of all your
dreams,
But he cannot make for you a loving home.

The preacher may speak to you of the depths and wonders
of scripture,
But he cannot enter them into your heart
And give to you the peace that passes understanding.

Rest assured you have done your job, and done it well.
I pray no misgivings of what-ifs and would-haves
To ever cross your thoughts by day,
Or trouble you at night.

It's my turn to shoulder the burdens
And lead the people.

I will pick up the torch and carry it home.

CHAPTER TEN

WAKE UP, EVERYBODY: EXAMINING BILL COSBY'S PLEA FOR RESPONSIBLE FATHERS

There we were—clueless, nervous college freshmen on the first day of class. We all crowded into the lecture hall, looking for familiar faces, wondering what difficulties lurked in college-level courses. This one was called Philosophy 101, and the professor was a black man named Lawrence Thomas. As he stood at the front of the room, Professor Thomas gazed out at us and began by posing a question.

"Why have black people in this country languished while Jews have flourished?" he said.

We all looked at one another for a moment, making sure we heard him correctly. I saw students scrunch up their faces in alarm. Did he just say what it sounded like he said? Noting the hesitation and indecision in the room, Professor Thomas repeated his question. It was confirmed—yep, that was what he said. Different hands started going up around the big assembly hall, slowly, uncertainly. One student said that it was an unfair comparison, because the Jews were persecuted in Germany, not in the United States. Another student said the system continues to discriminate against blacks. Another student started talking about how the Jews got their reparations in the form of an entire country called Israel, and we were still waiting on our forty acres and a mule. People started making comments all across the lecture hall. I noticed the only people raising their hands and making comments were the black students. The white students remained quiet; they were not trying to touch that one.

After the class, black students got together and talked in study groups, still amazed and outraged that a black professor would ask something like that in a classroom filled with white students. Some students got personal, calling him names like "sellout" and "Uncle Tom." But soon I began to notice something: The black students remained totally attuned, engaged, and involved in his class for the rest of the semester. There were a few cats from D.C. who knew one another, and when we got there on the first day, they were all slouched back in their seats on the side of the room, their feet stretched out in the aisles and over the seats in front of them. But after that first class, they were a different group of guys. They moved to the front row; they had their notepads poised next to them at the ready; they were raising their hands, fully participating. It was as if every black student in the class, including myself, had been awakened with a jolt. I wound up getting an A in the class, and I think most of the other black students got very good grades as well. The more I thought about it, the more I suspected he might have done that on purpose, specifically to motivate the black students on the first day of school. I asked around and talked to some upperclassmen who had taken his class. They all confirmed that he had done the same thing with them. I was amazed. That was genius! He had managed with one simple question to transform every black student in the room, to motivate us, to wake us up—and it was done right in front of a roomful of white students who had no idea what was happening. In fact, the rest of the subject matter for the course wasn't even connected to his question. I wrote him a letter toward the end of the semester, telling him my feelings about everything that had gone on. With a smirk, he told me he read it. That was all he said. The man was brilliant.

I began thinking about Professor Thomas when I observed the black community's reaction to Bill Cosby's critiques and criticisms over the last few years. It occurred to me that in publicly taking black people to task for what he sees as a growing lack of responsibility and maturity in the community, Cosby was doing exactly what Professor Thomas had done to us. He was challenging and motivating on the sly. It didn't necessarily matter whether the community agreed with him or not—he had issued what amounted to a wake-up call, which led to national debates, essays, books. Just like with Professor Thomas, some critics attacked him personally, called him some of the same names that students called Professor Thomas. I think Dr. Cosby exhibited the same kind of brilliance that I saw in the classroom at Syracuse. But the question remains, Is it having the same motivating effect on the black community as Professor Thomas's question had on his black students?

Speaking for myself, the Cosby controversy came along just as I was getting used to the idea of someone calling me "Dad." The huge weight of responsibility I felt for my son's life was changing me, forcing me to look at the world around me in a way that was radically different. When you consider your surroundings as a parent, you quickly begin to do the math, projecting and forecasting. *If things are this bad now, what will they be like in fifteen years, when my kid is in high school, in twenty years, when he's an adult, in thirty years, when he's a parent himself?* Suddenly, everything mattered in a way it never did before. When you're a parent with a son and daughters, you have to care about how the family next door and the one across town raise their kids, because they're eventually going to be your kid's peers, classmates, possible love interests. The living manifestation of that dad's failure to properly raise his son could one day be knocking on my door, talking about, "Is Imani ready to go?"

I understand how Cosby's comments and tone could have

offended some. Although I definitely did not agree with everything he said, much of his message was right on point. It certainly shook me up, made me think about issues I hadn't given a lot of thought to. He didn't mince words, sugarcoat the message, tone it down so he wouldn't make people feel bad. He said and wrote what he felt.

> *If the Ku Klux Klan were coming again, what would we do? We'd grab our children, throw them under the table, put them under the bed, put bodies on them, get the guns, and be ready. But how do we respond to a crack cocaine dealer? How do we respond to a dysfunctional school system? How do we respond to the criminals in our midst? How do we respond to those people who are unraveling the moral fiber of our village? . . .*
>
> *We have to begin by taking back our neighborhoods. We have to be involved. The people who need help are right here, right now, standing on that corner. We need a revolution in our minds and in our neighborhoods. We have lost many of the kinship bonds that historically held us together as a community. . . .*
>
> *We have to take our neighborhoods back. We have to go in there and do it ourselves. We saw what happened in New Orleans, when people waited for the government to help. Governments don't care. People care. . . .*
>
> —*Dr. Bill Cosby,* Come On, People

As I have expressed many times in this book, my children are little. I still have most of the thorniest child-rearing challenges in front of me. I can't wait. And I'm not kidding—I'm really looking forward to the challenge. But I am humble enough to realize that I don't come equipped with all the answers. So I decided in this chapter to talk to men I admire, to get their thoughts on the Cosby controversy, the community's reaction to it, and the challenges facing parents like me.

This first piece, a vehement defense of Dr. Cosby, comes from a man who knows him better than almost anyone on the planet—**Malcolm-Jamal Warner**, who played Theo on *The Cosby Show*, a character that Cosby himself has said was modeled after his own son. As you might imagine, Malcolm was not at all pleased by the attacks on Dr. Cosby. He uses this essay as a chance to respond to all the Cosby critics.

Dr. Cosby's initial speech was given at an event for the NAACP commemorating the fiftieth anniversary of Brown v. Board of Education. *His point was, Why are we patting ourselves on the back when there is a 50 percent high school dropout rate among our inner-city children? His question was "Where are the parents raising our children?" He wasn't speaking to kids. He wasn't "airing dirty laundry" or speaking rhetoric to a white audience. He was talking to black people at an NAACP event. What better place to discuss the issues at hand? When you listen to the speech, you hear the audience agreeing and applauding. You hear a man who is incredibly frustrated with the state of our inner-city communities. I liken it to the grumpy grandfather venting about "these young whippersnappers," and he broke it down straight, no chaser. But his beef about these kids was aimed more toward the parents of these kids, who have failed at instilling any level of self-respect in them, let alone respect for anybody else. A few individuals probably didn't like his tone, took some snippets out of context, turned it into "Bill Cosby is dissing the black community," and the message about taking responsibility was trivialized. But what you don't see or hear about as often in the press is how many people in the community agree with him. You can go into any 'hood and will definitely hear more people saying, "You know, he really is right," than we are led to believe.*

I read Michael Eric Dyson's book Is Bill Cosby Right?: Or Has the Black Middle Class Lost Its Mind? *In the book, he spent way too much time trying to discredit Dr. Cosby, and unfairly, not to mention inaccurately, tried to paint a picture of a man who is out of touch with what's happening in the community, while also perpetuating the laughingly asinine notion that Dr. Cosby has done the black community a disservice by portraying roles that don't reflect the struggle of black people in America. Though Dyson may have had some valid points with regard to numbers and statistics in his book, the spirit and energy with which he so vehemently disagreed with Dr. Cosby made it feel more like a deep-seated personal attack.*

When you are talking about self-accountability and responsibility of self, there is no room to discuss the responsibility of others. None of his detractors take into account the context in which he gave the speech. Think about it: Why would he need to cite society's past and present evils to anyone at an NAACP event? He went in as hard as he did because he was addressing a crowd and an organization that were already well versed in prejudice and racism on every level.

Look at Dr. Cosby's career span. His choices of roles, as well as his public persona, have always been a positive portrayal of black men, even during the racist climate of the sixties. He came up during the civil rights movement, was down with Sidney Poitier and Harry Belafonte, so he has always been a very conscious cat. He may not have been at the rallies, marches, and press conferences, but you have to remember and respect that the work of rich and powerful black men at the time was intentionally not high-profile. This is a man who has been on a long-standing crusade for education, from Fat Albert and the Cosby Kids *to being the entertainer who has given the most money to HBCUs. (Between the millions of dollars he's given to schools, and the individuals outside of his immediate family that he has put through college, he is personally responsible for hundreds of college educations.) And, of course, he gave television the globally phenomenal* The Cosby Show, *which forced America, and thus the world, to recognize the black middle class, which had been previously regarded as nonexistent. He changed the way white and black America saw black people. A* Different World *spawned a generation of young black people who wanted to go to college. And through all of that, when he looks out he sees an overwhelming number of young people who, in his eyes, seem not to care about anything but hanging out, getting high, making babies, and being badass enough to go to jail. He is part of the generation that has every right to ask, "This is the result of all our hard work? This is what people marched for? This is what Medgar, Malcolm, and Martin died for? This is what we have to show for it?" His speech was supposed to be a wake-up call, because while everyone was celebrating the* Brown v. Board *decision from fifty years ago, no one was addressing the present state of affairs with regard to our inner-city schoolkids. So though you may disagree with what he said or be mad because he didn't sugarcoat it, you cannot overlook or ignore his accomplishments and the positive effect he has had on black culture. Nor can you disagree with his overall point that there is still much more work to be done (by the NAACP, us, and the parents in these inner-city communities). Vilifying him is an erroneous distraction.*

On a personal level, working with Dr. Cosby, needless to say, was nothing less than an incredible experience. From checking me at my Cosby audition when I was trying to be the typical smart-alecky, precocious black TV kid, to checking the writers who were trying to write the show as a typical black sitcom, Dr. Cosby has always been about using his craft of entertainment as a vehicle to educate—even on something as seemingly simple as breaking away from stereotypes. His career—from his acting roles to his stand-up comedy—has never been predicated on being black. He's been criticized by Dyson and many before him as not being black enough, but the real lesson when you look at his work is that you don't have to "act black" to be black. Though he may use profanity in real life and discuss real issues pertaining to being black in America, these things have never been a crutch for him in his material as they have been/are for the majority of black comedians. One of many of the lessons I learned from him is how to navigate through this industry while keeping my integrity and dignity intact. He has been a friend, mentor, and colleague for more than half of my life, and to this day we are still very close. He has a lot of knowledge and experience and is willing to share with anyone who is willing to listen. I've always listened, and thus, between him, my mother, and my own father, to this day I still get some pretty solid guidance. He may talk for a long time and go on tangents, but if you stick it out, you will always get the gem he is destined to drop. So because I greatly respect this man who has done so much and been more active in "the struggle" than most naked eyes can see, I do get protective and defensive. You can disagree with him all day long, but when you go on an unfounded attack out of ignorance or publicity hunger, that's my dude and I'm going to call you on it.

When I hear people say he's out of touch or doesn't love black people, I have to laugh. I would say that those critics are the ones who are out of touch. Let's just start with the fact that he has been the only person to care enough to boldly point out the elephant lounging in the living room and say, "Hey, guess what; black folks are part of the problem, too." His "attack" wasn't on kids. If anything he was riding the parents who clearly aren't parenting. His points cannot be better illustrated than by the "callouts"—a program he's been doing for I don't know how many years. He goes to the poorest schools in the poorest communities across the country and holds assemblies. He talks for a bit, but who does the most talking are the young people he brings with him. These are all young adults who, as kids, have had just about every "inner-city hardship" thrown at them, from nonexistent parents either dead from drug overdose or violence, in jail, or just plain neglect; to physical or sexual abuse; to teen pregnancy; you name it. But instead of allowing these things to act as barriers or excuses, these kids made their way through school via graduating or getting their GEDs, and carved out lives for themselves. The message is: You may not have control over your circumstances, but you do have control over the choices you make. And that message is not just coming from this "black elitist"; it's coming from the kids who were faced with the very issues as the kids of which Dr. Cosby speaks. They are the ones saying there is no excuse, because they are living testament. So not only was he courageous enough to address the issue concerning our children, but he's in the trenches, in the communities, interfacing with these students doing the work and making a difference. The book he wrote with Dr. Alvin Poussaint, Come On, People: On the Path from Victims to Victors, *is presented as something of an inspirational guide, in which they discuss the prevalent issues in the community, and also present actual cases and statements of young people who have managed to shine despite their circumstances. He's not just pointing fingers and laying blame. He's walking his talk. I must ask of his critics, "You've got a lot to say against Dr. Cosby, but what solutions are you offering?"*

Blame is a big issue in our extremely litigious society—whenever something goes wrong, we want to look around and find somebody at whom to point a finger. It's something of a delicate issue in the black community, because, while we need to prepare our children for the challenges they will face because of bigotry, we also can't allow them (and ourselves) to be hamstrung by an unwillingness to accept responsibility for their actions. This was a big theme of mine when I went into the schools and correctional facilities. During the eight years I played for the Washington Wizards, I made it a practice to visit the places nobody else wanted to go—the worst inner-city schools and the youth correctional facilities. In fact, the woman in charge of community relations for the Wizards, Sashia Jones, would sometimes get flak from team officials because of the places I wanted to go. They would ask her, "Why does he only want to go to those places?" But I was adamant, and she had my back.

She told them they should back off and allow me to go where I wanted to go. I wanted to tackle the kids who were the castoffs, the ones too many people had already given up on. Some of the schools I walked into in Baltimore and southeast D.C. nearly brought tears to my eyes, they were in such bad condition. I wanted to scream out, "How can you expect anybody to learn in this environment?" But once I got in front of the kids, I tried to be as honest as possible with them. I wanted them to know how much the deck was stacked against them. I would break down the No Child Left Behind school reform law, and how the school system doesn't place a value on the education of our children. I would make the point to them that you can't blame the children if their test scores are not high; you have to look at what they are being taught, and that the quality of education in most inner-city and lower-economic schools should be unacceptable. I would explain how politicians take the money out of public schools, cut programs, implement the farce of programs like No Child Left Behind and then don't properly fund it, which only makes the situation worse. Then I would break down how the system gives our kids standardized tests and, when their scores aren't as high as the schools in the suburbs, they criticize them as being inferior. Then politicians push to end affirmative action in universities, claiming it gives our children an unfair advantage—as if they were given an equal education in the first place.

I would reference esteemed author Jonathan Kozol's *The Shame of the Nation, Savage Inequalities,* and *Death at an Early Age* often in my talks. I would recommend that they read these books themselves so that they can see in more detail everything I explained to them about the school system.

My reason for making them aware of this is because I want them to know that the second they walked into the front door of their school, they were already behind—so they had no time to be relaxing, chilling, goofing off, or any type of foolishness. They had to do extra, do more, go beyond the assigned work, go ahead to the next chapter, read an additional book. I would tell them how motivated I was when I was their age, and would hear adults say things such as that *Brown v. Board of Education* didn't matter to us anymore. The way I see it, many times it's not that the students are no longer concerned with *Brown v. Board of Education*; it's that the system isn't. But having that knowledge of how the system was set up for me to fail inspired me to work harder. My hope was that this information would have the same motivating effect on them.

So when you look at education, it is my belief that it is there with a very ugly head. However, it is also my belief that this is not the first time my race has seen systemic or institutional racism. There were times, even worse times, when lynchings were acceptable. Sure, the newspapers wrote about it, but it happened. Juries were set and freed the people who did the lynching. Therefore, we knew how to fight, we knew how to protect our children, protect our women. Today, in lower economic areas, some people—not all—some people are not contributing to that protection. Therefore, when you see these numbers, you see numbers and the character correction has not happened. Many times it's the TV set, a BET or videos played, kids look at it and they admire it.

—*Dr. Bill Cosby,* Come On, People

Growing up in Boston, CNN anchor **John King** says his father taught him and his siblings by the example he set, but he also wasn't shy about confronting John and setting him straight when the situation required. One of his most important lessons was for John to take responsibility for his actions and for his mistakes—a lesson that Cosby believes strongly, but which doesn't seem to have much traction in our society these days. In the following piece, King talks about growing up in his father's house and hearing many of the same messages Cosby has been preaching.

I think what Bill Cosby was saying was what my father said to me when I was younger: You're going to have problems in life, but when you fall down, you're going to have to get up. The first person responsible for that guy in the mirror is you. Take personal responsibility for your own actions. As the circle gets bigger, the next group you reach out and touch is your family. I think Cosby's core message was that personal responsibility has to be priority number one. The strength of the family starts at home, first with individuals, then the core family, and you keep drawing circles into a larger family.

Cosby ran into trouble, I think, because some people felt what he was saying was insulting, or that he didn't understand. Without a doubt there was a generational aspect to it. It caused some ripples in the African-American community. He was talking about not liking the names people were giving to their children, these nontraditional names. You had a guy from a more traditional upbringing, from an older time, who couldn't quite understand why things are so different now. And part of it was that he was deliberately poking people to start a controversy. Comedians do that: tell outlandish jokes to get people to talk about the issues. It starts from, "Oh, my God, did he really say that?" But then five minutes later they are having a casual but detailed conversation about the issues the comedian raised. That's the way it works.

One of the things he talked about was the dropout rate. It is horrible, and a cultural and community challenge. The president of the United States talked about it in his State of the Union address. There are a lot of problems now coming out of the recession. Communities are laying off teachers; they don't have the money to fully staff the schools. This is a nationwide problem. In the middle of that, none of us parents have much influence over that. We can vote, pay our taxes, and go to school board meetings, but beyond that, what can we do? I have a seventeen-year-old son applying to colleges, and it is so much more competitive now than when I did it thirty years ago. That tells me what the economic environment is demanding now. There was a time when you could come out of high school and get an entry-level job and work your way up. These days, people with high school degrees can't get jobs, because the guy with the college degree has it. So dropping out of high school is a dead end.

When I was a kid, we didn't have much money. My dad was a jail guard, and for a while when he was unemployed we were on food stamps. Somehow he scraped up the money to send us to Catholic school for six years, because the public schools in Boston were horrible. There was an examination public school—if you took a test, you could get into Boston Latin School. It was drilled into me, "You will pass that test, because you have a younger brother and sister behind you, and you've got to get out of the way." My dad didn't go to college, but he was determined that we were going to college. It might sound corny, but that was the American dream. You can't go to college if you drop out of high school. It was true then that dropping out was a dead end. In the environment we're in now and probably will be in for the next six, eight, ten years, all of the choices you face are so much tougher than the choices you have if you don't drop out.

My dad was an example to me—I never knew anybody who worked harder. When he had a heart attack and couldn't go back to the job as a jail guard because of the stress, he did plumbing, electrical work, carpentry. He was a handyman, and he paid the bills. He set a powerful example with his hard work. It said to me that if you work you will do okay; you should always try to get better. Dad didn't have a college education, but he read two or three newspapers every day; he was always reading books; he watched news on television. He was involved politically; he was involved in his community. He felt you had to step up every day and do something. And he had the power of persuasion. I was not a perfect child. He would take you and look you in the eye and straighten you out if you needed it, in a forceful way that said, "You will live up to the example I'm

*setting, and you will make yourself better. Yeah, you're allowed to
fall down a little bit and screw up a little bit, because every kid does.
But I'm watching you, and you'd better get your act together." He
gave discipline when you needed it, but I think you need less of it
when you have a powerful example to follow.*

When I talk to high school–age young men, I hear echoes of the
same things I heard when I was in high school from guys who were
heading in the wrong direction: "Why am I sitting here in class,
studying biology [or math or social studies] when I could be out
there working?" Even when I was a teenager, I knew this was silly
talk. You didn't have to look very far in our neighborhood to find
compelling testimony for the ridiculousness of this argument—
everywhere you turned, you bumped into high school dropouts
whose lives had gone nowhere, if the dropouts were still alive at all.
It was just like the scene in *Lean on Me* when Principal Joe Clark,
played by Morgan Freeman, confronts the boy who uses the same
argument to justify why he's going to drop out. "You'll be dead in
a year," Clark says. It may sound harsh or extreme, but if they're not
dead, their life chances have certainly been snuffed out. The dropout statistics are still mind-boggling and almost unconscionable—in
this economy, with opportunity being denied even college gradu-
ates in many cases, how in the world are you going anywhere without even a high school diploma? What planet must you be living on
to think there's any future in that—any future beyond a prison cell
or pine box?

I got serious as a student in middle school. That's when the bulb
turned on for me. Interestingly, because of my basketball talent, I
sometimes had the opposite situation from my peers—I had adults
trying to convince me to curtail my academic ambition. In high
school, when I was performing on the speech and debate team and
traveling out of state for tournaments, even once to Harvard University, my basketball coach wasn't a big fan of the time I was devot-

ing to it. At Syracuse it was even worse. Even though I didn't like math at all, I was determined to complete a business degree, which entailed courses like accounting, finance, statistics, and economics. My plan was to go into the NBA, so I wanted to know how to manage my money, how to properly invest. Sure, you can have people advise you, but I didn't just want to take the advice of somebody else—I wanted to know, to understand it myself. So I struggled through the math. Those classes kicked my behind. I liked economics, but I did not like the others. My basketball coaches at Syracuse didn't seem to get it. At different points, every single one of them wondered why I was killing myself—especially with calculus, for which I had a tutor I was seeing three or four times a week. The message was, "We're glad you're working hard and everything, but why are you doing this?" If I didn't have a serious reason to apply myself in those tough classes, if I hadn't seen a goal line at the end, I wouldn't have done it. But I was adamant that this was something I needed to do. I was convinced that I wouldn't go to the league and see my money squandered because I didn't know how to manage it properly. I didn't want to be one of those negative stories I talked about in chapter seven. If I could insulate myself from that with some hard work in college, that was what I was going to do. The key was having long-term ambitions—something that is too often in short supply in too many neighborhoods.

These next thoughts come from a man who is known for speaking his mind, radio talk show host and author **Russ Parr**. Mr. Parr is brutally honest about the need for the black community to look at itself in the mirror—and for the community to stop avoiding the truth in the statements Cosby has been making.

Bill Cosby took a lot of heat for putting it all out there, but I agree with almost 90 percent of what he said. I think we have issues in our community with misplaced blame. When things don't go our way, we look for a convenient scapegoat. And it's usually not the individual we see in the mirror. I feel that blaming somebody other than ourselves has held us back for a long time. I see so many men having children with people they don't know. That's the real crux of the problem. When they figure out who the women are, they're sitting there going, "Oh, man, let me skirt my responsibility."

Now, some men do want to take care of their children. But then they get caught in that catch-22, where the mother is thinking, You can't do anything for me; I don't want you in my child's life. Or, You got a new girlfriend; I don't want you in my child's life. We use these children as pawns. But then to blame white people for our woes, to me, is counterproductive.

People got upset at Cosby for "airing our dirty laundry," but we have to stop using white people as our modicum of success. I don't worry about what white people think of me unless they're writing me a check for a million dollars. Cosby put out the truth, but no one wants to hear the truth. People say, "Oh, we should keep it quiet, behind closed doors." I'm sorry, but there's ignorance being publicly displayed. We can't pretend the ignorance didn't happen. They didn't like Cosby because they thought he was selling everybody out. This man has been on the earth for seventy-odd years; he's earned the right to be able to say whatever he wants. We don't have to agree with everything. That's a problem—we all think we have to think alike, be Democrats (though I am definitely a Democrat), share the same views, pick one side and all stay on that side. That's ridiculous, and makes us very boring as a group of people. To evaluate ourselves based on what the white man might think of us, what they're going to say about us, continues to put us underneath a rock. I think when Cosby threw all of that truth out there, white people were the farthest thing from his mind. The overall message was intended for black folks.

The message was that we need to be held accountable for our actions, be responsible and stop looking for excuses. The white man is a convenient excuse. Racism is a convenient excuse. Yes, it hap-

pens. I deal with it every day. But I know how to play the game,
choose my battles. You can't go around demanding respect if you
haven't earned it. My philosophy is, Who wants respect? I don't
need people to say they respect me, because even when they say they
respect you, they don't. You can't cash respect. You can't eat respect.
I will do what I have to do to feed my family. I hear people say,
"This is my neighborhood and you have to respect my neighbor-
hood." Well, I'm sorry, but you're renting. You can't go to your new
job and the first thing you want to do is find out when's your vaca-
tion. You can't go in there and curse everybody out, then come home
and tell your children, "We can't eat tonight 'cause I cursed out the
boss." We can't burn all our bridges. I'm not saying you have to
be an Uncle Tom, shucking and jiving. But when I walk up to a
place of business, I think, Who do I have to get on my side to make
my money? You might call it kissing ass, but the only person who
has to know is that person whose ass I'm kissing and me. I'll do
what I have to do to get ahead.

Another thing that is too often in short supply in our society
these days is guys taking responsibility for their sexual behavior. I
can remember those adolescent days well—the boasting, the longing. Young boys live and breathe sex, talking about it far more than
doing it, but never allowing their minds to stray too far away from
it. With my father not really in the picture, my mom tried to fill the
void. As I discussed before, she showed me horrible pictures of sexually transmitted diseases, told me all the relevant facts. But when I
got a little older, I couldn't really talk to her about sex. It's just not
a conversation an adolescent boy can comfortably have with Mom.
So instead, I turned to my boys. We all lied to one another, pil-
ing misinformation on top of fabrication, the clueless leading the
blind. After coming through all that, the one thing I know is that I
don't want my son to have to rely on his clueless boys to get this
information.

Gangsta rap makes young people tough, but not tough enough to walk through walls. It can jazz them about sex, but it can't begin to make them good fathers. . . . The more socially impotent the man is feeling, the more he will rely on sexual conquests to prove his manliness. There's a lot of bragging that goes on among black men when sex and paternity are their main claims to fame. Some will see getting a girl pregnant and having a child as proof of their virility. But what it really proves is their insecurity.

—*Dr. Bill Cosby,* Come On, People

You should not have to rely on your homeboys to teach you how to treat a woman. You should not be getting the information from music lyrics and videos either. It needs to come from Dad, from watching, from emulating, from listening. I have some good stories that I can't wait to tell my son, Malcolm, mistakes that allowed me to grow, sometimes painfully.

For instance, I will tell him about one of my high school girlfriends. She was easily the finest girl in the entire school—captain of the dance team, smooth chocolate skin, piercing eyes that somehow made her look both sweet and edgy, a tantalizing smile, and an incredibly curvaceous body. That's all I saw. She was fine. I had absolutely nothing in common with her—as became all too clear after a short time. But, again, she was fine. I knew the only reason she was into me was because I played basketball and was popular. My boys were all hyped for me. They couldn't stop talking about how fine she was. But after a while, I saw there was nothing to our relationship; it was hollow. It wasn't the kind of relationship I wanted. I'm so glad I learned that lesson in high school. Beauty isn't enough. A lot of grown men I know still haven't discovered that one.

NBA legend **Kareem Abdul-Jabbar** has been speaking his

mind for a long time, so it seemed right to turn to him for some wisdom on the topic of men and responsibility. In this piece, he talks about the failures he saw among the men he grew up with, and the crucial lessons in manhood that he got from his own father.

Dr. Bill Cosby started a very heated debate when he challenged black Americans to achieve a definite description of parenthood that would take hold with black youth. Too many young black men see fatherhood as being a sexual conquest only. After the sex is enjoyed, these youth reject any more involvement.

I have known an old acquaintance of mine since I was in the eighth grade. We knew each other as part of our neighborhood group of buddies and maintained an ongoing friendship well into our twenties. This guy always saw himself as a ladies' man and had the good looks and charm to pull it off. Women were for him a challenge to overcome. Having the opportunity to be sexually intimate with a woman was for him a goal, and he proudly added each woman to his list of conquests. He never felt any responsibility for the results of his conquests, and the children that he fathered were left to be raised by their mothers. His attitude seems to be reflected by successive generations of black youth: the pride of conquest followed by a total lack of responsibility for the children they produce. The individual I knew from adolescence has fathered some five or six children, and none of them has been supported by him. Any achievements they have gained were accomplished without any help from their dad. He was not even thinking of them in any terms but that of a sexual conquest. This attitude has devastated many lives in the black community. Young men are so eager to be fathers in one way only, that of being a sexual stud. The important part of fatherhood—the duties of a parent—are totally beyond their comprehension. Providing a home, seeing to their children's educational needs, and being a mentor who teaches his children about morality and responsibility are not re-

motely possible for these individuals. Their manhood ceases to exist after they have experienced their orgasm. For those young men caught in this mind-set, another, more responsible lifestyle is beyond their reach. They lack the education and moral backbone to live any other way. Their children take the same attitude in their approach and produce children with the same amoral approach to life.

Because of my own opinion of what I should be, I always chose to take a different path. I wanted to be for real, somebody whom everyone should be able to take at their word—particularly some female I was interested in. I wanted her to know I was the real item, not just talk.

Dr. Cosby was alarmed that so many young men in the black community settle for an outcome that leaves them with no input into raising, guiding, supporting, and nurturing that child. A responsible parent will be there for his children through thick and thin for as long as necessary. That parent sees the need to be there for the long term. Growing up, I always had my dad as a positive image to follow. My dad was a police officer, and people absolutely gave him a lot of respect. He earned it; he sacrificed a lot. He was one of the first African-Americans to become a transit police officer in New York City. It certainly was not common to see a black face in a police uniform, so they had to deal with a lot of scrutiny. He dealt with it and did a great job; he made it to lieutenant before he retired. His work ethic was formed when he was a kid, delivering ice on an ice truck to help feed his mother and siblings. His father died when he was ten, a month before the Depression started in 1929.

We must find a way to get the message to all young men that their children need so much more from them and that their responsibility lasts until that child has the tools to live a meaningful life. We must find a way to overcome the legacy of powerlessness that has caused many generations of black children to suffer from neglect and abandonment. We can do it by really caring as a community. Our children deserve no less. If this cycle is to be broken it will take the entire black community's effort to effect change. The values of family education and personal responsibility must somehow be taught to our young people.

I learned them through observation. Talk about the strong, silent type—that was my dad. He didn't say much. I went to Catholic school, where I got a strong dose every day of morals and lessons in how to conduct myself. I got a job at a toy store and then at a dry cleaner's right there in the neighborhood, because that was the only way I was going to have any money in my pocket. But I was able to stay away from the negative forces in the neighborhood, because I kept my eyes on the prize. I wanted to go to college and get my degree, and I knew basketball would get me in that door. Colleges were writing me letters starting in tenth grade, saying I could attend their schools on a full scholarship. I always got good grades and knew that if I got in, I could get through. And I did.

I think people got upset in the black community with the statements Dr. Cosby made, because they want to put all the blame on racism. Certainly there's a whole tradition of racial discrimination and lack of opportunity here in America. It's the real thing. But if we just accept that, then we never move beyond our status at the bottom of this society. I don't blame young black men for being irresponsible and not having any work ethic, because racism in America had so much to do with creating the thing they're fighting. But it can be overcome. Black Americans have done it throughout the history of this nation when things were a lot worse.

I can't wait to tell my son, Malcolm, about how I met his mother on the first day of school at Syracuse. Coach Orr introduced us. I knew within a few weeks of dating that this would be the woman I'd eventually marry. It was an intense feeling I got, a sense. I want to teach my son about the importance of that feeling, the importance of finding that special someone. I will tell him I knew before his mom knew; I knew even before I got the stamp of approval from my mom. Now, I've talked about my mother in glowing terms throughout this book; I've made it abundantly clear how important she has always been to me. But I have to say, it took a while for Mom to let her baby go. She was real protective. I'm not saying she was quite Marie Barone, the overbearing mom in *Everybody Loves Raymond*. Not quite. But she didn't immediately greet my future bride with open arms. Still, I knew beyond a doubt that this was the woman for me.

As I look ahead to the challenges of raising two daughters in this oversexed society, where we see little girls walking around in clothes that they must have boosted from a stripper, I am so glad that I have my wife, Nichole, on my team. In her, my daughters have an ideal model of how a woman values herself, how she conducts herself, how she shows the world what a lady looks like. I feel fortunate to have that model living in my house, demonstrating these lessons to my girls on a daily basis. I got lucky. I can't thank Coach Orr enough for the introduction. He hooked me up. I'm definitely going to be relying heavily on Nichole to help me grapple with my girls' sexuality.

For a father, confronting the sexuality of daughters has to be one of the toughest things he will face in the fatherhood realm. With a teenage girl in his house, BET anchor **Ed Gordon Jr.** can speak about the topic for days. This is when one of Dr. Cosby's basic lessons, about how a man needs to protect and watch over his children, definitely comes into play. A teenage girl needs to know her father has her back—even if she sometimes acts like it's the last thing in the world she wants. In this essay, Gordon offers up some wisdom on the joys and struggles of raising a teenage daughter.

I started a campaign called Daddy's Promise because I got tired of hearing about deadbeat fathers. It came out of an article I wrote for Essence. *I knew deadbeat dads were a huge problem in our com-*

munity, but I also knew men out there who were doing the right thing, being great fathers in their daughters' lives. It was an opportunity to give a nudge to those brothers who weren't doing the right thing to come on board and do the right thing.

I jokingly told my daughter that when I imagined having children when I was younger, I always imagined having a little boy. I envisioned him playing sports, being popular in school, dating girls. But it didn't work out that way. My brother, who has a daughter, told me that this little girl will love you in a way no other woman in the world ever will. Unconditional love. It's different from wife love. With daughter love, you become Superman. The one thing you don't want to do is disappoint her. To a great degree, her image of you is what you aspire to. I play the role of protector, sheltering her, keeping the boys away. I think that's an important aspect of nurturing that comes from men. Men nurture in their own way.

My daughter is sixteen now. When she was getting phone calls from a young man at an hour that she shouldn't have been, I told her, "This is unacceptable." And then I called him and told him the same thing. I said, "This is a friendly call. You don't want to get a second one." I think he respected that. I tell my daughter all the time that you want to be respected by young men.

Too many girls are being disrespected by young men in our community. My issue is, it doesn't have to be that way. A lot of that is taught behavior. When I watch 106 & Park, I see these images being shown to them. They are constantly being bombarded with sexual images. When do we start instilling in them the idea that this is not what they should be conforming to? I think you start from the first day you meet her, the day she comes out. Everything is learned behavior. I watch my daughter and I see nuances of me in her. Her mannerisms. Our children pick up who we are and what's around them. It's far easier for them to see things than when you and I were growing up. Sometimes you have to balance all that *they see by sitting with them, talking to them. "Baby, this young lady may be dressing a certain way, but if you dress this way, you will be perceived in a way that I don't think you want to be perceived." My daughter is tall, so she grew out of children's clothing early. We had to go to the women's section. I vetoed dresses. She said, "You want me to dress like Saddam Hussein!" That's what she equated with the Middle East. But in the back of her mind, I think she understood.*

They will make mistakes; they just need guidance. That's where my generation has fallen down. I want to be my daughter's friend, but I have to be her parent first. Sometimes you can't be friendly. But along with the chastisement, the punishment, you must always let her know she's got your love.

With teenagers, you have to ready yourself. We used to spend a lot of time together. I used to tell her, "One day you will not want to hang out with your daddy." She would protest and say that wasn't going to happen. Now we laugh about it, because that day has certainly come. I know it's not personal; it's just the maturation into adulthood. The hardest thing for fathers is to know there are these little boys around who like your daughter and see her in a certain light. As my friends tell me, I'm being paid back. But I talk with her ad nauseam about sex. I'm frank. I tell her, "Understand that Daddy has lived his life. If you became pregnant and had a child, we would be there for you. My life would stay the same, but yours would change dramatically." Too often we tiptoe around it. But we have to be honest with them.

It certainly raised my eyebrows when Ed Gordon says that he vetoes his daughter's dresses. Something tells me my daughters, Imani and Sierra, will one day regret my encounters with him, because I am definitely going to borrow that policy. All dresses must go through Dad! I can already predict I'm going to have a problem with the clothes. I'm six-ten and Nichole is six feet. My girls are going to be tall and are going to develop quickly. My son, Malcolm, is already a head taller than his classmates at age five. I would be perfectly fine with outfitting the girls in full Muslim garb, the burqa, head wrap, and everything, until they head off to college. But I know that's not realistic (I don't think). However, I will be teaching them about what's appropriate dress and what's not. I anticipate there may be occasions when they might disagree with me. But I will have Nichole as my copilot, and we will present a unified front. My homeboys and I have already started joking that when our daughters start dating, we will gather the crew and all go to the door to answer it together, like Will Smith and Martin Lawrence in *Bad Boys II*, only worse. One of us will have a bat, another a crowbar, the third a chain. In one of *The Cosby Show* episodes, Bill Cosby said a father's job was to chase all the boys away like Old Yeller. He said every time the boys would come around he would bark. You do it enough times and eventually the boys will say, "I'm not going up there, 'cause Old Yeller lives up there." That's what you want, frightened boys!

But in all seriousness, I want Imani and Sierra to find that special someone. The person whom they will spend the rest of their lives with. I want them to be able to experience the type of love that Cicely Tyson and Dr. Maya Angelou described in *Madea's Family Reunion*. In this breathtaking scene Cicely Tyson expresses: "I have had an opportunity that few people ever get on this Earth. God has blessed me to share time and space with a man that he designed himself just for me. I have not only been blessed, I have been divinely favored." That's what I want for both Imani and Sierra, and that's what any father would want for his daughters.

What makes a good father? What makes me qualified to write this book? The fact is, I don't know if I'm qualified. I worry all the time if I'm being a good father. If I'm giving Malcolm enough time. If I'm building the security and confidence in Imani that every little girl needs to grow to be a confident and secure woman. If I am being affectionate enough with Sierra so she feels that closeness to her daddy, even if he is busy writing a book on fatherhood. I worry. And all I can do is try to do the best I can.

This book has been a blessing to bring to the world. This is the book that I wish I had had when I was growing up. Even as an adult, writing this book and hearing from the various prominent men speaking on different aspects of fatherhood has been a great learning experience for me. And I hope it has the same lasting effect on everyone who reads it.

I want to end this chapter with a prayer that I wrote for my children. As fathers we all strive to do the best we can and be the best fathers we can. Sometimes all we can do is pray and give it our best effort.

A Father's Prayer

My Children

I want to be embedded in your character
A permanent part of your soul
I want to be there for you whenever you need me
well into the days you are old

I want to pour into your cup until it runneth over with knowledge
Giving you the power to pursue your hearts' desires
The courage of your convictions
I see you as a bright shining ray of light in the midst of darkness

It has been said that "a child is not likely to find God unless he finds
*   something of God in his father"*

I yearn to be the just man walking in my integrity
So that my children will be blessed after me

Anointed with a sacred privilege
A struggle and a challenge have managed to grace me with the
    heritage of the Lord
A heavenly gift I'm responsible for
Help me to make my home a natural dwelling place for the
    presence of the Lord
I want my choices to be aligned with Thee
I thank You for blessing me with the companion You have assigned
    to me
And together I want us to rear our children in the way they
    should go
I want to be a father who will do my best to instill godly character
    in my children and trust the everlasting Father to complete
    the work
I pray that once I have done all that I can that God will do
    whatever I cannot

There are great rewards in rejoicing as a father of the righteous
I might just imagine standing back like a proud father, watching his
    children go farther than their wildest dream
And thank God for allowing them to reach their destiny

I want you all to be prosperous
For you to have enough of God's provision to complete His
    instructions for your own lives
While upon reflection of all of the blessings bestowed you remain in
    submission to the Most High
I want you to recognize His grace and continue to be thankful
Embrace humility

To understand that those in high places can easily be brought down
    when they fall out of line with God
When they deviate from their appropriate place
The daily influence of a degenerative society will constantly have to
    be erased
I want my children to be able to chase away the demons that will
    parade across their daily walk

You are the seed that decides the harvest around you, so
Be careful of the company you keep
Satan's favorite entry point is always through someone close to you
I want you to still be blessed although you will be walking in the
    presence of the ungodly
While not departing from the way you were trained
But embracing the lessons learned from an early age

Malcolm
My firstborn Simba
Named after my biggest influence
You're an illuminate image of a blessing
I couldn't be prouder
You shower me with joy with every ounce of development
You're never settled but have a familiar thirst for knowledge
As long as you keep God first you're sure to be special

Imani meaning faith
In all things whatsoever you shall ask in prayer, believing
    you shall receive
The evidence of things not seen
A shield
By which you will be able to quench all of the fiery darts of the wicked
Faith

Even as minute as a grain of a mustard seed
Can move mountains and conquer anything

Sierra

A smile that melts my heart
You've started your journey with curious eyes
Watching your siblings' every move
I see you absorbing
I hear the heartbeat of a warrior fighting injustice with a countenance
of compassion
I can see you rebelling against the norm, refusing to eat the king's meat
but seeking to never conform to the ways of the wicked
Dodging the influence of misguided misfits
With your allegiance fixated on the most high

Your brother and your sister can't wait to teach you all they know and
show you the keys to their passion
I tell them that you'll be ready to make your own path highlighted by
the bread crumbs left behind by big brother and big sister, and they
smile with anticipation
They pray for you every night, as do I with every waking day

Lord
Anoint my words with wisdom
Not planning on sparing the rod to spoil my children
But giving them strict discipline through directions of love
You told me that foolishness is bound in the heart of a child, but the
rod of correction shall drive it far from him
Help me to send forth that message properly
To chasten my young while there is hope, and let not my soul spare for
their crying
I'm trying to teach them the right way

I'm more than willing to do something I hate to create something
     You love
Please help me to be that beacon of light guiding my children
     along the way toward You
I don't want to steer them wrong

Please help me listen to Your voice
Hear Your command and follow the instructions that would be
     pleasing in Your eye
I've tried to do right
But Daddy's not perfect
I have many bags of rocks to carry
A burden that refuses to remain buried
Trying to defeat Goliaths with a handful of stones

Leading by example
I try to examine myself
Admit my mistakes
And turn away from the transgressions of my past
But they haven't been erased from my reality
As I still carry my burdens like a recurring dream I can't seem to rid
     myself of
I know nobody's perfect
But continuing to walk along the right path is the goal I'm
     reaching for
Constantly repenting on bended knees for forgiveness
If I told you I am without sin I would be lying
I want the best for each and every one of you
My everlasting desire is to be Christlike
I'm not there yet but I'm trying

In this final piece, the esteemed writer, professor, and thinker Dr. Cornel West gives some context to Cosby's campaign to wake up the black community—and he also offers some profound musings on the true nature of fatherhood.

CONCLUSION BY
DR. CORNEL WEST

We are living in a time when the very concept of fatherhood has been devalued in our society; in some ways, it has even been demeaned. I would like to salute Etan Thomas for having the vision to do a project like this one. He is a warrior, doing mighty work.

It takes tremendous courage to be a great father, a sacrificial father, a father who is always there. It takes courage to have longevity, to always keep track of your precious children, your precious spouse or significant other, over a long period of time. We live in a society that is so obsessed with fleeting pleasures, instant gratification, and short-term thinking, with being titillated and stimulated at the moment, rather than a persistent, recurrent courage to love, a courage to support, a courage to be there and always serve as a rock for your children and loved ones.

Just as justice is what love looks like in public, tenderness is what love feels like in private. To be a great father, you must be a militant for tenderness, an extremist for love, a fanatic for fairness, and, in the larger society, a drum major for justice. What does that mean? It means that tenderness, kindness, sweetness, a loving touch, a hug, finding joy in loving others, are all elements of being a great father. I was blessed to have a great father, so I'm just describing the late Clifton L. West, my dad. I lost him seventeen years ago, but that's really who he was. He had the maturity to be sweet and kind—he listened to and really heard Otis Redding's "Try a Little Tenderness." He knew tenderness was always a sign of a secure man, just as domination is a sign of an insecure man. We need these kinds of standards of excellence among men and fathers, so that we all see more tenderness and kindness and sweetness and joy. We need men who have a real, genuine delight in producing smiles in our children and wives and loved ones. That is real fatherly greatness for me.

A few years ago the great Bill Cosby raised awareness about the problems of parenthood in the black community, about the need for African-Americans to take more responsibility for our difficulties. First of all, let me acknowledge the comic and artistic genius of Bill Cosby. His contributions are immense; I can't think of anybody at the same level of comic genius other than the inimitable Richard Pryor. Second, I think Cosby is absolutely right in talking about how central personal responsibility is. No one would disagree with the centrality of responsibility if one is going to be a mature person, including a mature father. I think the problem was, the message Cosby was putting forward, especially as seen by young people, seemed to be a message of correction, but the compassion wasn't explicitly felt by those who received it. Anytime you want to correct others, the compassion must be felt in order for the correction to be effective. You can say the exact same thing in a critical mode, and if they feel the love they will listen. But if you say it and they don't feel the love, they will feel as if they are being demonized, degraded, isolated, targeted. With Cosby, I wish more of the compassion could have come through more strongly up front. Tell the young folk, "The reason we are so concerned about the way you wear your pants, about your not doing your homework and not being disciplined, is because you are so priceless and precious and we love you, and this criticism comes out of love."

Poor young brothers and sisters of any color, but especially black and brown, are already demonized by the mainstream press. They are already criminalized in terms of the targeting of police, the war on drugs, the expansion of the prison industrial complex, which the attorney and writer Michelle Alexander calls the "new Jim Crow." They are very suspicious of any kind of targeting of them and their behavior. We have to make clear to them that Cosby is right when talking about responsibility; he's right when he's talking about discipline; he's right when he's talking about deferred gratification.

If Etan Thomas, or rappers like Ice Cube, Chuck D, or Talib Kweli all said exactly what Cosby said, young people would respond differently. That doesn't mean that Cosby doesn't love them; it just means that the love was not made as manifest as I think it should have been. And let's not forget the role of the white mainstream press, which has not shown a deep love for poor black brothers and sisters, which then projects Cosby's message and misconstrues some of what Cosby himself believes. The press interprets it in a certain way for their own purposes, and the young folks feel even more isolated and targeted in a negative way. There is a very important difference between criticism that is enabling and negativism that is isolating. All of us experience this distinction in our own lives. If our mama tells us something that sounds like a criticism, we know the love is there and so we respond appropriately. If somebody else tells us the exact same thing and we know they don't love us, we're ready to fight.

The timing of this book is perfect, because a lot of the dust has cleared from the Cosby controversy. Now we want to tease out Cosby's insights and tease out his critics, like Michael Eric Dyson, and say, "Look, the bottom line is not about Cosby or Dyson or anybody else; it's about how we are going to help these young brothers and sisters lead a life of decency and dignity. That's the bottom line."

I also need to add something else—something that's extremely important to this discussion. When we talk about personal responsibility and the criticism of any sector of the society that is acting irresponsible, we need to be consistent. For example, let's look at Wall Street. We had all this predatory lending, fraudulent activity, and gangster behavior, yet no one takes responsibility when they get in trouble. We want our young people to know that when we talk about responsibility, we're not just talking about them; we're talking about everybody in the society. If we're going to tell our young people that we want them to be responsible and we put the focus on them, we also want to connect that with a critique of the most powerful in our society, who have tremendous influence over the institutions and structures that generate high levels of unemployment, dilapidated housing, disgraceful school systems, various stereotypes in television and movies that do, in fact, reinforce the worst of young black men in regards to how they view themselves and how they view others. Anytime I talk about the lack of responsibility of our precious young folk, I also connect it with the lack of responsibility of Wall Street oligarchs and corporate elites. When they get in trouble, nobody takes responsibility; nobody goes to jail. Even though the world economy nearly collapsed, there are hardly any prosecutions, hardly any investigations. The same is true of those who are torturing and committing crimes against humanity in the name of the American people. Not one person has been prosecuted or convicted. Not one person has gone to jail for wiretapping. All of these are against the law. It's hard for us to tell our young people to be responsible without also letting them know that we know some folks at the top who have tremendous power also need to be responsible. There should be a moral consistency to our concern about responsibility.

Young people who are living with despair and a deficit of hope about their future need to take their cues from the mythical Sankofa bird, which looks back while flying forward. They have to look back in order to move forward. We need to say to them, "You come out of a tradition of tremendous foremothers and forefathers, grandmothers and grandfathers, who, in the face of incredible adversity, were able to step forward with style, with dignity, with decency, and actually make themselves a way of life the whole world has taken note of. Be a count like Count Basie, a duke like Duke Ellington. We have Muhammad Ali, Martin Luther King, Fannie Lou Hamer, Louis Armstrong, Curtis Mayfield, Luther Vandross, and President Barack Obama—a whole crowd of witnesses."

Our young people need to focus on those persons in our past who, by example, will empower them to be able to transcend and transform their circumstances. Men like Etan Thomas. There's no Etan Thomas without his precious mama and community and church, which all had a part in making him the dynamite brother he is. That history is inside of him, so that he has been able to use that history in such a way to make it his own, but at the same time building on the shoulders of those who came before him. Our young people need that Sankofa bird mentality, to know that there's a connection to the past that is vital. It is not abstract. I'm not talking about digging through history books—I'm talking about people they know in their own communities, their own families, who have forged ahead through tremendous struggle and have been able to preserve their sense of who they are.

Our young people also need to know that so many of our transformative leaders came from circumstances no different from their own. If they want to know whether they can rise above their poverty, above their fatherlessness, we tell them about how the great W. E. B. Du Bois didn't know his father. And there is no greater scholar in the twentieth century than W. E. B. Du Bois. We tell them that John Coltrane's father died when he was very young, leaving him there all alone with just his mother and his cousin. And there is no greater artist in the twentieth century than John Coltrane, except maybe Sarah Vaughan and Vladimir Horowitz. We tell them of how President Barack Obama was raised by a single mother and met his father only once or twice. He didn't allow that to lead him down the path of a self-destructive and unproductive life, but he was able to make it to the highest position of our society. I believe if they begin to learn these things, they begin to see past their own depressed circumstances. They begin to see hope.

I am so thrilled that Etan has undertaken this project. It is so crucial. And what's wonderful about what Etan is doing and how he's doing it is that his love comes through so clearly. There can be no doubt about his love.